KU-018-994

THE
NANNY
STATE
MADE ME

Also by Stuart Maconie

Cider with Roadies
Pies and Prejudice
Adventures on the High Teas
Hope and Glory
The People's Songs
The Pie at Night
Long Road from Jarrow

THE
NANNY STATE

MADE ME

A STORY OF BRITAIN AND HOW TO SAVE IT

STUART MACONIE

EBURY
PRESS

1 3 5 7 9 10 8 6 4 2

Ebury Press, an imprint of Ebury Publishing
20 Vauxhall Bridge Road
London SW1V 2SA

Ebury Press is part of the Penguin Random House group of companies
whose addresses can be found at global.penguinrandomhouse.com

Penguin
Random House
UK

Copyright © Stuart Maconie, 2020

Stuart Maconie has asserted his right to be identified as the author of this
Work in accordance with the Copyright, Designs and Patents Act 1988

Quote from *Fight Club* by Chuck Palahniuk reproduced by kind
permission of the author.
Copyright © Chuck Palahniuk, 1996

First published by Ebury Press in 2020

www.penguin.co.uk

A CIP catalogue record for this book is available from the British Library

Hardback ISBN 9781529102413

Typeset in 10.5/14 pt ITC Galliard Std
by Integra Software Services Pvt. Ltd, Pondicherry

Printed and bound in Great Britain by Clays Ltd, Elcograf S.p.A.

Penguin Random House is committed to a sustainable
future for our business, our readers and our planet.
This book is made from Forest Stewardship Council®
certified paper.

For my Mum and Dad, who grew up in a different country.
And Noah and Arlo, who still might.

INTRODUCTION

London's skyline bristles with towers. Old and new, bloody and sleek, sandstone and silicon, monuments to kings and to commerce. From the Amazonian giants of the City's money jungle to the high-rise canyons of Camden. Visitor and native alike marvel at them, orient by them, lifting eyes from book or phone or feet, as the train exhales into Euston, as the bus crests Muswell Hill, as you jostle through the West End.

Whenever I pace the narrow lanes of Bloomsbury and Fitzrovia, I look up for one in particular. It's a Grade II listed building, much more familiar and human in its dimensions than the boastful monoliths of Canary Wharf. It's had many names and many lovers. It looms over works by Ian McEwan, The Goodies and Alan Moore. It is part of our shared national iconography. It is surely a symbol of something. Glamour, vision, adventure, the white-hot future that was coming.

Early in the twenty-first century, around about the time we were realising that that particular future wasn't coming for most of us down below, I had lunch at the top of that tower in the restaurant that used to revolve, the restaurant of failed dreams, with a man who helped build it. I was filming an interview with Tony Benn, grand old firebrand of the Labour movement, about the building's history. In 1966, along with holiday-camp magnate Billy Butlin, as Postmaster General he opened what was then called the GPO or General Post Office Tower, a new and thrilling addition to the London skyline, commissioned by the state, designed by civil servants, the draughtsmen and architects of the Ministry of Public Buildings.

Neither of those positions or organisations exist now. When a new Britain began to emerge at the end of the 1970s, as one of the first of what would become countless privatisations, the GPO Tower became first the Post Office Tower, then the Telecom Tower and finally the BT Tower. As Tony Benn and I sat talking in the quiet restaurant eyrie, closed to the public for decades on the vague and spurious grounds of it being a terrorist target, I could sense the mounting anxiety of the slick, besuited PR man lurking nearby. Eventually he sidled over to our table.

'Stuart, Tony, hi. I can't help noticing, guys, that you're referring to the building as the GPO Tower,' he laughed, nervously. 'It's not been that for a long, long time, guys. Can I just remind you, it's the BT Tower. As in British Telecom, who own it.'

Benn fixed him with a stare that combined pity and scorn. 'Excuse me. I oversaw the opening of this building. It was built using British labour and skills with the money of the British people who paid for it with their taxes. It belongs to them and always will. Margaret Thatcher took it from them and gave it to you when it was not hers to give. This is not your building. It is theirs ...' – he pointed to the streets below and the busy, swarming, preoccupied workers – '... and it was stolen from them.'

The PR man, wilting and tasting defeat, moved silently back into the shadows. Benn turned to me, rolled his eyes and winked. At that point, the seed of this book was planted. What happened to the GPO Tower was the start of a story.

This is it.

This is my story, your story and how it was stolen from us.

I am a child of the state. You are too. That's my guess.

We were born into the stern but loving embrace of one of its hospitals, redbrick, concrete, or steel and glass, raised in one of its compact, sturdy little houses and educated in its solid, unshowy but decent schools. Our minds were opened and filled by its silent and magical libraries, its draughty museums and echoing galleries, places of wonder travelled to on buses and trains that were unsexy and asthmatic but ran on time and went regularly to all the places we wanted to go. We ran and laughed and grew healthy and fit and were hale and naughty in its little local parks and huge national ones and its swimming baths reeking of chlorine, its muddied sports fields, on its putting greens and the cracked, weed-choked asphalt of its municipal tennis courts.

I have lived most of my life a happy and grateful citizen of the state. I will die in its arms.

If you are one of those people who styles themselves a 'libertarian' or 'contrarian', this may make me appear an unthinking automaton, a gulled and brainwashed serf. But perhaps only to those who have lived or who desire an entirely privatised life, born outside the NHS, educated at a private school perhaps, a stranger to public transport and recreation, living somewhere, perhaps even gated, far from the towns and streets most of us knew. These people are fewer than you might think. Most of us will never come into contact with them, never clink a glass with them, never dance with them, never wet their babies' heads or put a consoling arm around them. They are few and they are untypical. But they wield a power far in excess of their number, far in excess of what is right for a healthy society. Right now, they are more powerful than they have ever been.

In his column in the 3 December 1965 issue of the *Spectator*, the Conservative MP Iain Macleod fulminated against those milksops in the Department of Transport who wanted to introduce, of all things, a speed limit on British motorways. Predating by some four decades our current crop of professional white male fulminators (we shall not name them here, as Gandalf used to say of Sauron with a shudder), Macleod went on to grumble at this manifestation of what he termed 'the nanny state'. Thus was minted a phrase which soon became part of our cultural lexicon and political discourse. It crept into our national conversation, via tabloid leaders, letters pages, pub arguments and golf-club chat. It became a shorthand for a way of thinking that's inflicted on us real and lasting damage, a dull pain that we have almost grown used to. It's why I've written the book you hold in your hand.

The 'nanny state' has become a glib dismissal for all that is seen to be bad, weak and misguided about once-proud Britain. The term is now the blowhard columnist's friend, blamed for everything from teenage pregnancies to the erratic form of our fast bowlers. It has become a byword for failure. But I want to tell you that it was the spirit of our finest hour, the backbone of our post-war greatness, the guiding principle of our brief 'New Elizabethan' heyday, our 1960s cultural domination of the globe. Between the end of the Second World War and the early 1980s, Britain produced some of the greatest, most imperishable, popular and pioneering art, science, literature, pop music, comedy, film and sporting achievements the world has ever seen. To a major degree, these were achieved by generations of children of the state. Having defeated global fascism, a ruined country rebuilt itself from rubble thanks to the most progressive government in our history and the talents of its children, kids raised by and large outside of the establishment and the elite on a diet of orange juice, free school milk, NHS specs, *Watch with Mother*, public libraries, art schools, galleries and all the other benefits of a forward-looking state and a commitment to the public good not the private profit.

For forty years now, we've been sold – literally sold – a false and damaging narrative by a powerful and self-interested few. They've sought to convince us that the state was a bloated dinosaur, a scroungers charter, an outdated and creaking handrail for 'losers'. By contrast, they told us the private sector – bold, dynamic and free – was a thrusting cure-all for our national ills. To put it bluntly, this was a con. It was a lie invented and promoted for their benefit only. It's proved an ideological blind alley that has, far from making Britain fitter and stronger, left it weaker, less happy, less productive and a much duller and nastier place to live.

But what was quite so bad about this poor old nanny state, mocked and vilified by rich men in the Sunday papers for money. What was so terrible about properly funded hospitals, student grants, decent working conditions, affordable houses, trains that ran for convenience not profit, water that poured from the tap whose function was to slake your thirst not to make shareholders a dividend. What exactly was so wicked about public libraries, free eye tests and council houses? We may be coming to realise that the people who complain about the nanny state are the people who had nannies.

Our story is different, and our side of it is worth telling.

*

'I wanted to join the Margaret Thatcher Society, but it turns out there's no such thing'

Moose Allain

There is such a thing as society. If you doubt that, you probably aren't going to enjoy or even agree with what follows. But then with respect, if you dispute the existence of society, how are you reading this book? How has it arrived in your hands? Did it fall from the sky? Was it given to you by a fair maiden riding on the back of a unicorn? Is it magically written in rainbows in the azure skies above you? Did it grow out of the rich loam like a potato?

If it did, marvellous. But I think it probably arrived in your hand via a series of industrial processes that started with me at a desk in an upstairs room or on a train tapping at a laptop and then passed through a complex nexus of editors, designers and printers, people packing boxes in warehouses, people sorting stuff and selling stuff, all working collectively in an organised and co-operative way. If you got it out of the public library, or at college or a drop-in centre or such (I once picked up a copy of Terry Wogan's autobiography with a sticker that said 'Not To Be Removed From This Hospital'), then you also have the state to thank. Maybe even that much-maligned beast 'the nanny state'.

Let's begin with that term. Nanny state. It has its origins then in Conservatism, and is still used largely by those of a right-wing bent or possibly that shrinking sector, the older, blue-collar left. In this it has something in common with its newer companions 'PC gone mad' and 'fake news' in political origin and in the way it's deployed. The nanny state is hardly ever used complimentarily or even objectively. It's a usefully blunt instrument wielded to shut down any competing view. It serves to close down and enrage your opponent and to rally the like-minded to you.

Two types of professional language-user keep it handy in their rhetorical quiver. Firstly, it's a convenient straw man or Aunt Sally for the pundit keen to create a lather of faux outrage. We know who they are; plying a lucrative trade in the Sundays and tabloids, pitching up with wearisome regularity on *Question Time* and Sky News. They style themselves as 'contrarians' and 'provocateurs', though they operate from positions of total security, a sprained wrist from too vigorous a bashing of the keyboard or reaching for the green-room canapés the only hazard they face. Then there's the politician or economist espousing the virtues of 'standing on one's own two feet' or 'pulling oneself up by the bootstraps', two kindred dead phrases that do a similar job, emphasising a vague notion of self-reliance and sneering at the supposed excesses of the welfare state and what the Americans call 'big government'.

What's especially interesting linguistically is how a term of highly niche resonance has gained such traction. Most people have a nana or a nan but not a nanny. The very fact that a term of such limited cultural reach – consider perhaps some equivalents; the chauffeur state or the butler state – has gained such regular currency shows how powerful certain small groups are in our society. It's a soft power perhaps, but reflects what sociologists call 'hegemony', the dominant cultural mores of the era usually imposed from an elite. Oddly, though many of these had nannies to which they remain weirdly attached – Jacob Rees-Mogg springs to mind, albeit in a vampiric, cadaverous 'spring' – they seem to have very negative feelings about the word, unlike most regular folk. Working-class people, in fact most people, the many not the few, have neither sneering contempt nor quivering fear of the nanny state. You perhaps had to have had a nanny to feel this way. We had 'Nan's' and 'Nana's' and they were not, in the main, remote, frosty authority figures but Irish 'shawlies', loaf-haired chatterboxes, old ladies with budgies and Werther's Originals and Parma Violets whose small, warm, smelly, lovely houses you went to on Sundays for tinned John West salmon and Eccles cake and who would push fifty pee into your hands when you left with a conspiratorial wink and squeeze. Jackie Ashley, writer and academic, has remarked that the 'tens of millions of people for whom state intervention was most needed would have never come across "nanny" in their lives, except perhaps as "nan", as in granny. As for the millions who came across them only through popular culture, nannies were mostly a benign fantasy – sweet-voiced Julie Andrews sweeping in with a dose of sugary medicine and a sparkle of magic. Today … if "nanny" conjures up anything, it is a keen, confused, homesick teenager from Bratislava.'

The aforementioned Jacob Rees-Mogg, a kind of alt-right Harry Potter and poster boy of extreme Toryism and much in the news as I write these words, still has a nanny. She was his own nanny when he was a small boy and now she is nanny to his six children. He calls her 'nanny' quite unselfconsciously in his near constant TV appearances, his interviews with Andrew Marr, Kay Burley and the rest. There will be those who find this quaint and comforting, delightfully redolent of *Mary Poppins* or *Bedknobs and Broomsticks*. There will be others who feel it fantastically alien and arcane, not to say downright creepy, in the mouth of a fifty-year-old man.

The election of December 2019 may suggest that Britain has lost its moral compass and its clarion voices. Those voices are harder to hear sometimes than the clamour of the pontificator and the bully, but there is I think a deep and insistent bottom note of anger and longing in the big symphony of our national life.

An editorial in *New Statesman* of early 2019 echoed this. 'There is no appetite in parliament or government for Thatcherism 2.0. Far from the age of big government being over, voters now long for its return. The 2018 British Social Attitudes Survey found that 60 per cent of us favour higher taxes and spending, the highest in fifteen years.' Other recent polls suggest that an astounding 83 per cent of us are in favour of re-nationalising water, 77 per cent in favour of this for electricity and gas and 76 per cent in favour of rail returning to public ownership. As Will Hutton has written, 'It is not just that this represents a general fall in trust in business. The privatised utilities are felt to be in a different category: they are public services. But there is a widespread view that demanding profit targets have overridden public service obligations. And the public is right.'

In August 2018, the government had to step in to take control of Birmingham's Winson Green prison from the private company G4S after inspectors found it in 'an appalling state' with widespread violence, drug use and negligible discipline or control exercised by terrified staff. This state of affairs culminated in riots. Humiliatingly for the privateers, it had been the first prison to be given over to the private sector in 2011.

Some of the rebellious inmates may well have been sent there on evidence that passed through the labs of the private forensics company Randox. That was at the centre of controversy in 2018 over data manipulation affecting 42 police forces and 10,000 cases. The *Yorkshire Post*'s headline ran, 'Privatisation in the dock after the biggest forensic science scandal in decades'. The Conservative government had closed the state-run forensics agency in order to provide 'innovative services at the lowest cost' despite opposition from the vast majority of forensic scientists at the time who believed, rightly, that it would lead to an increase in miscarriages of justice.

Over the last few years, the state (and the taxpayer) have had to take on board dozens of failing private academies, 'free schools' and 'studio schools' at an estimated collective cost of £48.5 million. This was 'a monumental waste of taxpayers' money at a time when schools are severely underfunded,' said the National Education Union's Mary Bousted. 'Although it trumpets the market as a model for education, no business would continue to throw good money after bad at what is clearly a failed school experiment.'

In May 2019, the probation service was taken back into the public sector after a disastrous privatisation instituted by one of the least competent politicians of modern times, Chris Grayling. Against the pleading and advice of experts, probation officers, union reps and even offenders, Grayling pushed through in haste an entirely unpiloted, half-baked scheme in time for the 2015 election. The debacle has cost me and you £500 million. Nick Hardwick, former Chief Inspector of Prisons, has said that Grayling 'should be ashamed to show his face' in public.[1]

It goes on. We picked up the tab when Virgin and Stagecoach made a colossal mess of running the East Coast main line. When the Royal Bank of Scotland, and indeed the entire banking system, trembled on the verge of collapse, we lost millions from our public purse. While the bankers responsible still pocketed huge bonuses, it was our libraries, nurseries, Sure Start schemes, surgeries and community centres that closed.

Most spectacular of all these failures of privatisation came in January 2018 when the construction giant Carillion collapsed under the weight of an enormous £1.5 billion debt, triggering the largest liquidation in British history, a result of their 'extraordinarily negligent planning', said Frank Field MP. Debt this big is beyond the conception of you and me. We can feel the heat of an unpaid tenner to a mate or a student loan or, in the biggest instance, a mortgage. But once you bloat to Carillion levels of incompetence and greed, you know that you will walk away unscathed, maybe with a bonus if you're lucky, shielded from the chill winds of economic reality – the ones they're always claiming they have expert knowledge of – by the taxpayers' largesse. Once you're up to your neck in it to the tune of a billion-plus, the figures don't matter, unless of course you're one of the tens of thousands of cleaners, porters and maintenance workers who lost their jobs

---

[1] Grayling really should be on the cover of this book, so emblematic is he of the privatisation disaster. As well as the above, most Graylingly of all, he lost us £50 million when he awarded Channel ferry contracts to a company with no ships.

because of this squalid mess or you were relying on the hospitals and schools that were left half-built, useless and flooded.

A parliamentary report found that Carillion prioritised shareholder dividends and executive bonuses while failing to properly fund the staff pension scheme. Between 2012 and 2016, they paid out £217 million more than they generated. Carillion's borrowing, ultimately responsible for its crash, was not to invest and improve performance but to pay shareholders. The same parliamentary report put it starkly and damningly; Carillion's directors were guilty of 'recklessness, hubris and greed'.

Carillion's collapse in turn sent Interserve, another private company with huge government contracts, into freefall with debts of half a billion pounds. Few people had heard of Interserve until the extent of its incompetence and power – always a lethal cocktail – became apparent. It's 16,000 shareholders lost their investments, which concerns me less than the small businesses and workers thrown on the scrapheap while, astonishingly, CEO Debbie White enjoyed a pay packet of £525,900 for four months' work (including a 125 per cent bonus) and kept her breathtakingly lucrative position.

The Economist magazine, not famed for its statist zeal or Marxist rhetoric, said that Interserve's fall 'reflects the humbling of an entire sector. Britain led the world in government outsourcing, whereby public services are contracted out to private companies.' Meanwhile the *Today* programme asked, 'Is this the end of outsourcing?' If it is, many will think it's not a moment too soon. A *Which?* survey grading customer satisfaction for the UK's top 100 companies found that Npower, BT, EDF Energy, British Gas and E.ON (each one a provider of essential utilities which were publicly owned before Margaret Thatcher's 'reforms') all appear in the Top Ten Worst Companies according to the British people. The capitalist myth of the swashbuckling, risk-taking, dynamic and virile entrepreneur – hiring and firing, living on his wits as an alpha-male king of the boardroom jungle – is just that; a myth. These are supposedly virile alpha males very much reliant on the Viagra of the nanny state via grants, subsidy and bailouts.

For the most part, outsourcing has been a calamitous, universal failure. It has damaged our social services, eaten into taxpayers' money, made life generally harder for most of us. And yet in this country, almost alone in the West, we cling to it as a religion. This religion still has its pulpit-bashing zealots and though they are still powerful, their sermons are starting to ring shrill and hollow. For most of us, it was starting to look very much like, as far as schools, hospitals, the law, power, transport, energy and even finance were concerned, Nanny knew best.

Some people are sounding distinctly rattled by this kind of talk, a possible groundswell of public mood turning against our privatisation culture. *The Economist* ran an editorial claiming that 'if England's water utilities were renationalised as Mr Corbyn intends [a move supported in polls by the vast majority of us] they would be unlikely to be shining examples of local democracy'. This is very odd stuff indeed. We don't need water companies to be 'shining examples of local democracy'. We have local democracy for that. We want water to come out of the pipes safely and reliably for the public good not the profit of a few.

In truth, the state is usually the source of innovation and creativity in business, science, tech and the economy. In her excoriating study, *The Value of Everything*, economist Mariana Mazzucato finds high drug prices particularly enraging and immoral since the majority of fundamental research in biochemistry, crucial to pharmaceutical innovation, is funded by the state. And Owen Jones, baby-faced standard bearer of the new left (who I often utterly disagree with), spent a few coldly analytical pages of his book *The Establishment* nailing this canard, summarising his arguments in a *Guardian* article. 'It is yet another example of socialism for the rich, capitalism for everyone else. Britain's private sector is utterly dependent on state largesse to make money. They depend on the state to invest in infrastructure; in research and development; in education to train up their workforce; in law and order to protect their property.' Modern capitalism, he argued, is based on a myth: 'that thriving private entrepreneurs generate wealth through their own hard work, innovation and get-up-and-go. In fact, the state subsidises the entire system, nationalising the risks but privatising the profits, while allowing its beneficiaries – our shameless, profit-obsessed elite – power without accountability.'

So we have every right to be losing patience with this false narrative, this pervasive lie that's held sway for forty years. This is the lie that has it that outsourcing, selling off and privatisation are always for the best, that the businessman is king, and the state is not to be trusted. On the contrary, I think most nurses, teachers, doctors, care workers, emergency-service personnel and the rest *can* be trusted with our children and our lives. In fact, that's exactly what we do every day. Recent history tells us again and again that, more often than not, it's those in the boardroom, the smooth ennobled fellow or his wideboy chum, who can't be trusted.

Even Francis Fukuyama, the US intellectual who, dizzy with excitement at the collapse of communism, wrote the once much lauded but latterly mocked *The End of History* (a confident assertion of the triumph of Western capitalist democracies and neo-liberalism), now says that public ownership is no bad thing.

> If you mean redistributive programmes that try to redress this big imbalance in both incomes and wealth that has emerged then, yes, I think not only can it come back, it ought to come back. This extended period, which started with Reagan and Thatcher, in which a certain set of ideas about the benefits of unregulated markets took hold, in many ways it's had a disastrous effect ... it's led to a weakening of labour unions, of the bargaining power of ordinary workers, the rise of an oligarchic class almost everywhere that then exerts undue political power ... At this juncture, it seems to me that certain things Karl Marx said are turning out to be true.

To which the only considered intellectual response is, blimey
Francis, that's one change of tune.

This then is a book about 'The National'. Not the brooding
American alt-rock band but the notion of shared endeavour, the
common good, fairness, fun and social justice, and how the state
should bolster and celebrate that. One of the reasons I love the
National as a band name is that it seems to speak of something
grave and trustworthy, serious and proper, maybe even a little
mysterious and severe but always on the side of right or, rather,
good. The National Health Service, the National Coal Board, the
National Theatre, the National Trust, the National Forest, National
Parks, the National Curriculum, the National Gallery. That last fine
London institution has a Sainsbury Wing, which I don't mind at
all. I don't actually want to see every Sainsbury's branch razed to
the ground and replaced by a collectivised state food outlet.[2] Billy
Bragg summarises this well in his pamphlet *The Three Dimensions of
Freedom*: 'Capitalism is like fire. Controlled it can give us heat and
light. Uncontrolled it destroys everything in its path.' That's why
I'm strongly in favour of what used to be called a mixed economy,
a system in which individual and private business enterprise is
allowed and indeed encouraged but regulated and exploited not
just for private gain but the common good. It's an eminently
sensible state of affairs. We leave the dehydrated curries and the
clothes and cars to Vesta and Vivienne Westwood and Volvo, but
the water supply and the prisons and the teaching kids to read and
the skilled life-saving operations to the government and its
appointed experts. That's the thing about brain surgery. It actually
is brain surgery. It's really difficult. It's best left to brain surgeons
rather than somebody off *The Apprentice* with a shiny suit and
no socks.

*

---

[2] In October 2019, Owen Jones advocated just this, a state-run fast-food outlet
chain. This would seem to me a classic example of proposing a solution to a
problem that doesn't exist, at least so long as there is Gregg's.

A kind of paternalistic capitalism and 'One Nation' Toryism was taken as a given for most of the twentieth century until the Thatcherite revolution of the late 70s, in its own way as much a fundamentalist ideological uprising as underpinned the Ayatollah and the Mullahs seizing power contemporaneously in Iran. Paternalistic Toryism was embodied by men like Harold Macmillan and Ted Heath, decent types, products of a very English education and military system and often war heroes, ironic given that Thatcher regarded their sort – fair-minded if supportive of the status quo, approving of the welfare state and a kind of social justice – as wet and gutless. Storming beaches under gunfire at Normandy was clearly less the kind of bravery she and her academic advisors admired than the 'courage' to cut kids' milk and nurses' wages.

For the historian David Edgerton, what ended with the coming of the Thatcher revolution was not just a particular era or mindset. Edgerton contends in his 2018 book *The Rise and Fall of the British Nation* that 1979 spelt the end of just that: the nation itself. He argues pugnaciously that modern Britain was born in 1945 out of the travails of war:

> The British nation, as I define it, was not a natural state of affairs. The British nation was created: it emerged out of the British Empire and out of a cosmopolitan economy, after the Second World War … a British nation was created …

This new self-made Britain was a rejection of the mouldy Churchillian imperialism that's made a queasy return in the last few years. Instead this was the dawn of a new progressive country, self-reliant but outward-looking, requiring 'economic development of unprecedented speed, of the creation of an economy more focused on industry than ever before, of a developmental state, a warfare and welfare state'.

Oxford Professor of Economics Paul Collier echoes this. For him, as he told the *New Statesman*, the period of social democratic hegemony that lasted broadly from 1945 to 1970 was 'glorious ... it was when it all came together,' he said. 'We inherited a huge asset – a shared sense of purpose coming out of the Second World War, a sense of common endeavour. But it was a wasting asset that needed to be renewed. And both left and right failed to renew it.'

To have forged modern Britain at all so quickly and determinedly was remarkable. To have done it in 1945, bloodied, broken, bankrupt and half-starved, was astonishing. Those of us who think that this peacetime victory too was one of our finest hours are sometimes dismissed as centrist romantics. But it's in the Spirit of 1945 where the beloved, beleagured nanny state begins.

CHAPTER 1

1945 AND ALL THAT

'War? What is it good for?' asked Edwin Starr in 1970, gruffly. Without waiting very long it has to be said, he answered himself: 'absolutely nothing'. Edwin meant well but he was clearly wrong. Culture Club's Boy George may have been on more solid ground when he declared that war was 'stupid'. But he was erroneous too. Stupid it may be, George, but war gets results, just not always the intended ones. Even if we reject the old cruel philosophies about 'thinning out the population' and 'the purgative fires of war', there's no doubt that structurally and politically war, or at least the end of war, can change a country for the better. Greater suffrage is often extended after wartime, women are at least partly emancipated and free medical systems are often implemented in the aftermath of conflict. This happened in Rwanda, Nepal, South Sudan and elsewhere as part of a 'peace dividend', or a move towards a new social order. In Britain, the Second World War brought a kind of national transformation that has become mythic.

'War did not revolutionise the British. But it did radicalise them,' was Paul Addison's view in his book of the TV series *Now the War Is Over*. The Second World War had been a harrowing experience for the British people but it had been one that they had borne largely collectively and that was to prove a catalyst for a social sea change to come. Class differences were moot and meaningless in the air raid shelters and the ruins, the experience of rationing was largely felt by all and the great national ruptures and traumas of Dunkirk, the Battle of Britain, the Blitz and evacuation bonded us all. Tom Hopkinson, editor of the influential popular magazine *Picture Post*, said, 'we would go on to fire-watching at night and a managing director would fire-watch with an office boy and the junior typist, five or six people, and they'd all doss down in great discomfort in one of the offices with the rugs that were provided for the purpose. And the visible signs of any kind of class difference would disappear.' To borrow the phrase that George Osborne used after the 2008 economic crash, we were all in it together. The difference being that, in 1940, it was true.

There had been a growing national sentiment from about 1940 on, from J.B. Priestley's fireside 'Postscript' talks on the BBC Home Service to the progressive leanings of the radical press like *Picture Post* and *Daily Worker*, even to a smaller number of Liberal and Tory voices like Keynes and Rab Butler, that if the war was ever won (and that was far from certain) a new Britain had to emerge from the ashes. When Ernest Bevin, Minister of Labour, went to Portsmouth to visit the soldiers on the eve of their embarkation for France, he was asked, 'Ernie, when we have done this job for you, are we going back to the dole?' He knew and Britain knew that the answer had to be no. His colleague Herbert Morrison, as quoted in David Kynaston's *Austerity Britain*, could sense change in the air in the spring of 1944, and in the attitudes of the British: 'a genuine social idealism' reflecting 'the altered moral sense of the community'. He felt that we 'were moving into an altogether different form of society working in an altogether different atmosphere of ideas'.

We like to invest dates with meaning, and the more portentous the better. Thus a couple of 66s nearly a millennium apart (10 and 19) are potent reminders of humiliation and triumph in Hastings and Wembley. In 1605 and 1976, anarchy is evoked and almost loosed upon us thanks to the incendiary dreams of Guy Fawkes and Johnny Rotten. The years 1945 and 1979 are significant markers for this book though, with that first a date as resonant of people's victory for some of us as 1415 (Agincourt), 1805 (Trafalgar) and 1815 (Waterloo) are for others. This was not just a battle. This was winning a war, abroad and at home.

More doctrinaire leftie types than myself often accuse my variety of being hopeless romantics about the 1945 Labour government. I can only respond that if there is anything in our recent history to feel unashamedly, unequivocally proud and romantic about – more than football matches or Eurovision Song Contests or 'taking back our country' in referendums – then I'd say it's surely two things: the victory over fascism and the setting up of the welfare state. Both come neatly packaged together for we softies in the 1945 Labour government. This justly famous administration of all the talents (Attlee, Bevan, Bevin, Cripps, Greenwood, Morrison, Wilkinson; drawn from across the movement's political spectrum, take note) swept to power in a landslide, unseating Churchill, determined to make a new Jerusalem of a wounded and exhausted country ... and succeeding. Peter Wilby put this into context well in the *New Statesman*.

Since the Brexiteers' rhetoric suggests they think they are re-fighting the Second World War, Rees-Mogg's 'think tank', as it generously calls itself, should study the record of the wartime government. As early as November 1942, an official commission under William Beveridge set out a blueprint for a welfare state. Another report that year proposed the 'green belt'. White papers on social insurance were published in 1943 and on a national health service in 1944. Also in 1944, parliament passed an Education Act promising secondary education for all. When Labour took office in 1945, most of the measures that made its name were already in draft form and public support well established. We should be thankful that Rees-Mogg and his ilk weren't in charge during the war. Their narrow, divisive and unimaginative outlook would have persuaded the British there was nothing worth fighting for.

Of course, some of the old guard weren't happy even then. Reeling from what he saw as a lunatic shift in the mood of the British electorate, Churchill gave a frenzied speech, plastered across the front pages of all his mouthpiece press titles, announcing that there would be a 'Gestapo in Britain if Socialism Wins'. It was a pretty disgraceful thing to say to a country that had just stood often alone against Nazism. Furthermore, it didn't work. As Jasper Rees of the *Telegraph* put it in his review of the BBC documentary on this momentous election, *When Britain Said No*:

> Here, to recite the charge sheet, was a Victorian aristocrat with blood on his hands after Gallipoli, detested by the miners whose labour powered his beloved Empire, who once admired Mussolini, Franco and even Hitler, abhorred the semi-naked fakir Gandhi, and believed Native Americans and Aboriginals had been displaced by 'a higher-grade race'. His celebrated though interminable broadcasts were clearly delivered when drunk ... Indeed, the only reason history has stuck him on a plinth is because Churchill wrote the history himself ... [The day before polling] Churchill addressed a baying crowd at Walthamstow dog track. 'Have another good boo,' he retorted, shielding his eyes with his hat. Leaving the stadium he wound down the car window and made V signs. The next day, the electorate made one back.

As for all the scaremongering by Churchill and his cronies in the press, if there were any fears that a Soviet-style Britain was now about to emerge, with five-year plans for grain harvests, giant portraits of Attlee on Leeds Town Hall and rocket launchers trundling down Oxford Street and the Royal Crescent every May Day, these were unfounded. Our revolution was kinder and gentler. Some would say it did not go far enough. But it went as far in the right direction as any British government has ever gone before or since, or seems likely to. In her history of the British working class, *The People*, Selina Todd states 'between 1945 and 1951 the lives of working-class people greatly improved. Labour took power committed to maintaining full employment and collective bargaining and to introducing cradle to grave welfare provision'. There were caveats, of course: 'For those who were used to a comfortable way of life, the late 1940s were an uncomfortable period of privation. But for those who had grown up in the depression and survived the blitz, the immediate post-war years heralded the start of a new life.'

In 1945, more than 70 per cent of the population could be described as working class, employed either as rural labourers or industrial workers. Over the next decade, they would grow in prosperity and status. As Nicholas Spice put it in his review of Kynaston's *Austerity Britain*, 'if the people put up with the inequity of post-war Britain and soldiered on through years of discomfort and privation, they did so not out of a supererogatory deference to the existing order, but because Butler and Beveridge and the Attlee administration brought about a quiet but enduring revolution'. Kynaston detailed these as 'free grammar school education, universal healthcare, a comprehensive system of national insurance, family allowances, food and housing subsidies'. He also noted that large-scale nationalisation and full employment had 'shifted power significantly towards the workers'.

Selina Todd though, like many on the modern Left, is critical that Attlee and the Labour Party of the time did not go far enough. They accepted Beveridge's idea that the new welfare state be paid for via a National Insurance system rather than redistributive tax hikes on the rich. Many in the highest echelons of Labour still clung to the idea that those in the senior professions and at the top of management should be rewarded more highly in order to encourage 'hard work'. In truth, this was a view fairly widespread amongst the British people themselves, who have been disappointing left-wing intellectuals since Marx with their distinct lack of revolutionary ire. Sadly for the them, we are the only electorate they have.

What we Brits have always had though, in our own minds at least, is a desire for justice and fair play; that feeling that 'we are all in this together', before George Osborne reduced that phrase to a hollow joke. This was an especially pertinent notion when forged through six years of war. In those years, collective national spirit and endeavour had been not just a nice idea but a prerequisite for survival. The 1945 Attlee government, with its commitment to 'a social contract with the people', was welcome and invigorating. That contract was to hold for thirty years until it was gleefully broken by those who'd never had much time for ordinary British people anyway.

The 1970s, in many ways, were the last Golden Age for the benevolent state and the British working people. You wouldn't know that though that if you trusted only to the rote dismissals of right-of-centre pundits or only read and watched the reductive, misleading boilerplate pop culture documentaries on the era. Cut and paste the script template of 'bad hair ... flares ... terrible music' and dig out the footage of football hooligans, picket lines of hard-faced Norman Hunter lookalikes warming their hands on a brazier, bin bags piling up uncollected in the streets and Sid Vicious eating a bogey to bolster a very partial view of the era. Dominic Sandbrook in his book *Seasons in the Sun* argued that 'Britain's fortunes seemed to have reached their lowest point since the Blitz' by the mid-70s. In a *Spectator* article entitled 'Britain was utterly wretched in the 70s', Brexit's most zealous architect, Daniel Hannan, bemoaned 'a world where 'Women's Libbers break up beauty pageants; where Ulster is gripped in para-military conflict; a world which is still truly postwar ... the sheer awfulness of the 1970s: the power cuts, the strikes, the inflation, the sense of constant crisis.' Daniel must have been a particularly sensitive and observant child since he was only born in 1971 and a far-sighted one too, since he as born and grew up in Peru among wealthy expats. One pictures him in a nursery in Lima, breakfasting on ceviche and Farley's Rusk, nervous about the escalating internal tensions in the IRA as he watches a dubbed version of *Andy Pandy*. When Grace Maxwell, wife of musician Edwyn Collins, read Hannan's piece, she responded with a typically vigorous and insightful tweet. 'In 1975, aged 17, I sailed off to Glasgow University from my council house, in a steelworkers town, maximum grant, fees paid, part-time job in Woolworths, no burden on my parents, with a spring in my step, in glorious technicolour. Utterly wretched my arse.'

Unlike Daniel Hannan, but like Grace, I was there for a lot of the maligned 1970s, and I can tell you, some of it was bloody great. It may not have been a good or profitable time to be a major shareholder of Rio Tinto-Zinc or any of the other global corporations beset by currency fluctuations, oil price wars or the like, or the chairman of a failing multinational or an ageing and crazy dictator facing the wrath of his people or even a member of the British establishment. Happily, though, I was none of these. I was a young teenager embarking on the great adventure of adult life. My parents were in regular, reasonably paid work like many other factory and mill workers. We lived in a decent affordable house rented from the council. I had good friends and long golden days and evenings. I had prog rock, northern soul, glam, funk, dub, punk (and, if I'd have only known, some incendiary jazz fusion, innovative folk rock and thrilling modern classical music), I had Connors, Borg and McEnroe, the total football of Cruyff, Rep and Neeskens, the samba genius of Pelé, Tostão and Jairzinho. There was *Python* and *The Goodies*, *Play for Today* and *World in Action*. Should this appear trivial (though it isn't) there was also the Pinter of *Betrayal*, *No Man's Land* and *Old Times*, the novels of John Updike, Hunter S. Thompson, Thomas Pynchon, Iris Murdoch and Anthony Burgess, the poems of Elizabeth Bishop, John Ashbery, Ted Hughes's late, rainy masterpieces and Maya Angelou. We celebrated *The Joy of Sex*, *The Dice Man* and *Zen and the Art of Motorcycle Maintenance*. Hollywood was experiencing a Golden Age of Easy Riders and Raging Bulls and even in Britain we had the bleak brilliance of *Get Carter*, *The Wicker Man* and *Don't Look Now*, *A Clockwork Orange* and *The Go-Between*. It was a whole lot more than deeley boppers, pub bombings and Angel Delight.

Recent British history is routinely mashed into a thin, easily digestible narrative gruel by a succession of right-wing press barons, cynical politicians, populist historians and TV clip shows. This reductive view of post-war Britain goes roughly like this. The 50s: stifling social conformity, tail-end of rationing, Brylcreem, Teddy Boys. The 60s: free love, drugs, kaftans, the Incredible String Band, Julie Christie walking down the King's Road in a miniskirt swinging a handbag. The 70s: strikes, Abba, clackers, platforms, strikes, Chopper bikes, terrorism, Basil Fawlty, Johnny Rotten, strikes, strikes and more strikes. But none of these gives a very accurate or nuanced view of any of these decades. In particular, the 70s emerges as a sort of East Germany of the mind: nasty, brutish, shortages. But that isn't the full picture.

More considered opinion is available. Historian David Edgerton refutes the usual story of decline and unrest. He argues that British industry grew and flourished in the late 1950s and early 60s spurred on by British knowhow and developments in chemicals, technology and transport infrastructure like motorways. 'In 1950 the United Kingdom was still the same coal-fired, food-importing area it was in 1900,' he wrote. 'By the mid-1970s it had been changed into an electrified, motorised nation which could easily feed itself.' He believes that in the 1970s, 'British social democracy and the welfare state were to be at their peak'. Trade union membership rose to its high-water mark; inequality was at its lowest. Gross Domestic Product doubled between 1950 and 1973. In the 60s, there were regular growth spurts of 6 per cent a year, and the record high remains 1973 – for monetarist naysayers supposedly the heart of our economic darkness – when it hit a magnificent 7.4 per cent. The popular notion that the 1979 Winter of Discontent was an economic nadir for Britain that propelled Thatcher to power is something of a myth too. Almost 30 million working days were lost by strikes that year, but 20.7 million of them came after the election when the Conservatives were in government. British decline, as journalist Neal Ascherson has pointed out, 'shows not a steady descending gradient but a sudden cliff-edge'. That cliff edge was 1979. We shall return to this infamous year.

Andy McSmith, writing in the *Independent*, laid into the myth of the 'wretched' 70s with gusto.

> Much has been written about the inefficiency of state-owned utilities. British Gas in particular was a favourite target of the consumer TV programme *That's Life*, fronted by Esther Rantzen. However, because the utilities were state owned, the government could keep fuel costs low. After 1979, British Gas raised its prices by inflation plus 10 per cent for three consecutive years, so that it could be sold as a profitable monopoly, enabling its chief executive, Cedric Brown, to enjoy a 900 per cent pay increase.

In his pithy and polemical *That Option No Longer Exists: Britain 1974–76*, John Medhurst says, 'It was not a grey decade of decline, defeat and power blackouts. Bursting with cultural experimentation, sexual liberation and industrial militancy, the 1970s saw the ruling elites of Britain challenged at every level, most especially by a Labour left led by Tony Benn which aimed to effect a "fundamental and irreversible shift in the balance of wealth and power in favour of working people"'. The academic Tim Jackson from Surrey University assembled what he called a Measure of Domestic Progress, a calculation based on including factors like economic growth, inequality, government spending on health and education, crime, family breakdown, road accidents, noise, air pollution and the environment, to try to compute whether life in general had improved or worsened. His conclusion was that in the last thirty years of the twentieth century, the year in which the greatest progress had been made was 1976. In a separate study early in the 2000s, the respected New Economics Foundation created a measure for overall economic, social and environmental wellbeing, and concluded that, again, 1976 was the best year in modern British history.

In truth, for most of the 1970s, for most people, for most of the time, this most disparaged decade was just fine; increased social mobility, decent housing, good wages, the chance of further education for you and your kids, new foods, exciting music and compelling if dirty football. They were also a bracingly non-judgemental time with a decent set of priorities, a decade when a pregnant woman could have the odd Babycham or half a lager and lime without being treated like the Antichrist and when the destruction of working-class lives and communities was more decried than the odd chubby toddler or hurt feeling. Later it would become lazily fashionable, on the strength of a few bad perms and crimplene trouser-suits, to dismiss it idly as 'the decade that style forgot'. Even if this is true, and from Borg's Fila top to Agnetha's blue satin hot pants (and that's just the Swedes by the way) I'm not at all sure it is, then so be it. There are more important things than style. There's substance, something the 70s had a great deal of. By the end of the decade, however, some of the weightiest thinkers were not on the side of the angels any more, and the ideological gloves were coming off. Google 'revolution 1979' and you'll find it all there. How militant and ruthless ideologues swept aside the old guard and their liberal, permissive ways. How the people, initially thrilled by the steely allure of the new, eventually found themselves poorer, less happy, less free as the fundamentalists undermined and took control of every corner of the nation's life. As in Tehran, so in Teddington.

The election of May 1979 which brought Margaret Thatcher to power was the first that I could cast a vote in. With the typical enormous self-centredness of the teenager, I naturally thought this made it the most momentous and significant election since the war, indeed possibly since the advent of universal suffrage. But it turns out I was right. Just after the result was in and Margaret Thatcher entered 10 Downing Street as our first female prime minister, I came across a sticker which said, 'Don't Blame Me, I Voted Labour'. At the time I had a very cheap Zenta Stratocaster copy electric guitar which weighed as much as a block of obsidian and wouldn't stay in tune. I stuck this bold statement of allegiance by the pick-ups. It stayed there through my student days and into my twenties, becoming more dirty and ragged and relevant with every passing month and year.

Margaret Hilda Thatcher's election changed Britain in ways we still feel, and feel keenly. She was inculcated in many of her bedrock, catechistical ideas at the knee and bacon slicer of her dour grocer father Alfred and during her four visits each Sunday to the Methodist Chapel, albeit without picking up much Christian charity it seems. Here she developed her core beliefs: the virtue of self-reliance, the sanctity of private profit and enterprise, a loathing and mistrust of the state and the public sector. These were the deep tribal roots of what became Thatcherism overlaid on which was an intellectual and theoretical framework taken from Friedrich Hayek's *The Road to Serfdom* and the Chicago School of Economics as developed by Milton Friedman. Essentially, Friedman espoused that the free market should be allowed to operate as it sees fit with minimal or no government interference. His doctrine was called 'monetarism' and meant strict control of the money supply and inflation even if this brought hardship, job losses and cuts in public spending. It was a way of thinking that sought to present itself as a bracing corrective to Keynesianism and the New Deal, theories which had held sway here and in the US for decades. It proved tremendously seductive to some people on the rise in British politics and a novel, fashionable talking point among policy makers and the media.

But it nearly all became merely an eccentric footnote. It is easy to forget just how close Margaret Thatcher came to being regarded by posterity as a failure. The two years pre-Falklands War, her first inglorious 700 days or so, were relentlessly grim; lengthening dole queues, flying petrol bombs, riots on the streets of our major cities, devastation to the industries of the north of England, Scotland and Wales. With unemployment soaring and the economy in free fall, her personal standing in the nation was low, so low that one point she confessed to policy advisor John Hoskyns,

'It's all gone wrong. I don't think it will ever come right. I'm the most unpopular prime minister ever. I will go down as a total disaster.'

But Edwin Starr was wrong again. War turned out to be very good for Margaret Thatcher. In the spring of 1982, the Argentinian junta invaded the Falkland Islands, a British colony that few other than ardent pub quizzers could place on a map, and Thatcher ordered the dispatch of a naval task force to regain the islands. Cast deliberately by her advisors as a kind of 'Britannia with battleships', once the war was won, she swept back to power in a landslide in 1983. In this she was helped by the first fruits of the discovery of North Sea oil and the dire, chaotic state of Labour under the derided Michael Foot. Foot's case is illustrative of the gulf that has always existed between the political class and the electorate. Like Enoch Powell, another remote ideologue, Westminster lore continually talks up Foot's spellbinding oratory and reputation as a great parliamentarian. Voters thought he was useless.

Thatcher went from strength to strength for most of the rest of the decade. The size of the 1983 victory and another in 1987, and the absence of any effective opposition, meant she could push on with her 'project' unopposed and with vigour. More and more elements of our welfare state and our public sphere were besieged and dismantled. Whole communities were scattered to the winds. The City of London was featherbedded and favoured over our manufacturing sector and our industrial towns and cities. According to the Sheffield Political Economy Research Institute, that mistaken prioritisation has seen us lose out on a 'staggering' £4.5 trillion (trillion!) over the course of two decades because of an oversized financial sector, inflating asset and property prices. Thatcher protected her class and her supporters with the entrenched and single-minded bias and self-interest of the most ardent trade unionist or class warrior. Dissent came in the form of strikes and riots, but not at the ballot box and not in the cabinet room. As pilloried on the long-running puppet satire show *Spitting Image*, Thatcher presided with cold impatience over a cabal of posh, cowed public schoolboys, adulterous grandees and general second-raters with the icy imperious mien of Ming the Merciless. Anyone who lacked her ruthless ideological rigour was a 'wet' and not 'one of us'. Resistance was futile.

There were, though, the occasional yelps of protest from within. According to her long-term chancellor Nigel Lawson, the nearest Thatcher ever came to a full-scale internal cabinet revolt was when her enthusiastic support for something called the Omega Project was leaked in September 1982. Geoffrey Howe, later to prove instrumental in her eventual downfall, was one of those who rejected this initiative from the Adam Smith Institute (the right-wing libertarian think tank backed by Thatcher's own economic adviser, Sir Alan Walters). Thatcher was all for the Omega Project, an appropriate name for a new series of savage cuts, hospital closures and compulsory private healthcare insurance that 'would of course mean the end of the NHS', to be replaced by 'more efficient alternatives from the private sector'. With her tone-deafness to public opinion and unblinking, undeviating missionary zeal, Thatcher had underestimated or ignored the public attachment to the NHS. She was forced to back down, indeed to declare 'the NHS is safe with us'. It was a lie and it remains one. Our public services, born of the optimism and community spirit of 40s Britain, are more under threat than ever.

You are a child of the state. I can tell. I am too. We were born not with silver spoons, but with golden futures and the best intentions, incubated and injected and immunised in a ward of bustling nurses to the ping and drip of the benevolent state machine. The love story begins here.

CHAPTER 2

I AM BORN

'A GERM-FREE ADOLESCENCE'

I was the 8,047,970th baby born into the National Health Service. I came into this world just as you probably did, in a manner rarely mentioned in literary memoirs and romances. Not in a lonely croft high on a windswept moor or a tiny cottage by the raging sea or during an air raid or on an ocean liner or any of the ways babies are born in yarns and tall tales. (Tom Waits claims he was born in a taxi – yeah, right, Tom.) I was born into a large, complex, impersonal government facility in Prescot, a nondescript suburb of Merseyside. A modern hospital ward, functional and austere but also sterile, well lit, decently equipped, safe and professional. I was born into the care of the state, and NHS baby 8,047,970, Maconie, Stuart John, is very proud of that fact and that number.

So far, and I am very grateful for this, I have not had anything like as much experience of the National Health Service as some. I've been lucky enough to avoid long stays in hospital or the need for serious surgery. That day will doubtless come and when it does I hope the NHS is still there waiting for me. But like every British person, I have brushed against the NHS down the years, here and there, part of the shared narrative of our lives.

At the edge of memory, I can dimly recall having my tonsils out. I remember it in the abstract; lights and beds and masks, a chloroform-scented dream. I was part of that generation, maybe the last one, who went routinely under the knife in infancy as part of a brisk, probably unnecessary, now disfavoured health strategy. No fuss, like car insurance always claims to be. The emphasis back then was very much on the pre-emptive whipping out and snipping off – I avoided that one, actually – of surplus tissue of all kinds ('Come on, stop crying, don't be a baby, you can have a Thunderbird 3 when it's all over') rather than have it become all complicated and messy and burst or infected later on. I can remember being wheeled into surgery on a gurney as a cheery orderly in a white mask loomed over me. 'If you can find this shilling,' he said, tossing one into the bedclothes as he slipped the black rubber gas and air mask on me, 'you can have it.' The next thing I knew I was waking up in a starchy bed with a glass of warm Ribena and a Thunderbird 3.

About forty years later, I was waiting quietly and anxiously in a 'relatives' room in the interior of Birmingham's City Hospital on the Dudley Road. It's been a local landmark in the decades that has seen the surrounding streets shift and bloom and wither and bloom again, from back-to-back terraces to rubble-strewn bombsites to foundries and corner shops and now to a crazy, lively mix of tattoo parlours, sari makers, kebab shops and mobile-phone repairers. It was quiet and tense in the room where I sat, though, as a young doctor, Malaysian/English I think, was telling me and my stepdaughter that my gravely ill ninety-year-old mother-in-law would probably not last the afternoon. However, he said, there was one slim chance of keeping her with us a while longer. It was tricky and risky and would involve him inserting a thin wire in a vein in her arm and trying to manually guide it up and into her torso via a maze of arteries and eventually to her heart where, with luck and skill, it would remove the blockage there. He made it sound a little like the fairground game where a steady hand around the curves of a steel pipe is needed to avoid setting the electric buzzer off. Except the price of failure was rather more serious than a mild jolt, of course. We told him to try, and away he went.

Forty-five minutes later, he returned, rolling his sleeves down and mopping his brow. 'Well, it worked,' he said, breezy and matter-of-fact. 'She's weak and very poorly but she's still here. You can go up for a chat in a minute. I have to go now.' With that, and the tired but satisfied air of a mechanic who had just replaced a fan belt, he strode away to perform another minor miracle. I thought then, as I do every time I recall that morning, that in those forty-five minutes that young man achieved more, did something more important, than anything and everything I will do in my whole life. Yours too, probably, if you'll forgive me. When I think about the NHS, I think about him, and then I think about those people not fit to scrub his hands who make his job and his life – and the jobs and lives of his tired, overworked, dedicated, brilliant workmates – harder every day. And I know whose side I am on, and who my enemy is.

The summer of 1948 was hot, tense and unusually busy all around the world. The Berlin Airlift began and Korea split into two mutually suspicious and antagonistic republics. A Cathay Pacific plane, the *Miss Macao*, became the first commercial flight to be hijacked. Columbia Records unveiled the 33⅓ LP record and the first monkey astronaut was launched into space. After years of conflict and negotiation, the state of Israel came into being, and the ramifications and shockwaves are still felt seventy years on.

In Britain the sun shone on a country gamely but gingerly still emerging from the long, dark tunnel of war. Dutch runner Fanny Blankers-Koen was the star of the 'Austerity Games', the London Summer Olympics staged at Wembley Stadium and the Empire Pool, London. The *Windrush* arrived with its cargo of 492 Jamaican immigrants who would change the look and tenor of Britain forever. In Manchester, 'Baby', the pioneering electronic computer that attracted Alan Turing to the university, ran its first program while on the Suffolk coast the first Aldeburgh Festival was held.

Even among such momentous events, one stands out. At midnight on 5 July 1948, the National Health Service began in

Britain. The NHS, as it quickly became known, was the result of years of research, argument, hostility, persuasion and campaigning. But the people of Britain were overwhelmingly in need of it and becoming increasingly vocal in their demand for it. Fortunately for us and them, help was at hand in the shape of a 'bard' and 'a warrior', to give the two very apt English translations of his name.

The 1945 Labour government was self-consciously a 'cabinet of all the talents', reflecting (and appeasing) the different wings and strands of thought within the Labour movement. It was packed with tough, smart, industrious, compassionate individuals, many of whom were also the kind of hustler, bruiser, charmer and schemer you need to be to make a difference in the febrile competitive British political system. Few would doubt, though, who the star was. That was the Welshman whom Labour historian Kenneth Morgan called 'a stormy petrel ... the most hated – if also the most idolised – politician of his time'.

Aneurin 'Nye' Bevan spent most of the 1930s as a backbench thorn in the side of his more moderate Labour bosses. He was even more of a nuisance during the Second World War to Winston Churchill's Tories, whom he once memorably described as 'lower than vermin'. In his turn, Winnie thought Bevan was a 'squalid nuisance'. Mention of Nye's name can still find grown men becoming thick of voice and damp of eye, prompting the kind of glazed remembrance that Bobby Charlton or Barry John or Fred Trueman does. He is one of the few heroes Ken Loach and Alastair Campbell probably have in common. I confess that I can be a sucker for a spot of Nyemania myself. I'm not wild about fannish cults surrounding politicians. I'd rather have the hard-working, principled, slightly dull Clem Attlee over sordid 'characters' like Boris Johnson any day. But if we're going to have cults, let's reserve them for people like Nye. When I have winced behind splayed fingers as Jeremy Corbyn has scuttled in disdain and fear from journalists' perfectly reasonable questions, flanked by minders who bleat about him being 'hassled', I wonder what Nye would have done. I think I know the answer. He would have wrestled the mike from them, jumped on the nearest table, dealt with any questions and still be talking now.

Harold Macmillan, a more emollient and thoughtful Conservative PM than Churchill, regarded Bevan, not unkindly, as 'an uncontrollable star ... almost a comet' who 'could not forget and never want to forget the sufferings he had seen in the mining valleys of South Wales'. Much of that suffering was down to poor health and the inability of Bevan's friends, family and fellow townspeople to pay for medical care in the scrappy, piecemeal and unfair public health system that prevailed in Britain before the Second World War. It was a wretched picture: consultants arriving for work in frock coats and top hats; GPs' surgeries having separate doors for private and 'panel' patients; flag days and charity; begging bowls in hospital wards; worried mothers with sick children counting the coins in their purse in doctors' waiting rooms; workhouse infirmaries; means-tested hospital beds; children regularly and unnecessarily dying of diseases like scarlet fever simply because their parents could not afford a doctor's visit. Bevan, taking his cue from but going further than Beveridge's famous report (discussed later), proposed, in the words of the famous White Paper of 1944, a National Health Service, that 'everybody irrespective of age, sex and occupation shall have equal opportunity to benefit from the best and most up-to-date medical and allied services available ... free of charge'.

Bizarre and dismaying as it may seem now to those of us who cherish it, which is still most of us, the NHS was not welcomed or wanted by all. For starters there was Winston Churchill and his Conservative Party, who voted against Bevan's NHS Bill every time it came to parliament. Then there was the press. 'Fight This Bad Bill!' trumpeted the *Evening Standard*, toeing the Tory party line. But significantly, there was sustained opposition from the very people who were key to making it work, Britain's doctors themselves, as expressed by their trade body, the British Medical Association. They were wary about becoming 'servants of the state', and panicky at the prospect of losing long-cherished status and income. As the BMA debated the proposed changes of the Beveridge Report on election day 1945, the news broke that Beveridge himself had lost his Berwick parliamentary seat. The BMA burst into a spiteful cheer. According to John Marks, who qualified as a young doctor on the very day the NHS was launched, there was 'no great enthusiasm for it. The vast majority of doctors regarded it as something they had to put up with. It was mainly the young and more left-leaning ones like me who wanted it ... I'd been brought up to believe that the world didn't revolve around money and power, so I believed in the concept of a welfare state.' Bevan had changed the funding model of Beveridge's original report from social insurance to general taxation. He intended to nationalise Britain's 3,000 hospitals and have them report directly to him, to sell their private practices to the state in return for a basic wage, topped up according to their patient numbers. In other words, to cease to be lucrative private freelancers and to become salaried employees of the state.

This was not what the doctor ordered. Not most of them, anyway. John Marks's less public-spirited colleagues were not giving up their enviable lifestyle without a fight. The BMA defended the status quo on what now seem ludicrous and specious grounds. They claimed that the warm and intimate relationships with their (largely well-off) patients would be sullied and ruined by becoming part of a national state system. (BMA propaganda films of the day paint GPs as part saintly old sage, part father confessor and part creepy marriage guidance counsellors.) They claimed that reducing the medical profession to 'a branch of the civil service' would not be conducive to good work. They fretted about the removal of 'competition', that great guarantor of good public service. Some even raised the spectre of doctors in uniforms marching to do the state's work. In November 1946, the BMA voted to boycott Bevan's plan. The country and the wishes of a free and elected parliament were being 'held to ransom' by the self-interest of a powerful, bullying trade union. But unusually this time it was perfectly acceptable to the powers that be.

A year and a half later, just three months before the target date for the setting up of the NHS, the BMA voted again, and again they rejected the idea of a National Health Service. As their position became more and more untenable, with a sick nation hungry for change, the old elite guard of the BMA obstructed and prevaricated at every turn, singling out and abusing the younger, more radical medical students as 'reds', 'commies' and 'traitors'. Bevan was resolute though. 'No matter what harsh words come from the words of the great, kind words come from the mouths of the weak, the sick and the poor who will now have access to what was formerly held from them. When I hear the cacophony of harsh voices trying to intimidate me, I close my eyes and listen to the silent voices of the poor.'

The silence had been broken though. By now the national mood had changed, and the swell and tide of public opinion was against the elite rump of the BMA. The idea of a National Health Service had gripped the public imagination and the British people did not view kindly the transparent self-interest of wealthy doctors at a time of national hardship and struggle. Reluctantly, the BMA began to bend to the national will. Bevan also sweetened the deal with concessions like handsome salaries. As he famously later remarked, 'I stuffed their mouths with gold.' Essentially, Bevan allowed doctors to be self-employed and run their surgeries as private businesses. This is still the case for GPs, unlike nurses, junior doctors, physiotherapists and the rest. Some think this means GPs are still wasting time on management and accountancy that could be spent seeing patients.

Whether Bevan was right in this is now moot. British people in their tens of millions were soon signing up for the new NHS and the last vestiges of doctor resistance crumbled. Six weeks before the launch, the BMA advised its members to join the new National Health Service. Thus, at one minute past midnight on 5 July 1948, an individual's health ceased to be a private financial matter and became a communal and civic concern. As Owen Sheers said in his seventieth birthday tribute to the NHS, *To Provide All People*:

... overnight, the shadow of poverty in Britain became a few shades lighter. It is hard to imagine what an equivalent cultural shift would look like today. A one-tier education service suddenly brought into being perhaps? Private schools abolished and the very best of education available to all, regardless of their social position or wealth ... somehow, a deeply socialist idea has become a cherished institution at the heart of a wider society which has, in the years since its birth, only ever travelled further in the other direction.

At just approaching midnight on 4 July 1948, in a cottage hospital in Glanamman, West Wales, Edna May, a young woman with six children already, was coming to the end of a long, difficult labour. With the end in sight, she was relieved when the attendant doctors and nurses began to gather with words of encouragement. But they were shouting and urging, not 'push', but 'stop, Edna, hold on'. They were conscious, even if Edna was not, of the clock on the wall. They knew that if she could hold on for another minute, her daughter would be the first baby born into the new National Health Service. At one minute past midnight, number one for the NHS, a mere 8,047,969 places before me, pop pickers, a baby girl arrived, utterly unaware of her significance.

'You must call her Aneira,' a doctor said, the female form of Aneurin. Years later, that baby recalled, 'I became known as Nye, just like him. When I was a child my mum would introduce me to people, saying, "This is Nye, my National Health baby" ... I never knew any of my grandparents because they died between the ages of thirty and fifty. But my mother lived until she was ninety-five, which she put down to the NHS. I am the youngest of seven children but was the first to be born in hospital, and it didn't cost my parents a penny. When my six older siblings were born at home, my mum and my dad, Willie, had to pay a midwife one and six [7.5p] to come and deliver the baby.' Aneira, though, was the first child of a generation who would never know that dark undertow of fear and constraint. Fittingly, she went on to work in the NHS for twenty-eight years as a nurse in a mental health hospital. 'It was very challenging, but the standard of nursing was great. You do feel sad for the patients but I was always upbeat. It was hard work, but I was born to do it.'

The hospital where Aneira was born has long closed and is now a derelict cluster of abandoned buildings. Filmed there by *Channel 4 News*, she looks to be wandering around a decommissioned Romanian chemical warfare research facility. It is a sad sight. But another seminal landmark of the NHS is still very much standing, booming in fact, even in the face of adversity and austerity. Worth seeing, I thought. Well worth the tram to Trafford Bar and the 256 bus to Collyhurst, a working-class suburb of Manchester with a claim to be the historic heart of the National Health Service.

We shouldn't let the memory of an inflated self-publicist like Boris Johnson dangling marooned on a zip wire high in the air, waving a little flag like Captain Mainwaring's halfwit brother, suggest that all instances of political theatre are foolish and wrong. Nye Bevan could surely have made even that daft stunt work, just as he made the opening day of the NHS a stirring national spectacle with himself, of course, at the heart. Bevan was there, alongside Matron Anne Dolan, to symbolically 'receive the keys' from Lancashire County Council and take charge for the nation of the Davyhulme Park as an NHS hospital. The Minister for Health and Housing had lodged with two local Labour councillors the night before and their daughter June helped serve him breakfast in bed. 'I remember him sitting up in bed in striped pyjamas with a shock of grey hair and my mother putting the tray on his knee and then off he went … I was small, the age you don't take it in, but I knew it was something momentous and my parents had explained what it was all about.' Fittingly, little June Rosen later went on to be deputy clinical lead therapist at cancer treatment hospital The Christie in Manchester after a working life in the NHS.

Later that morning in 1948, Bevan walked up the long drive to the hospital's grand frontage flanked by an honour guard of young nurses. In Ken Loach's passionate and partisan documentary *The Spirit of '45*, we see some photographs of that ceremony – because it really is a ceremony, Bevan saw to that – being passed around and discussed by three of those young nurses, now in their eighties. One of them eulogises Bevan as 'a visionary. Imagine driving a scheme like that through nationwide.' But of the day itself, she more vividly remembers the jam scones they were given for tea. 'Dear God, that was marvellous ... we were still on the ration, remember.' Britain may have been rationing its food, but it was not stinting where it mattered – on compassion and a belief in the public good. In these pictures, in the news footage, 5 July 1948 looks like a glorious morning across the terraces and avenues of Davyhulme, Urmston and Collyhurst, suggesting that God, as many have speculated, is faintly socialist at heart.

Seventy years later, almost to the day, God (or at least a warm front of high pressure moving in from the Azores) has seen to it that the sun shines on me too, as I arrive at what is now called Trafford General Hospital, but which still regards itself as the emotional as well as the physical birthplace of the NHS. I recognise the gates and the wide parade from the pictures of Bevan and the nurses as I stroll in on a crisp April morning. Down the road, the kids of St Anne's Primary file in chattering, swinging their *Paw Patrol* lunchboxes and little parkas. Stately homes and grand civic occasions never move me, but I can bubble up like a blocked sink at ordinary places where people's history has been made, the beautiful mundane. I nearly burst into tears in Paul McCartney's childhood council-house home in Forthlin Road, south Liverpool. I even 'teared up' a bit on the estate in Cumbernauld where *Gregory's Girl* was filmed. But if there was any danger of this happening this morning, it was soon dismissed by the brisk cheerfulness and purpose of my hosts, Matron Julie Treadgold and communications officer Lauren Flanagan, waiting at the door for me. Everything is lovely and welcoming, even for a hospital, and I can feel my loins gently ungirding.

They were previously very much girded because, at the risk of sounding ungrateful, hospitals are fairly low on my list of great places to relax and have fun in. Had I spent more time in them perhaps they would have lost their power to disturb me. As it is, a visit to a hospital generally freaks me out pretty comprehensively, even now when they look less like a clinical facility and more like the reception area of a motorway hotel or a high-street building society. There is still all that unsettling stuff, the signage, the shade of green, the rubber tubes, that smell. Also, there's a piece of writing I can never fully shake on these occasions. 'Ten Types of Hospital Visitor', by Charles Causley, a dark, witty poem by the West Countryman which, after providing pen portraits of the types of people you'll see clutching grapes in the wards and such, ends: 'The ninth visitor is life/The tenth visitor/Is not usually named.'

My relationship with hospitals, that cocktail of fear, curiosity, helplessness and mild titillation, is mirrored and amplified in the feelings of the nation as a whole, I think. All kinds of things are mixed up in there, from *Casualty* to *Green Wing*, *Angels* to *Doctors*. But our relationship with the NHS expresses itself best as comedy, usually black and visceral: Hattie Jacques and Dirk Bogarde, James Robertson Justice brandishing an evilly large hypodermic, Shirley Anne Field taking your temperature, jokes about bedpans, the smack of a surgical glove. In Lindsay Anderson's state-of-the-nation satire *Britannia Hospital*, it becomes a metaphor for Britain under Thatcherism itself in a film described by Danny Leigh as 'a J.G. Ballard take on *Carry On Doctor*'. Alan Bennett's most recent play *Allelujah!* straddled comedy and polemic and continues this conflation of the NHS with Britain itself in all its big-heartedness, mess and embattled chaos. The Health Service is a country of its own, or at least a state within a state, with its own fiefdoms, leaders, armies, capitals. As the General Medical Council boss Niall Dickson once observed, 'The NHS is so vast that you can say just about anything about it – good or bad – and it is probably happening somewhere.'

Our obsession baffles and amuses foreigners, especially Americans, who have managed to put a bloke on the moon without developing a grown-up healthcare system. US comic Erich McElroy, domiciled here for two decades, bases much of his act around a foreigner's shock at receiving 'socialised' medical care. 'I saw a doctor who gave me a couple of pills and sent me on my way. But I still hadn't really done any paperwork. I was like, "This isn't right!" So I went back to the same woman, and I said, "What do I do now?" And she said, "You go home!"' However, this is what his countryman, Nigel Cameron of the right-wing Washington think tank the Center for Policy on Emerging Technologies, had to say at the UnHerd contrarian website: 'The thing that makes Brits most *proud* to be British is the National Health Service. Their affection for it borders on a cult-like devotion … At the heart of the love affair is an obsession with keeping the private sector out. It has blinkered people to the NHS's failings, preventing much needed reform to raise standards. So the time has come to slay this obsession with public-sector delivered healthcare.'

Really? Sorry Nigel, but mess with the NHS, you are dissing and messing with Blighty in all its screwed-up, battered magnificence. The heath service is a secular sacrament in the UK. So much so that a bare-faced lie plastered on the side of a bus about money saved from 'Europe' that would go to the NHS – 350 million non-existent pounds of it a week, you may recall – may well have swung the referendum of 2016 towards the vote to leave the European Union. While the NHS's name is misused, taken in vain, traduced and exploited by Britain's political class and media chatterers, twenty-four hours a day, its workers like Matron Julie Treadgold do their job of keeping it and its patients alive.

'When I started in 1984, it was still Park Hospital, as it was when Nye Bevan came.' Julie stands before what is now Trafford General, beneath the clock tower at the end of the long drive, familiar from the Pathé newsreels and history books. 'A lot of the older generation still call it that. If you have someone in your care with dementia, say, it's often easier to call it Park. They know where they are then. They haven't got a clue where Trafford is.'

Over her quarter of a century here, Julie has seen successive waves of reforms and initiatives, some good, some less so, shape and occasionally batter the fabric of the NHS. Various reports such as Cochrane and Griffin, regular white papers, black papers and Royal Commissions have tinkered with the organisational and pay structures, introduced new layers of management and boosted consultant numbers, reorganised and re-designed hospitals and their wards, often without asking people like Matron Julie.

'These wards here, they're the new extension. Before that they were the long Nightingale wards.' She notices my blank expression. 'You know, the old-fashioned ones you see in the Florence Nightingale illustrations. Where you could see at a glance all the patients all the way down. No single rooms and they can shout you if someone's fallen. In 1994, they changed all that and made them into "hotel facilities" with carpeted bays, which is great ... ' a wry pause '... in a hotel. So then in 2002 we ripped them all out again having realised that it just wasn't appropriate in a hospital.'

Here is exactly the kind of thinking that has dogged public institutions for several decades now. Under the guise of 'reforms', of making them 'more agile' or 'fitter and leaner', the overstretched and underfunded public sector is subject to continual change and tinkering in the name of improvement, but really in the pursuit of ideological rectitude. The burden of these reforms is known to every weary and dispirited public servant; new computer systems that don't work and have to be scrapped having lost millions, marketing men put in charge of radio networks, accountants and 'change management' experts brought in at vast expense to ruin perfectly good school-meal systems or bus timetables or hospital rotas. 'If it ain't broke it, break it' has been the guiding mantra of British politicians since the dawn of the 1980s. This, I stress, is my opinion. If it's Julie's, she doesn't express it. She's too busy, probably.

'The average age of our patients is still around seventy-six. So
that feeds into our specialisms ... stroke, "neuro", orthopaedics,
dementia, complex health. We're in the middle of a working-class
community with a lot of elderly people, very much the same kind
of community and patients we had when Nye opened the place.'
Trafford General's awareness of its storied past is everywhere. It
wears its history as proudly, if less ornately, as any Venetian palazzo
or Berkshire stately home. Under glass on the boardroom wall is
the spade that dug the first of the hospital's foundations. Here is a
black-and-white picture of Bevan talking to the very first NHS
patient, a girl of thirteen in bed with acute and life-threatening
liver disease. Little Sylvia Diggory later became a talismanic figure
around the hospital, often called upon to share her memory of this
moment. 'He was charismatic and larger than life, very charming
and articulate, with the most attractive voice with a Welsh lilt. In
no time at all he had everyone in the hospital like a gigantic fan
club ... Mr Bevan asked me if I understood the significance of the
occasion and told me that it was a milestone in history – the most
civilised step any country had ever taken.'

Along many of the corridors where rows of patients wait, well,
patiently with their iPhones, Lee Childs and *Heat* magazines
(though sadly no small boys with saucepans on their heads) are
photographs of the staff. I spot Julie there, and she makes an
embarrassed face and scuttles on. Like the young Asian man who
hotwired my mother-in-law's heart, Matron Julie has all the virtues
I've come to associate with the NHS, a crisp but kindly competence
and a clear-eyed, compassionate grown-upness with none of the
drippy flummery and cant of various homeopaths, ear-candlers and
horse-whisperers I've encountered. Julie is not just staff. She had
her three daughters here, though the maternity unit is now gone.
The various changes at Trafford mirror the evolution, for good
and ill, of the NHS down its seven decades. Julie points to a little
sunlit courtyard framed with bouquets and memorials. 'That's a
sad reminder of when we had a maternity unit. Not every story
ends happily. There's the chapel of prayer. There's the new diabetes

centre. That's coping with what's a modern epidemic. All funds raised by one of our consultants. We did have a nurses' home until a week or so but that's gone.'

She nods outside to where diggers perform some noisy choreography on a patch of rubble. I let out a wistful sigh. Back in my early twenties, becalmed between college and getting a job at the *NME*, some of most enjoyable nights of that drab time were parties at the nurses' home at Wigan Infirmary, opposite the gates of Haigh Woodland Park. The hedonism and excess of these nights in those hallowed halls were legendary. Once, in the 1970s, an irresponsible junior doctor laced the punch with ethanol with fatal results. Even in the late 80s, when such craziness was gone, the 'liveliness' of get-togethers there was well-known. I once developed a fever after a tooth abscess and lay sweating, groaning and delirious on my bed at home for two days straight. A visiting friend who'd let himself in took one look at me, smiled, and asked, 'Nurses party?'

I don't mention any of this to Julie, although she looks to be having a little reverie herself, gazing through the mesh fence at the hi-vis, hard hats and JCBs. 'I was on the first floor. Room forty-two. Three floors. As you got more senior you got a double room. There must have been over a hundred of us in there. Neat little kitchen, toast and eggs, shared bathrooms, rows of showers. When they pulled it down I went down and took a little brick as a souvenir.'

Trafford General is not just a historic reminder of our once-visionary civic spirit. It's a vast, busy, working hospital, still 'the Park' to many of the big urban working-class community it serves. 'Our population hasn't changed much. But even here, there's been a bit of gentrification. House prices have shot up since they built the Trafford Centre and there's some nice big houses on the quiet side roads.' The hospital bustles as it has done for seventy years. But the challenges are greater than ever, and 'challenge' here is not just marketing consultancy or election leaflet guff but a daily reality for people like Julie.

'Every year more money needs to be saved. We have to do that without it affecting patient care, without the patient even noticing ideally, and that is very, very difficult. You saw the diabetes centre. That was paid for by the efforts of a member of staff. "Patient Choice" [and the way Julie says it you can just hear the capital letters and quote marks, another imposed strategy] means we have to accommodate all the people who want to come here. The people who've read the CQC[3] ratings report and say, "I want to go to Trafford," which is fine but it all costs money.'

That week in spring, the public institutions of this corner of Manchester have had two famous visitors. Prime Minister Theresa May, flanked by armed police outriders in a thundering motorcade, visited a local junior school. Here she met awkwardly with children who were specially selected and vetted by staff and instructed not to mention any recent political events or Jeremy Corbyn. More significantly for the people of the area, Sir Alex Ferguson had been admitted to Salford Royal with a suspected bleed on the brain. ('We're nearer,' smiles Julie, 'but they're a centre of excellence. He's absolutely in the right place.') While I'm at Trafford General, the visitors come and go, less famous but no less welcome. A young girl dashes in crying 'Grannie' and then, like all of us, is delighted by the unexpected arrival and wagging tail of a black Labrador. Rufus is the ward dog. Julie, bending to pet him, says, 'Without wanting to offend anyone I can definitely say that this is my cutest member of staff.' (I can confirm that competition is stiff in this regard.) 'He's very intuitive. He knows who to go to. On the neuro rehab unit often they're not very coordinated and so they can't stroke him properly. But he intuitively strokes and rubs their hand with his head. The kids love him. The staff love him. The stroke ward love him, which is appropriate,' she adds with a smile.

I notice both the time on the clock tower and the host of various people wanting to speak to Julie and Lauren, and decide

[3] Care Quality Commission, independent health regulator for England.

I've taken up enough of their time. 'Oh, we like showing off,' laughs Julie. 'We're very aware of our history, Stuart, and very proud of it.' So they should be. When the ministerial visits are over, when the awkward glad-handing is done, when the walkie-talkies have ceased to crackle and the sleek black armoured cars of the motorcade are roaring back to London full of bored, relieved apparatchiks, someone like Julie is stroking a worried damp brow, or wiping away snot or tears or blood, or watching closely a green blip move across a screen or a gauge or a dial while a black Labrador called Rufus gently nuzzles a mottled, shaky hand.

I'm not the kind of dupe who thinks Cuba is a socialist paradise or a model country. I hope I'm not that sappy brand of 'useful idiot' apologist whose love of Stalinism annoyed Orwell. I know that Cuba's economy is a mess (although being sanctioned and blockaded by the world's only superpower surely didn't help). I know that freedoms were curtailed and unsatisfactory and they had a dire human rights record. But I am curious of the one area where the Cubans look to have got it objectively and emphatically right, even in the eyes of a disbelieving world.

In 2006, according to a *Newsnight* report, Cuba's state healthcare system was one of 'the world's best public services'. In 2000, Secretary General of the United Nations Kofi Annan said, 'Cuba should be the envy of many other nations. Cuba demonstrates how much nations can do with the resources they have if they focus on the right priorities – health, education, and literacy.' Rich Warner, a PhD student at Anglia Ruskin University, Cambridge, made his points powerfully in an online magazine piece.

> The Cuban healthcare service has stood the test of time. It has afforded a foreigner like myself the opportunity to study a career free of charge while many of my colleagues are thousands of dollars in debt after attending medical schools in the US. It ensures that open heart surgery doesn't result in lifelong indebtedness. It has created

globally competitive biotechnology and pharmaceutical industries. It doesn't turn people away because of their socioeconomic status. It is a system that has been there for its people. Yes, it has its flaws and challenges which need remedying, but it is not merely a propaganda tool for the powers that be.

And its influence is felt in places far from Havana.

As a Lancastrian, it irks me to admit it – since it gives the locals one more thing to be bumptious about – but Yorkshire is a bloody beautiful county. The vexation is softened slightly by the knowledge that some of the quietest, most desolate, loveliest places lie near to 'our' bit, in the debatable lands between Lancashire and Yorkshire, that great band of lonely hills and moors that rise from Keighley and famed Brontëland, down over Halifax, Huddersfield and Barnsley to Sheffield. On a fine spring morning, if the traffic is light and the birds are singing, there are worse commutes than Manchester to 'Sheff' or 'Wakey' or 'Tarn' across this landscape, past the tough and tender towns and villages: Tintwistle, Edale, Stalybridge, Glossop, Chapel-en-le-Frith and the rest, overlooked by sombre ridges, nestled in those scooped Pennine hollows, dotted by dark, shining reservoirs.

The only hint that the gorgeous low farmhouse I'm approaching, perched high above this Pennine wilderness between the Woodhead Pass and Longdendale, doesn't belong to an old established farming family or local nobility is the Durham-issue truck piled with black coal proudly displayed on a raised plinth by the driveway. Bold and stark against the distant haze of hills and horizon, it's a reminder of how most people once made their livings here, hard and good livings, fought for fiercely down the years before king coal was deposed.

Margaret and Jim are the lucky folk who live here. They're at the door when I arrive down the long, rutted track, quick to welcome me in with tea and introductions to the family. I shake hands with a tall smiling young man with a mug in hand. 'His brother's upstairs on the PlayStation probably. Saturday morning, after all, but this one ... he takes after his granddad. Going to go into politics,' says Margaret Scargill with quiet pride.

The name 'Scargill' probably terrifies some people. Even shorn of any connotation, it sounds stark and forbidding, maybe a rough ascent route of a northern peak or a dark dale in winter. Then there are those connotations, a bogeyman from old scare stories, a name to be feared, a folk demon. Not so much by my folk though. Where I come from, in the towns and streets I grew up in, the name 'Scargill' draws a different, more nuanced response. Still problematic perhaps to some. But not to the many who, though memories might still be conflicted and raw, associate it with the values of community, the defiance of the ruling paymasters, the fight for working people's jobs and way of life.

Margaret Scargill is the daughter of Arthur Scargill, who led the National Union of Mineworkers throughout the bitter and momentous strike of 1984–5, and Anne Scargill, co-founder of the Women Against Pit Closures movement which approached the strike not as a demand for higher wages but as a struggle for jobs for kids and grandkids and the preservation of communities. They have since divorced, but their names are forever linked in working-class history. Both were products of that class at its most powerful and informed, thanks to the strong links between trade unionism – especially mining – and education. (Arthur Scargill studied economics and social history at Leeds University in the early 60s.)

Jim hands out strong tea. We take a seat at a sturdy farmhouse table and Margaret takes a thoughtful sip. 'I'll say one thing for my dad. He stuck up for me when I was told that I wasn't bright enough to be a vet or a doctor. My teachers said, "Don't aim so high, Margaret. If you must want to do this, apply to be a nurse." But my dad, credit where it's due, said we're not having that attitude.' Margaret went to Sheffield Poly then to the university for a Master's in research physiology. From there to Barts: 'where they took you based on your interview not your A levels ... then to

Leeds to train to be a GP. I worked with this old laid-back Asian doctor from Scunthorpe and he was great. He just cracked on with his paperwork and would tell me, "You see the next one," and then that would be the next and then the next … and so I became a career GP. Once I'd finished my training I thought about moving away but decided to stay and work at the local GP surgery in the area I was born. Kendray, central Barnsley, depressed, rundown, lots of social problems and a surgery that was operating out of a little terraced house back then in 1996. But that was all going to change. That's where I met Jim.'

It was my friend the actress Maxine Peake who suggested I get in touch with Margaret Scargill and Jim Logan, both of whom she'd got to know when writing a play about Margaret's mum, Anne. 'If you're writing about the NHS then you should go and see what they've done at their NHS practice in Barnsley. It's amazing.' Jim and Margaret are two of the chief protagonists here in a story about individual brilliance and innovation in the service of the welfare state. The other I guess is Fidel Castro. But let's start with Jim.

'I was underground at fifteen and a half,' says Jim. 'Grimethorpe. Left a bit of meself down there actually.' He lifts the hand not clutching his tea mug and shows me a right thumb that ends suddenly just after the knuckle. 'Worked my way up to underground manager. The Coal Board had a very clear and direct management structure. There were half a million men working in mining but the chain of command, if you like, was very short; coal-face, then underground manager, then manager, then regional director, then chairman of the NCB. Seven steps between the coal-face and the top of the organisation. You wouldn't get that anywhere now. We were brilliantly trained. Years at night school, constantly appraised, taught to understand mining and manage-ment as well as to be businessmen. So when Grimethorpe closed in '93, I had a set of very transferable managerial skills. And I decided to take 'em to the NHS.'

*

The scars of the mines ran deeper than on Jim's hands. When the last coal was cut from Grimethorpe in 1993 and the once proud pit (home of the world-renowned colliery brass band) closed, the heart was ripped from the area. Unless you've known the intense collective life and vivacity of a pit village in its prime, you can't fully appreciate the sense of desolation and abandonment that came over places like Grimethorpe (or Ferryhill or Easington or Knottingley) once those mines were gone. A year after the pit closed, an EU survey said Grimethorpe was the poorest and sickest village in the country. Unemployment throughout the 1990s stood at 50 per cent. Crime rocketed from 30 per cent below the national average to 20 per cent above.

Two things contributed to a kind of resurgence in pride and community spirit, if not in material wealth and prosperity. One was the success of the movie *Brassed Off*, celebrating the spirit of the pit villages here as embodied in the families of the Grimethorpe Colliery Band. The other came from further afield as noted in a mildly surprised but suitably impressed report in the *Independent* newspaper of October 2006. Under the headline 'A New Revolution in Grimethorpe; Cuban-style Socialist Health Care in South Yorkshire', it continued:

> A former pit worker is to bring Cuban-style health care, administered by Arthur Scargill's daughter, to Grimethorpe ... The Oaks Park primary care centre, built at a cost of £3m, is the phoenix that has risen out of the ashes of the closure of the Grimethorpe colliery in South Yorkshire. For the locals, its grand opening this month was an event to compare with the sudden rise to fame of the local brass band. Built with the backing and input of the Scargill family ... the Primary Oaks scheme is the brainchild of Jim Logan, Arthur Scargill's son-in-law and the one-time Grimethorpe colliery manager, who made a study of the Cuban health system. According to Mr Logan, Fidel Castro's health reforms provide a model

that the Health Secretary would do well to follow. The Cuban healthcare system is recognised not only as one of the best in the developing world, but also as better in some aspects than those in the developed world.

More tea, and Jim explains his unusual epiphany. 'The mining communities and NUM had always had links with Cuba, and through that I'd got to know a cardiologist there and clearly they were doing something right. I went to see him and he showed us everything they did at their hospital and all the polyclinics in every Cuban town and village. The GP sits in the centre of this hub and everyone else's room radiates off from him or her. They're the gatekeeper. They see him or her first but then he can say, you need kidney advice? Go next door. Your knees need looking at properly? Pop across the corridor. Direct referral. Everything under the same roof. It is a one-stop shop that they do better in Cuba than anywhere else. So I thought we should try it in Barnsley.'

Despite a struggling economy, thanks to those American sanctions and the end of Soviet aid, Cuba's healthcare system puts ours to shame in some respects. There's a doctor for every hundred and fifty people as opposed to our single doctor for three times that amount at least. It was the first Latin American country to legalise abortion and has significantly lower infant mortality rates and an increasingly favourable life expectancy compared to its wealthy neighbour, the United States of America. As stated, I'm wary of romanticising the Cuban regime and ignoring its many faults. But let's also be slow to automatically assume our superiority in all things. Sceptics and critics say that there is limited choice. At the risk of sounding like Fidel himself, I think choice might sometimes be over-rated. Private healthcare in Cuba is both illegal and, frankly, unnecessary.

Not everyone thinks like this, though. Jim's visionary plans met with resistance, and not just from the politically and ideologically opposed. 'GPs are naturally risk averse. Also, Jim's nickname is Mr Marmite,' says Margaret, not unfondly. 'He rubs people up the wrong way, especially middle-class health professionals and the new breed of NHS manager. He's a bluff northerner who's spent a working life underground and hasn't quite realised that you can't deal with them like you dealt with pitmen. And then after we'd got together, he'd come home and get it in the neck from me from the GP's point of view ... the other coalface, so to speak.'

In his own words: 'I made a nuisance of myself. People come into NHS management these days who know nothing about the organisation. I spent six months visiting everybody at every level. I sat in waiting rooms and talked to patients, talked to consultants, read every White Paper. If you're a boss in a mine ... well, put it this way, you can't lie to pitmen because you'll end up with a broken jaw. You learn to be brief and to be truthful. I believed in uniting all the services in one place, particularly health and social care. But they turned me down.' Undeterred, Jim drew up plans for a Cuban-style health centre in rundown central Barnsley and, by reaching out throughout the community, funded the project himself.

The results were transformative. As well as seven GPs, of which Margaret was the most senior, the new centre provided a whole suite of medical treatments: chiropody, dental services, ophthalmology, pharmacy, dietetics, midwives, community psychiatric services, physiotherapy. It caters not just for health issues but for connected wider social needs, such as housing and benefits. As a GP in a former mining community, Margaret knew all about respiratory diseases and heart problems. But these were just the obvious symptoms of a post-industrial community's problems.

'My surgery is often full of people with complex life issues – kids in care, drugs, unemployment, housing problems – none of which are treatable with a pill. These are social issues and they're depressed because of the circumstances of their life. How do we help them? We can give them Prozac but what does that do? But if I as a GP have that instant access under my roof, I can get social services involved to help them with their debt, we can help them through the maze of claims and benefits. We can get schools to help with their kids. They trust me to act as "signpost" (that's the buzzword) to avenues that they don't know about because they're in despair. I've been here twenty-three years. They've grown up with me. If Dr Scargill says it, it must be all right.'

'And it just felt good,' points out Jim. 'A big shiny new thing that's nice to be in. Plenty of light. Convenient. Everything under one roof. Everybody uses the same computers, telephones, canteen. Open seven days a week, twenty-four hours a day. It works.' TV companies and newspapers flocked to see it. New Labour were soon borrowing Jim's ideas. 'Tony Blair tried to do it on the cheap, though, and cosmetically,' says Margaret. 'Stick a café in and what have you. But Jim was a maverick. He designed it, funded it and built it with this community in mind. Their version was a mass-produced, "one size fits all" approach where you got the same building in Barnsley and Surrey. Barnsley and Surrey have very different needs, Stuart.'

'Just a bit,' agrees Jim wryly. Once Margaret's workload would have involved the usual mining community GPs' complaints: 'TB, chest infections, lung disease. Now it's drugs, obesity, diabetes. I even had a case of malaria this week.' They have also become a victim of their own success, bursting at the seams with patients and relentlessly, insanely busy. 'We're so trusted and liked that we've had to convert our emergency room into a mini-*ER* department. They come to us with heart attacks, strokes, anaphylactic shocks, everything, rather than go to A&E. They assume we can deal with everything. We got into the local paper the other day because we had to shock a bloke back to life. They come to us in states of major collapse and I do want to say, "Why have you come here? Get to the bloody hospital." But they just say, "Oh, I know you'll sort me out, Dr Scargill."'

Before I leave, I ask the question you read in every trenchant, pessimistic newspaper column and hear on every earnest discussion show: Is the NHS in crisis? Yes, answer both instantly, but their diagnosis is not what you might think. 'It's not necessarily underfunded. Just hugely mismanaged at every level,' says Jim. 'I've not met anyone with vision beyond their little empire. No sense of a bigger picture.'

'It's overmanaged,' says Margaret firmly. 'The money is going to all the wrong stuff. It's misspent. I'm well paid. I think I get a good wage and my colleagues feel the same. I don't want more money. I just want the freedom to treat my patients and longer to treat them. If a lass comes to me with bad shoulders and chronic leg ulcers, I've got ten minutes to help her. And that might just be the tip of her iceberg. I don't want a pay rise. I just want a manageable day.'

Margaret bemoans cultures of box ticking and overmedication and sees a very simple cause for the acute and chronic crisis in GP recruitment. 'Why would you join a profession when columnists will say that you're fat and cosseted and overpaid and just play golf all the time? Why do it when the *Daily Mail* calls you rubbish, incompetent or a child-killer every day? Why would you do that? Because of Shipman, we have a new system of an extra fifty hours of assessment and "education and self-reflection" to keep your ticket. Shipman would have passed that with flying colours because he was a psychopath! We face aggression and mismanagement and just a general lack of respect. One bloke said to me, "I'd love to have your job, it's a doss. All you do is just talk to people all day."' Jim quietly bridles. 'God, I'd love to live in his mind. What a simple little world that must be. She's in at five every day.'

Margaret smiles. 'The very least of my troubles is Dr Google. I don't mind that. At least it's funny. They come in with their notes they've made off the internet and I say, what do you reckon you've got then, lad, beriberi? Lassa fever? Let's have a look, then.'

I say my goodbyes and leave past the pit truck and into a golden morning over a quiet Woodhead and Longdendale. I remember that these generous, passionate and hard-working individuals, their colleagues and the communities they serve, were once dismissed and defamed by Margaret Thatcher as 'the enemy within'. If so, they are an enemy I am proud and happy to call friends.

But that's enough about all that. Let's get back to me.

In the grand scheme and the great narrative of the National Health Service, Whiston Hospital, Prescot, Merseyside, has the significance of neither Trafford General nor Glanamman cottage hospital where the NHS itself and its first baby were born respectively. But NHS baby 8,047,970, Maconie, Stuart John,[4] attaches great significance to 'Whizzy Ossie' (as the Scouse locals call it) since here's where I came into the world, in the same excitable summer of change that Kennedy was nominated for president and Benin, Burkino Faso, Ivory Coast, Chad, the Congo and Ghana all threw off the imperialist yoke. It was a big month for world affairs and in suburban Merseyside, I was doing my bit.

A popular online encyclopaedia informs me that Whiston started life as a workhouse established by the Poor Law Union in 1843, adding a cholera isolation ward in 1871. On the 1948 establishment of the NHS, it was known as 'The County' and accommodated 500 patients. It's now a major teaching hospital serving four million people across the north. In the year I was born, a burns and plastic-surgery unit was set up, now one of the best in Europe. But that is the only mention of any significant events in the hospital's history for 1960, I note, a little disappointed.

Now, for the first time since I left swaddled and dribbling that summer half a century ago, I am back. I can't tell you whether the old place has changed much but it certainly looks the very model of a major modern hospital, a grand, sleek, futuristic building,

---

[4] In fact, despite being told all my life that my middle name is John, there is no record of any middle name on my birth certificate. My mum recently said that she made one up when I asked as a child because she thought I 'wanted one'. Hence, my passport, credit cards and bank details are all inaccurate and probably illegal.

more like a huge, modernist hotel than a 'ossie'. There is a branch of Costa in reception, and on the signage that indicates the gastro-urinary department and the IC ward an arrow points up to the Spice of Life restaurant on the top floor. With that promising name, I'm looking forward to flock wallpaper, sitar music and chutney trays, but sadly, it's just a modern café/canteen albeit with panoramic views above suburban Prescot. I scan the rows of patients/customers and spot, through the kids in replica Everton kits and old chaps in dressing gowns, the man I've come to meet. A man who has done as much as anyone to champion the public image of the NHS in recent years and who also conveniently happens to live just down the road.

'I am totally a product of the nanny state,' says Frank Cottrell-Boyce – writer, dramatist, actor, and general all-round force for good – over his latte. 'State school, educated myself in libraries, never gone private for anything, full grants all my life. Those things that the state does for you, these are all the things that tell you you're valuable, that you're an asset. The nanny state. When they told us how awful the nanny state apparently was, they didn't tell us they were going to replace it with the Wicked Uncle Abanazar state, did they?'

I didn't watch the opening ceremony of the 2012 London Olympic Games as it went out. Opening ceremonies are all always a bit naff, daft and overlong aren't they, so to be honest I didn't expect much from it. Next morning over breakfast, I learned otherwise. I read in every paper, broadsheet, tabloid (left, right, centre or indifferent), that in fact the ceremony had been a scarcely believable triumph; warm, funny, joyous, powerful, intelligent and spectacular. In a chorus of acclamation, it seemed to have managed the impossible: to have genuinely celebrated the best of the nation, made us enormously proud in a uniquely healthy, respectful, unobjectionable way, put a spring in the nation's step and confounded cynics who had to rapidly rewrite their half-completed advance copy. I fired up the BBC iPlayer and several hours later realised, from the opening tableau of the forging of the fiery

Olympic rings in Britain's industrial furnaces, to the skilful nods to *The Tempest* and classic children's literature to a stunning and audacious tribute to the NHS, exactly what I'd missed.

Frank's friend and colleague Danny Boyle, the film director from down the East Lancs Road in Bury, had already conjured a potent image of British healthcare when he gave us Cillian Murphy waking up in a deserted London hospital in the zombie horror movie *28 Days Later*. But there the effect was chilling. When he wanted to celebrate the NHS ('the institution that most unites our nation') in the Olympic opening ceremony he enlisted his friend, Frank. Cottrell-Boyce is one of the country's leading writers for film, TV and children. He was the man who, when a writer on *Coronation Street*, made sure there was always a copy of *Living Marxism* prominently displayed in the corner shop. I imagine when Culture Secretary Jeremy Hunt learned that this was the man who'd be writing the opening ceremony that would have the eyes of the world upon it, he was so delighted.

This would be the first time since 1948 – the year the NHS was born – that Britain had staged an Olympiad. So it was appropriate that in the opening ceremony, alongside elaborate, brilliant celebrations of Britain's industrial heritage, music, literature and culture, Boyle and Cottrell-Boyce decided to stage an emotional celebration of the National Health Service itself. Six hundred actual NHS staff would take part in a choreographed display of pride, climaxing with the holding aloft of three huge illuminated letters spelling NHS. A billion viewers around the world saw it, many of them only dimly aware of what the NHS was. For their benefit, FCB wrote the broadcast notes for the different national broadcasters. 'We all reverted to core skills. I wrote Huw Edwards some bullet points and the press notes for the world's media that went to every single outlet. I just loved the fact that some chap from the Midwest would be reading all this stuff out verbatim desperately trying to keep up, telling great swathes of Middle America all this stuff about "treatment on the National Health Service is completely free at the point of delivery".

Essentially, a whole load of propaganda for the NHS, and he just wouldn't have the time to stop and think or censor himself.'

Bold and inspiring and unashamedly (though genially) political, it left no one in any doubt as to where the makers' hearts lay. But any critics poised to snipe were wrongfooted, disarmed even, by the overwhelming sweetness, integrity and wit of it all. 'Giles Coren [*The Times*] had already written an article saying how shit it was. Did you know that? He's very open about it. He wrote, "Depending what time you're reading this it's either Tellytubby pomp rock nonsense or the greatest night of our lives." Later he said, "You had me at 'Nimrod'." So fair play to him, I suppose. Then there was a Tory MP, Aidan Burley, who also weighed in. He said on Twitter it was, quote, "leftie multicultural crap", and then quickly realised he was on his own on this. My son Jo, my eldest, called me up and said, "You've divided the nation." I said, "Really?" And he said, "Yes, there's the nation and there's this one guy who didn't like it." As someone said, "Mate, if you think this is multicultural, wait till you see Team GB."'

'We put a lot of ourselves into it,' continues Frank. 'But it became much more than our script. It became the joy and pride of those volunteers who all worked in the NHS. Danny always says you can tell just by watching how a film has been made and what it was like to work on. And you can tell in the NHS sequence of our show how much people were loving being part of it, how much they relished the opportunity to stand up and say, "I love the NHS." They gave up a hundred hours each, but you can see the pride.'

It's not hard to find a sourish irony though in the fact that the chief musical element in the NHS celebration was an extract from *Tubular Bells* played by its creator Mike Oldfield. His mother was a nurse who later needed the long-term care of the NHS for mental health issues. *Tubular Bells* is a lengthy, entirely instrumental suite written and played by a troubled but precocious teenager, which could only find a home back in 1973 on Richard Branson's new Virgin label, itself a fanciful and fledgling hippieish endeavour.

Tubular Bells has since sold in excess of twenty million copies around the world and its success formed the cornerstone of the global capitalist conglomerate responsible for thirty-five or so divisions of business (one of which is a catering start-up competition called 'Foodpreneur', a name which makes me wish for the swift extinction of the human race).

In the past I've found myself oddly ambivalent about Richard Branson. Though I'm unlikely to ever be invited to Necker Island, I've met him and he seemed personable enough. As stated in the prologue, I don't think all entrepreneurs and business people are the very embodiment of human evil because, well, because I'm a grown-up. Also, I can't quite cast the man who sold the twelve-year-old me those terrific, mind-bending Philip Glass, Henry Cow and Gong albums for a pocket-money-friendly 50p as a rapacious anti-social villain who's trying to destroy our beloved NHS. The evidence, though, seems to lead to that inescapable conclusion.

True, the NHS has never been as utterly and purely 'free' as we might romantically think. Some services, like dentistry, optical care and the pharmacy, have had substantial private sector provision for decades. Both the Blair and Brown governments increased the use of private providers into the NHS on the typically Thatcherite grounds of 'choice' and 'competition'. Car-parking services were farmed out to the private sector and have since become a controversial cash cow for hospital trusts and their shareholders, seen by some as a 'tax on the sick'.

But since the return of the Conservatives alone or in coalition, first under Cameron, then May and now Johnson, the drive towards privatisation seems to have gained pace, while being at the same time publicly denied. The Health and Social Care Act 2012 extended market-based approaches, emphasising again spurious competition and equally spurious notions of choice. Certainly no patient or taxpayer chose some of the fat contractual offers that ensued: £1.2 billion offered to deliver end-of-life and cancer care in Staffordshire, £800 million paid out to provide services for older people in Cambridgeshire and Peterborough. Private providers salivated at the thought but after much criticism, both tender offers were dropped.

Similar controversy followed the franchising of Hinchingbrooke Hospital, Huntingdon to a private operator called Circle. In January 2015, Circle announced that it would hand management of Hinchingbrooke back to the NHS as a result of financial pressures and the hospital having been put into special measures. This is the classic failure narrative of privatisation, seen in schools, law enforcement, finance, transport and more; hand the contracts out to privateers, and when it becomes apparent that they cannot or will not do the job – usually because it's harder or less profitable than it looked on the boardroom spreadsheet – hand the mess back to the state and the taxpayer to sort out.

Even so, according to the think tank the Centre for Health and the Public Interest, over a quarter of NHS provision is now in private hands, far higher than the official figure of around 9 per cent. The 2012 Health and Social Care Act obliges – forces in other words – NHS clinical commissioning bodies in England to tender out to the market any contract worth more than the weirdly specific figure of £615,278 or more. This has meant a huge and lucrative increase in contracts awarded to profit-driven firms like Richard's Virgin Care and Care UK. Virgin Care alone has won more than £2 billion in contracts from the NHS over the last five years and holds more than 400. Worse, Virgin Care won undisclosed damages from the NHS in 2017 after it sued them, citing concerns over 'serious flaws' in the way a children's care contract was awarded in Surrey. If he was behind this, well, frankly, I don't care how good the Gong albums were. He can go to hell.

Alongside the Chinese People's Liberation Army, the Indian railways and the Walmart supermarket chain, the NHS, with 1.64 million workers, is one of the largest employers in the world. It shares the bureaucratic complexity and missionary zeal of the first two and, increasingly, the marketplace ethics of the latter. From those seedling beginnings in a working-class Mancunian suburb in a ravaged and weakened nation, the NHS now casts its net of care wide across the United Kingdom. Its furthest outposts reach as far as the kingdom itself, from Dr Herdman's surgery on Main Street, Belleek, Fermanagh, in the west to the one on the flat road to Lowestoft Ness in the east, from the community hospital on King Edward Lane, St Mary's, on the Isles of Scilly to the far north of the Shetland Islands and the health centre with, as Dr Susan Bowie will happily tell you, 'the best view from a desk in the world'.

Look past the Anglepoise lamp, the stethoscope holder and the blood-pressure monitor, and there is the beautiful, curving crescent of Hillswick Bay in the far Northmavine of Shetland. On this fine spring evening, the breakers are rolling in over white sand, over shingle and seaweed and jagged rocks. To the right in the sparkling air, I watch the white horses dash and foam at the base of the high and rugged crumbling ochre cliffs where, remote and mysterious, Eshaness Lighthouse stands. Here the land opens into the maw of the ocean in sudden and vertiginous 'geos', bays and inlets, and during the 'White Nights' of June, the sunset lasts forever.

It's seven o'clock when I arrive, after the last patient has gone and the last note and prescription has been written. If it goes dark at all tonight, it won't be till two or three in the morning and even then it'll be a thin covering of night, the 'simmer dim', thrown over the spectral bay for an hour or so before the sun starts its slow climb again over the most wild and beautiful part of Britain. 'I call this my happy valley. Look at my commute. Look at that view. Is that not stunning?' smiles Susan as I stand gazing mutely out to sea. 'I never tire of it. It's always amazing, and when a big storm builds and starts to roll in, it's incredible.' What she doesn't say until later, over a glass of wine (me not her) in the panelled wood dining room of the St Magnus Bay Hotel, is that it was these reddish, sheer granite cliffs that she dangled over on the coastguard's rope during her training for a doctor's life here on the edge of the world.

Dr Bowie, a warm, funny Glaswegian, has run the UK's most northerly health centre for twenty-five years. She'd come to Shetland originally when a medical student, taking summer jobs in the fish factories of the capital Lerwick. 'I had a pal who came here and she said, "Come up, you'll love it," and I did. It was quite well paid, two hundred and eighty pounds a week, no tax, and you got free kippers. So I came for quite a few summers in the 1970s. I made loads of pals here and then when I qualified as a GP in Glasgow and was getting away from a guy, one of those pals called and said there's a job in Shetland. So I thought I'd come for six months. That was in 1984.' She and husband Tom did move to the Highlands of Scotland for a few years, 'but it was the kind of place where you had one playgroup for the locals and one for the offcomers so I thought, fuck that, frankly. So I came back as locum in Brae and we were given an old ruined croft in '94 and we've been here ever since.' Her children were raised here. Two of them are training to be doctors. One has just graduated from Aberdeen and is back in Hillswick. 'Tonight she's gone down to the carnival at the village hall dressed as a bear or something ... I don't think we'll see her till morning,' she says with a smile. Her son James was a contestant on *The Great British Bake Off* and has written a cookbook with dad Tom called *Shetland: Cooking on the Edge of the World*.

For Susan then, the love affair with Shetland began in the unpromising environs of the scale and slime of the fish-gutting floor. For me, it was the half-hour drive from Sumburgh airport to Lerwick, north through the quiet magnificence of the summer landscape, the crystal blue and green of the seas, sometimes dotted with orcas and basking seals, the awesome rolling ridges and hills, massive and deserted but benign, the scattered brightly coloured homesteads, the painted boats, and the gloomy distant hulk of Foula, the loneliest of the Shetlands' hundred or so islands, mostly uninhabited like tiny Mousa off the other coast with its gigantic Iron Age tower or 'broch'. The feel is not Scottish, certainly not British, more Scandinavian (which it was part of until 1469), but it is in the end, utterly 'Shetland', which you soon learn is a magical and indefinable thing of its own. I'd been invited to play a show at the fabulous Mareel arts centre, built like so much of Shetland on oil money, and I was in love before I checked into my hotel. I may not have actually moved here like Susan, but I come here whenever I can. I have fallen just as hard.

Susan has 800 patients spread over 77 square miles of moorland, heath and shore. It's by no means a small amount and there are very particular health issues here: high rates of inflammatory bowel disease, obesity and rheumatoid arthritis. She allows fifteen minutes per consultation, as opposed to the brief five or ten you'd get with a doctor in most urban practices. When other doctors or locums arrive, she hands them an OS map covered in thirty or so dots to represent the elderly or housebound patients dispersed across this beautiful but empty, high and remote northern edge of Britain. Knowledge of Shetland's lonely valleys and bays and the twists and straights of its unlit single-track roads is vital, since the 'White Nights' of summer are soon over and October brings endless dark ones with just the lights of isolated homesteads and the dull glow of Europe's largest oil terminal, Sullom Voe, to navigate by.

Susan loves this place and the people of the Northmavine adore her, it's clear. But a doctor's life this far north can be tough. There have been good times and bad. The good times came shortly after Susan came to Hillswick in the late 90s and early years of this century when Tony Blair's currently much maligned government oversaw a huge improvement in British healthcare. In 2002, Chancellor Gordon Brown increased National Insurance by a penny to pay for the largest-ever increase in NHS funding, and in the years that followed, patient satisfaction reached record levels.

'It was a good time,' she says. 'It was a gilded age really. The Labour government pumped in lots of money. We had a great primary care service in Lerwick. There were funds. There was optimism. We called it the Golden Years. Then from about 2004, things began to change. There were a series of complicated new contracts. Then we were all assessed by Deloitte, the accountants.

They didn't even come round. They looked at a map and decided how much doctor time this practice needed. And they decided it needed zero-point-eight of a doctor.' If you want a snapshot of the brazen wrong-headedness that has characterised British policy making and the national political culture in the years since 1979, here it is. An accountant in London in clothes that probably cost more than Dr Bowie earned in a month sitting in judgement on men and women like her, consigning the sick to yet more pain and inconvenience with the stroke of a Mont Blanc pen.

'I was earning thirty thousand pounds a year and living in a ruined croft. I thought I'd have to give up the practice. I had five sleepless weeks of worrying about how to tell the staff [she employs six part-time workers], but then I realised that my old contract still held and was still valid, and out of that came a pay rise that meant I could buy and do up the old manse house here.' It's just down the lane from us here, on the thin strip before the headland, sea on two sides, set in a wild and tropical garden, and I won't tell you how much Susan and Tom paid for it because a) anyone reading in a small flat in Streatham would hurl the book across the room in tears of rage and b) I don't want any more people going to Shetland. Selfish, yes. I don't care.

Susan tells me much about the technical side of the employment structure within the NHS; conditions of service of locums, the weird pay anomalies, the details of the new contracts, the responsibility for the running of the practices and such. But the overall picture is that of so many in the NHS and the public sector in general. This is a woman who loves her job, who rolls her eyes at the madness in the managerial sector, and gets on and serves her community willingly. Since the setting up of the National Health Service, GPs have been essentially sub-contractors running their own businesses. But the strain of that has meant that many have given them up, or gone bust, and handed them into the direct care of the NHS. There are ten practices in Shetland. Eight are now run by the board. Susan's remains in her care at great personal cost to herself. 'I still do my own "out of hours", because I live here and work here and I'm part of the community and I'm not going to sit drinking a nice glass of wine if someone's exsanguinating next door. My "out of hours" remuneration is five grand for twenty-six weeks. That's not a great wage, is it? If I worked for the board, I'd get a hundred pounds an hour. I'd get eight hundred pounds a weekend.'

She continues, 'We have terrible problems with recruitment, with retirements, with people going abroad. Did you know that half our trained and qualified doctors go to Australia and New Zealand where the life and the system is a lot easier? I'd stop that. I'd make it like military doctors. You should have to work five years here before you can go anywhere else. We spend half a million pounds a year training doctors who then immediately go away.' In Scotland alone, whose jurisdiction Susan's Shetland practice comes under, in the decade up to 2017, of the 5,044 doctors who registered, 2,895 are no longer connected to a UK 'designated body', meaning most probably that they have gone abroad.

'There's a real crisis happening in the NHS. We're trying through various methods to stop the rot: the Rural GP Association "Save Our Surgeries" campaign, Facebook and Twitter, all that, just to say, yes, we are really worth preserving. Essentially, there's a great view, and beautiful landscapes, we're a lovely team and there's orcas and puffins and lots to do. But the money is elsewhere ...'

Later, at the St Magnus Bay Hotel, a wonderful, eccentric wooden hostelry built for the Orkney steamers a century ago, we're joined by Tom, who writes and broadcasts (check out 'The Beatcroft' online) from this fabulous place. It's a convivial evening of food and chat and Susan is just about to dip a spoon into her cullen skink, the warm, reviving fish soup of the north, when the young waiter comes to her table with phone in hand. 'Dr Susan, I think you're wanted ...' Susan picks up her car keys and slips away to a call-out which is thankfully neither too long nor serious and is back at the table within the half-hour, watching the rest of us dive into another bottle of wine. Without fuss, the bowl of skink is returned from the kitchen where it had been discreetly magicked and kept hot without us noticing. I get the feeling this happens a lot.

'I don't want to live in a community where I couldn't or wouldn't help at night if someone was sick. The patients here only call me if they need me. They don't bother me for nothing. But they know that if they call I'll come. We have a volunteer fire brigade, a volunteer mountain rescue. You live collectively because you can't live any other way here.'

At just gone eleven, long after daylight has gone and the blinds have been drawn down against the night in London, Birmingham, Manchester and even Glasgow, it is still bright and sunny in Hillswick and the sun still bathes the dark and towering cliffs of Eshaness. Saying goodbye to the good doctor and Tom, I weave, a little unsteadily, down to the beach. I'm thinking of those last words of Susan's about community and the absolute necessity of pulling together, here at the edge of the world. You often hear about how isolated rural communities breed a certain hardiness, all that rugged individualism and self-sufficiency. Largely, this is rot; macho romanticisation beloved of beardy guidebook writers and the like. In places like the Northmavine, you cannot live like that. The thin weak skeins of pure commerce couldn't hold people together here for long. There's an excellent shop in this far-flung settlement. Fresh fish from the nearby Voe on Mondays and Tuesdays, good bread on Wednesdays. But it's a community shop. People volunteer, kindly business rates are negotiated and sometimes deferred, shifts are worked for free. Home deliveries are made when people are ill, prescriptions picked up. There is more at work here than the raw, cold business of making money.

Heading to take a last look at the blood-red sun low over the Heads of Grocken and Tangwick Haa, the path to the white sand and crashing surf passes a small walled cemetery. A sign, still readable with midnight not far away, says, 'This cemetery contains Commonwealth War Graves'. It's another powerful reminder that this is a community, a real one. The cemetery is full of dead young men from Shetland and Norway who gave their lives so that the young 'uns of this age can go down the road dressed as bears to the village hall and dance all night to the flying fiddles.

Hillswick may feel so wild and northerly that it has nothing to do with Britain or the office-bound bureaucracies of the state. This is Ultima Thule surely, the edge of the world – that is its joy and magnificence. But no. Susan Bowie works for the NHS. Tom works for the BBC and a state tourism agency. As well as being part of the community they are part of a nation that pulls together, or should do, in good times and bad. There is such a thing as society. If you don't believe that, then fine. I hope you never need the volunteer fire brigade who are ready to get out the engine in the quiet little garage by the cemetery, or the mountain rescue to bring you down safely from Eshaness, or young men and women like those who lie in the lonely cemetery by the endless crashing waves at the edge of your country. You are not a rugged individual. You are not, like Shetland, an island. You are part of a society. You have responsibilities and duties to those around you. This, as well as how to be a unique and special individual expressing yourself freely and creatively, is just as important, if less cosy. We should teach it in school.

CHAPTER 3

I GO TO SCHOOL

'PUT THE TEACHERS ON THE TOP'

What's the first thing you remember? What's your first memory of being here, in the world of people and shapes and exterior things? Some people claim they can recall the womb, a warm amniotic sea rocking them gently to the tide of a mother's heartbeat. Some say they remember being born, ejected explosively and bloodily into a carnival of lights and faces. I tend to scepticism here, just as I do towards those people who swear they were visited in their gardens by white-robed aliens then taken to Venus in a spacecraft to meet the Grand Galactic Council of Wompum El Bagnok. There they were given the secret knowledge of the universe, but apparently still can't match a shirt and jacket properly.

George Orwell said that only by resurrecting our own childhood memories can we realise how distorted a child's view of the world is. I've always maintained that I can remember my first day at school. But can I? The memory is fragmentary and mosaic as if seen in a shattered mirror or glimpsed through the twists of a kaleidoscope. In a room of peeling green-painted wood and high windows, there is a sandpit and sitting in it is Steven Horrocks, pale and blond and grubby. Twist and there's chubby, obstreperous little Martin Hock pacing the floor in his shorts and snake belt. Twist again and here's Steven Barry, inconsolable against Miss Reddington's legs, a huge tear rolling from his green eye (singular, the other having been removed by a ricocheted air-pistol pellet one winter afternoon). Miss Reddington herself is stern in a grey wool skirt with her silvering hair braided. Miss Hart and Miss Leadbetter, younger, nicer, but somehow strangely scarier, have miniskirts and make-up and dark eyes. Twist again and here's Karen Carter, or Anne Rudd or Denise O'Neill, doing handstands against a wall, pleated skirts falling scandalously over their heads and showing their white knickers to the jostling, yelling mass of the playground.

School, said Émile Durkheim, is our first introduction to the 'austerity of duty'. As any sociology student worth their GCSE will tell you, the transmission of knowledge, the inculcation of lists of formulae and South American capitals and elements of the periodic table, is only one part of a school's role. It is also a tremendously powerful and vital agent of 'socialisation'. What Durkheim means is that it represents our first slightly bitter taste of compulsion, coercion and responsibility. We have to be there whether we like it or not. We have to take our place in a world of strangers who demand things of us, rather than the indulgence of the family's bosom. It is our first real introduction to the hell (and heaven) that is other people.

My first school was St Joseph's Roman Catholic Primary, Caroline Street, off Miry Lane, Wigan. That address – Miry Lane – makes it sound as if I waded through cart ruts filled with dung to a school in Cheapside during the Middle Ages. In fact, it was near the town centre of a busy, thriving Lancashire industrial town in the mid to late 1960s. Despite this, and my extreme youth, a perceptive (and attractive) child such as I could tell the place was a relic of a bygone age. St Joseph's was already ancient when I passed through that stern entrance marked 'Boys'. You could feel the sooty, collective weight of history in the walls and doorways, a thousand crowded schooldays of working-class kids with scabbed knees and dirty faces, only the fashions changing from clogs and mittens to pumps and pinafore dresses. Ceilings were high and vaulted, the furnishings antique and dreary save for the odd splash of colour on the posters declaring that A is for Apple and B for Ball. I swear there were slates, miniature blackboards for the tinies to chalk on, each with a little rag strung on to erase their childish mistakes. There was an outside redbrick boys' toilet that was merely a stinking wall to be wee'd up at competitive heights. The approach to the school came via 'the brew', a slope formed of what I remember as coal dirt and asphalt. Behind that the terraced streets stacked and fanned away.

I'm looking at an old black-and-white photograph of the main school hall that an ex-pupil has posted on the parish website. The picture dates from a decade or so before I lined up there every morning but the shock of recognition is instant and powerful. This is where our small, wiry, perpetually belligerent headmaster Mr Kane would pace the room, scanning our faces looking for signs of guilt after a broken window, swear word, bloodied nose. 'Some boy ... or girl ... in this ... school has been ...' Half a century on, I can feel the quiet fear seeping along and into every one of us, whether you'd done anything wrong or not. And you would have, because our church taught us that we had all done something wrong, however secret we kept it.

What anyone would notice immediately is that in a room the size of a squash court, there are no fewer than four statues of the Virgin Mary. Above our heads, on door lintels, on bookshelves, on cupboards, on the teacher's desk dwarfing the globe that sits alongside her. This is where we would mutter our way through rosaries and catechisms, heads bowed and palms pressed. This is how we were schooled: in draughty halls beneath the melancholic faces of the martyred saints and the scarlet of the sacred heart in Jesus' chest to the sounds of bloodthirsty hymns like 'Faith of Our Fathers' sung in lusty uncomprehending voices and erratic playing on clanking, never-tuned pianos; on muddied fields in stinging rain, legs mottled and goose-pimpled, the heavy wet oval ball flung from hand to fumbling hand, pretending we were Billy Boston or Eric Ashton; in rooms heavy with chalk motes at creaking desks with jaws of iron, the pots gone from the inkwell but in the gnarled wood the names of long-dead scholars scored blue by fountain pens given as prizes and Christmas presents. Across the road was our church, also St Joseph's, named after the saint which we knew with some pride was Jesus' step-dad of sorts and thus proper inner-circle celebrity. We crossed that road most days to come inside this chilly, eerie place for one of the many ceremonies that mark the Catholic life: communions, confessions, benedictions, novenas to Our Lady of Perpetual Succour and the rest.

But when I was about seven, all that changed. In common with the shifts and movements that were happening to working-class communities all across industrial towns and cities in the north, most of the Catholic families who'd lived in the grimy and dilapidated 'back-to-backs' on Miry Lane and Wallgate were moved to big new housing developments. My new home was south-west of the town centre in an area called Worsley Mesnes, an exotic and storied name that we'll return to. We abandoned the old church and school (the school is now a retail park but the church is still there derelict, home to a city of pigeons and haunt of the odd urban explorer; the most recent pictures of the place gave me the willies for all kinds of reasons) and we all moved with glee to a new parish with a new church and school; St Jude's, named without irony after the patron saint of lost causes.

There was nothing lost about our cause. We were giddy with anticipation. The new church was crazily modern and strange. I could see that, even at my tender age, though my vocabulary wouldn't have stretched to celebrating 'the tactile richness of Hans Unger and Eberhard Schulze's Expressionist design' or noticed that 'the mosaic crucifixion combining glass tesserae and smalti (opaque glass handcrafted in Venice)'. I didn't know that this (from the official declaration at the time quoted on the Mosaic Matters website) was the kind of stuff some smart people were actually saying about the little church on a drab corner of an identikit northern council estate. But I note that it's now a listed building, which is oddly gratifying.

The school was not quite so noteworthy to the architectural connoisseur of the future, but the consensus of us kids was that it was 'ace'. This was our highest accolade, our most laudatory utterance of praise along with 'belting', 'lush' and 'shit-hot', though the latter was only used by the most outrageous iconoclasts. St Jude's RC Juniors was a single-storey cluster of open-plan rooms with glass walls and sleek tray-storage systems and central heating and taps that worked. My school was heavily yoked to the church, but it was still within the auspices of a state that cared about ordinary people, thought they deserved both the spectacular and the functional in their everyday lives; modish sculptures and challenging mosaics as well as properly equipped clean modern schools.

British education was changing in the 1960s, faster than at any time in the preceding century. The first Labour government in over a decade was bent on driving through a new kind of education system, classless, egalitarian and hugely controversial. Comprehensive education would replace the three-tier selective system based on exam results at eleven with, in theory, a universal and identical educational experience for all British schoolchildren regardless of income, class or region. It was, depending on your point of view, a grotesque piece of leftist social engineering or a first and most crucial step towards a fairer society. The thrusting new Labour government's mantra for education might have been, 'Hey, teacher, don't leave those kids alone.' From the late 1940s onwards working-class kids were the guinea pigs for this radical new system. By the 60s, it was entering its most ambitious and extensive phase; a provocative blueprint for a new Britain beginning in Huddersfield, Tividale, Coventry, Wigan and elsewhere, but firstly in the misty north-western corner of a Welsh island.

In the becalmed dead centre of a chilly, damp afternoon on Anglesey, sea fog rolling in, giving only the occasional misty glimpse of craggy Ynys Badrig rock and the green bulk of the now dormant Wylfa nuclear power station, you wouldn't think that the coastal town of Amlwch has ever been anything but a sadly overlooked sort of place and a dire Scrabble hand. A peculiarly

North Walian variety of surly melancholy seems to sit on the town. 'You can't park there,' barks the landlady of the Queen's Head helpfully from the doorway where she's enjoying a quick smoke between pulling pints. 'There' is a perfectly legitimate unoccupied spot just by the curry house a good hundred yards from her pub. Still, I don't argue.

The Visit Anglesey website tries gamely to talk up Amlwch's attractions in a plucky but slender paragraph thus: 'The town of Amlwch, on the north east coast of Anglesey, is a major draw for those interested in industrial heritage. Walking around this peaceful town, with its three windmills, it's hard to imagine that in its mining heyday, it was one of the busiest ports in Wales, and home to nearly 10,000 people. The old harbour at Port Amlwch is well worth a visit with its new Copper Kingdom visitor centre.'

Peaceful is fair I guess. Moribund might be nearer the truth. Amlwch maintains its bona fide pub-quiz fame as the most northerly town in Wales and its striking Futurist-style Catholic church is genuinely amazing. But the town's heyday passed with the decline of what was once the biggest copper mine in the world. Shipping, beer and tobacco had their day in Amlwch too. More recently has come the dire news that the town's plastics plant is to close, a victim of our growing ecological conscience, and that the nuclear power plant is not to be reactivated by a Japanese concern as was hoped. For now it looks like Amlwch's future might be its past, perhaps in the undoubted attraction of Parys Mountain, the gaping and rugged multicoloured canyon that remains of the copper mine, and possibly in the exceptionally niche sector of educational history tourism.

I'd been spending a summer week at a big house on a nearby headland, walking the coastal path, eating chips in Cemaes Bay, swimming in the harbour of the abandoned porcelain works at Porth Wen. One night, doing some reading for this book, I'd been surprised to learn that Anglesey had effectively been the laboratory for comprehensive education in Britain. Ysgol Gyfun in Llangefni and Ysgol Uwchradd Caergybi in Holyhead had both been pioneering institutions here. In the case of the latter, that was thanks largely to headmaster Trevor Lovett, a comprehensive education evangelist who was convinced that selection of children for streamed schools was unfair and destructive. But these were ideological changes to existing schools. I read on to learn that the first purpose-built comprehensive school in Britain was Ysgol Syr Thomas Jones, Amlwch, which is why next day, with the school holidays fading, I ended up rather furtively mooching around its deserted grounds.

In my defence, let me say that I didn't pry too much or make myself a nuisance. I took nothing but notes and would have happily declared that it was a fair cop if challenged and that I was just engaged in a little book espionage. But the gates were open and, apart from a delivery truck whose driver passed me by with a mildly curious glance, I saw no one. The kids would be down at the beach or on holiday abroad, the teachers would presumably be buried away somewhere with a pile of marking and preparation with one anxious eye on the calendar. That didn't matter. I just wanted the feel of the place. In Britain, we are annoyingly keen at putting up plaques and venerating our castles and grand old houses, our emblems of military power, dynastic might or conspicuous wealth. But real history, as opposed to the fancy, frivolous, dressing-up version beloved of TV documentaries, happens in quiet, uncelebrated places like Sir Thomas Jones school, Amlwch.

Clean, white, functional buildings radiate from a fine central stone clocktower which would not have been out of place in the Ynys Mon of a thousand years ago. In the spacious airy hall with its large glass panels, chairs are arranged as if for an exam, an arrangement that brings a little chill. Somewhere in here once sat, if briefly, Glenys Kinnock, Lemmy and RAF kid Dawn French. (Yes, Amlwch has a French connection.) But like a football ground or a gig venue, there is always something disconcerting and odd about a place that should be crowded, vibrant and noisy caught in its downtime of desertion and silence. Before somebody asks me what I'm up to, I'm off back through the gates and back into the town's small centre to run the gauntlet of the landlady of the Queen's Head once more.

Beyond headmaster Lovett's personal convictions, it's not immediately obvious why Anglesey was chosen as the Petri dish for the experiment that was comprehensive education (or multi-lateralism as it was also called in its formative early years on Anglesey). In attempting to find out I tracked down online a research piece called "'Britain is watching this school experiment, Anglesey leads the way." A forgotten pioneer? Anglesey's comprehensive system, circa 1953–1970' by an academic from Manchester Metropolitan University called Dr Anna Olsson Rost. Exhaustive and readable, it still left a non-specialist like me wondering 'Why Anglesey'? So I emailed her. She got back immediately.

> Hi Stuart,
> Thanks! On the whole, not enough people get excited about post-war education on a small north-Walian island … so I'm really pleased that you found the article useful for your chapter! The LEA had been in favour of 'secondary education for all' since the 1930s really – this was partially due to practicalities. But I would argue that there were also more ideological reasons behind this: a reluctance to divide pupils into different types of schools after the age of 11. The fact that Anglesey was a small, rural, and considered a not very radical LEA, most probably helped to get the Ministry of Education to approve the Development Plan in 1948 as well.

That was the situation then on Anglesey, and the British educational revolution began to spread further when Labour gained power in 1964. Far from Holyhead, Llangefni and Amlwch, at the Westminster vanguard of all this was a Labour cabinet minister and socialist intellectual called Anthony Crosland, one of the big beasts of Harold Wilson's cabinet. In the days before self-righteous moral orthodoxy was the operating system of the Labour

Party leadership, it was seen as undeniably a strength to have a range of opinions in government. Thus Crosland, a centrist moderate, could quite happily if combatively share a cabinet table with radical left-wingers like Tony Benn and John Silkin as well as the emollient Roy Jenkins. He was privately educated, undeniably upper class, haughty and often contemptuous of colleagues and opponents alike. He was mildly sybaritic in lifestyle, loving food and booze and once declaring 'Total abstinence and a good filing system are not the right signposts to a socialist utopia'. But for all this, there was one point on which Crosland was as adamant and zealous as any Bennite. According to her biography of him, he told his wife Susan, 'If it's the last thing I do I'm going to close down every fucking grammar school in England. And Wales. And Northern Ireland.

Had he succeeded, it might very well have been the last thing he did. Crosland died suddenly in 1977 aged just fifty-eight from a cerebral haemorrhage. But by then he had helped at least partially revolutionise Britain's school system. I say partially because it was always piecemeal, never achieved a consensus, reached various areas at wildly different times and has been subject to dismantling in the post-Thatcher years. But it became the experience of life for most British kids. But not all. For instance, it missed me. Just.

I belonged to the last school year in my district to take the eleven-plus exam. This was a series of tests in maths, English, verbal and spatial reasoning which would determine whether you would attend a grammar school or a secondary modern. Five lads and slightly more girls from my class passed for grammar, including me. This was the best my little council estate school of St Jude's had ever managed, but it was nothing to the enormous pass rate of St Cuthbert's across the main road, which sent forty or fifty kids to grammar school a year. Darkly though, they were rumoured to do little else but 'cram' with past papers for the last two years of 'Juniors' like hothoused automata.

At St Jude's, home of lost causes, we took a more relaxed view. Even so, I can remember all of us feeling the approaching menace of the test, throbbing in the distance like the music from *Mastermind*, getting nearer all term. People would be promised new bikes, shoes and Scalextrics if they passed. The test itself was like a quiz – albeit a quiz on which a great deal of your future depended – and thus I loved it. There were the usual array of knotty anagrams and the decantings of liquids between bottles of wildly different sizes for no obvious good reason. There were the endless competitive races between A, B and C, the latter of whom would always be labouring under some bizarre handicap. Also, there were essay titles such as (these are genuine examples) 'Eggs', 'Everest', 'The Gothic', 'Queen Salote', 'The Maoris', and 'What life must be like as a cat'.

Because I passed, I've never much dwelled on what might have happened had I not. I blithely went on to St John Rigby RC Grammar School, Orrell, Wigan, there to be given the strap by Christian brothers (who seemed about as Christian as Pol Pot to me), smoke Embassy Regal behind the art room listening to the chart rundown on Johnnie Walker's Radio 1 show and pick up some basic education. Most of that came later under my own steam in libraries and the like. But for others – like my mate Eddie and my brother-in-law David – not being particularly good at anagrams or caring much about Queen Salote that single afternoon as an eleven-year-old marred them a little and screwed up the next bit of their life, at least until they became old enough to shape their own destinies.

The debate about selection and streaming, grammar schools and 'comps', refuses to recede into the obscurity of history. The issue is far from settled – there are still 163 state grammar schools in England, though none in Scotland or Wales – and the pros and cons are still contested. For every educationalist and politician who argues that grammars were a powerful force for social mobility, a ladder up for working-class kids, others think that the system was stigmatising and limiting, labelling kids as 'failures' at eleven and relegating them to a lesser set of life and career options. Deflatingly for a polemical book, I can see the truths in both sides of this argument. But then I only know it from my limited experience of the slightly odd and rarefied, not to say warped and violent, world of the Catholic grammar school. I wanted to speak to someone who had experienced life at a comprehensive. Fortunately, I knew just the person and exactly the right 'comp'.

Simon Armitage is wrestling with a dilemma when I FaceTime him in his New York apartment. Formerly Professor of Poetry at Leeds University and Chair of Poetry at Oxford, the soon to be Poet Laureate. This semester he's the Holmes Visiting Professor of Poetry at Ivy League bastion Princeton. But his immediate thought is how much he's willing to pay to hear 'Rocket Man' and 'Candle in the Wind' warbled in a faux Deep South drawl by a bespectacled man from Pinner. 'Elton John's playing at the theatre at the bottom of the street tonight. Thinking of going. Might be fun. Two hundred and fifty dollars a chuck, though. Bloody 'ell. Will it be that much fun?'

I was a fan of Simon's long before I was a friend. I've always been a poetry geek, so when he emerged as part of the New Generation poetry promotion in the mid-90s – a kind of verse version of Hirst and Emin and the YBAs – my first reaction was fervent admiration tempered by sheer envy. He was brilliant, he was northern and he was a couple of years younger than me. The sod. I'm over that too, now. As you might have guessed from that reference to the cost of an Elton John ticket as well as his vowels, Simon is from Yorkshire. Specifically he's from, as he has called it, 'the flat mud of the Colne Valley'. It was in that valley, nearest big town Huddersfield, that another state education landmark occurred. Colne Valley High School was the first purpose-built comprehensive in northern England, founded in 1956 on thirty-eight acres in the Yorkshire village of Linthwaite. It cost a hefty £350,000 and was staffed largely with young and idealistic teachers fired with passion for comprehensive education. Ex-English teacher Charlie Adamson told the *Yorkshire Post* on its fiftieth anniversary:

> In the early days it was an adventure going into the unknown. The staff were young, the school was young.
> In the Colne Valley in the 1950s education had been

fragmented. Some went to junior school, some went to Harold Wilson's old school, Royds Hall. People went all over. The Calder Valley was an area which lent itself to the idea of a comprehensive school. Our first headteacher, Ernest Butcher, staged a number of meetings with parents around the valley. He was so convincing that there were parents who could have sent their children to grammar schools but decided to send them here.

Another former teacher, Andrew Pearson, said, 'Opponents of comprehensive education wanted the school not to succeed. We were damned if this was going to happen. We had visitors from all over the world, it was a bit like being in a goldfish bowl.' People came seeking to learn about how this experiment in non-selective, non-streamed, mixed ability teaching was working and some came to see it fail. There was distinct vocal opposition from some quarters. In 1961 the school's head of religious education, E.J.R. Cook, told a public meeting that 'religion is not chained to the Bible in this school'. It was also claimed that extracts from Marx had been read at the school assembly. There was a considerable local uproar. But an inquiry by the school governors concluded that they were perfectly happy with Mr Cook and the ethos of this young school and its staff. The significance of all this was largely lost on the young Armitage.

'I didn't know that it was the first. I knew it was very early in that system. And it certainly felt experimental at time. For one thing, it was absolutely huge. When I went to university, I remember people I spoke to being astonished that I didn't know the name of all the teachers at my secondary school. There were staff you'd vaguely seen knocking about during your seven years but you didn't know who they were or what they taught. To me though it was just a bog-standard comprehensive with an enormous amount of kids.' 'Bog standard', he's at pains to point out, is not meant as an insult but merely a hint at its ordinariness. Even he sussed that there was nothing standard about the 'two amazing things' about the school that still have him chuckling in his Manhattan kitchen.

'For one thing, it had a farm. An actual farm. Apparently they had some huge financial bequest and had to choose between a swimming pool and a farm ... They chose a farm. It wasn't unusual to see a kid on the bus with a piglet or those wellies with turn-ups on or a lad in the corridor with a couple of chickens. We intellectual English lit and sociology types in our dads' old jackets, we definitely saw this as the lowest option: Farm Studies. Double digging, it was known as.

'Then there was "the flat". The school had an actual flat on the top storey of a five-storey block, with its own little balcony and kitchen and bedroom. Truly extraordinary. If you were unfortunate enough to do domestic science, which I was, at some point over that two-year period, you had to live there for a week with another pupil like Eric and Ernie,[5] in this flat overlooking the school. You had to cook meals for teachers, get them their lunch and invite them round, then wash up and vacuum up with one of those little Ewbank things. The idea was to introduce you to adult life beyond school. Sort of a halfway house, like they'd give to a crack addict. I think it was looked on by the authorities as a treat as you were off timetable. But of course it was excruciating. Immediately you were marked out and declared "gay", obviously. Plus you were obliged to wear non-school uniform. So there's me on the balcony of an afternoon with a cocktail in my purple velour suit. You may as well have worn a target on your head. There'd be nineteen hundred kids looking up at you taking aim and pelting you with potatoes from the farm.'

Despite the twin eccentricities of the farm and the school, Simon recalls that 'it was certainly a kind of collective education in all that is good and bad about that. You had to bump along with everybody. It was not in any way selective or elective. It was

---

[5] In their beloved comedy shows, Eric Morecambe and Ernie Wise were seen to share a house and indeed a bed, an arrangement which Britain seems to have accepted quite happily and without comment.

co-operative. The English teachers were great and sort of cool and flamboyant with their own staff room and the school was always full of piles of books. Everyone would have their own copy of *The Comedians* by Graham Greene or *1984* handed down from one generation to the next. There was that level of decent provision then.'

He remembers another detail. 'Also there was a school song. Never knew what it was called. We called it "Adventure On" as they were the only words we knew. You were just were expected to know it the moment you arrived as if it were in your DNA. But no one did, so you would mumble through it at assembly until everyone would join in with this fascistic bellow of "ADVENTURE ON!!!"'

I quote him the correct words of the song, which *is* actually called 'Adventure On', probably written by a teacher, although the author of the lyrics seems to have been lost in the mists of time:

Let us adventure on, through these our days of youth,
In endless search for Beauty, Knowledge, Justice, Truth.

In a New York apartment, preparing for his next Princeton lecture, ex Colne Valley High School pupil Armitage S., soon to be Poet Laureate, smiles. 'Well, there wasn't much beauty. But there was a lot of truth.'

Like many of the pupils of the new comprehensives, Simon Armitage was barely aware that he was a foot-soldier in an ideological educational war that was being fought up and down the land. Nowhere was the fighting fiercer than in north London. In the 1970s, the postal districts ('packed like squares of wheat' as Larkin had it) around Hampstead, Islington, Tufnell Park and even Camden were the heartland of artistic, intellectual left-wing London. It had become the preferred patch of the capital for writers, film makers, actors, musicians, politicians, boho flâneurs and writers for the new 'Sunday Colour Supplements'. Most of these were zealous advocates of comprehensive education, determined to make the schools of these boroughs a radical and egalitarian alternative to the fustian private school sector, following the lead of Holland Park Comprehensive ('the Socialist Eton') across town.

They were not hypocrites, not by and large. They sent their own kids to these schools. They organised petitions and protest marches. They debated in rooms above pubs. You would hear it discussed in the Coffee Cup in Hampstead where you might be asked to budge up over your veal paillard or tiramisu to make room for Michael Foot, David Owen, Peter Sellers, Fay Weldon, John Fowles, Judi Dench, Margaret Drabble or Salman Rushdie. And on 'the heath' you might have bumped into two Cumbrians deep in conversation, getting in a little low-level ambling that would have to suffice here, miles from their beloved Haystacks and Grasmoor.

One was Wigton's Melvyn Bragg, the other Carlisle's Hunter Davies. The former, the novelist and broadcaster, would end up in the Lords as a Labour peer. The latter, one of our most prolific non-fiction writers and columnists, has always described himself as 'not political'. But in the early 70s, he was one of the most passionate of creative north London's campaigners for what he saw as the social necessity of non-selective comprehensive education and the end of the grammar schools. He even went as far as to spend a year incognito in one such comprehensive as a teacher, writing a book called *The Creighton Report* about his experiences. I'd met Hunter before at his lovely house in the Lake District's Loweswater and shared a glass of wine and a bowl of tatie pot in his local up there, the Kirkstile Inn. But as of 2019, following the death of his wife the novelist Margaret Forster, he was now permanently domiciled in the north London house that had been his home since 1963. 'Come down and talk,' he enthused by email. 'Come to London! See my Beatles and football treasures and have lunch at an amusing bistro by the Heath.'

Today, he ushers me into the kitchen, kicks open the fridge and fills two glasses with alarmingly generous slugs of white wine 'Would you like a drink?' I hesitate a little. 'You're not teetotal, are you?' he asks, seemingly horrified. Satisfied this is not the case, we are off around his lovely house. 'And the next question always is how much ... and the answer is five thousand pounds, at which point people are usually sick.'

Hunter is a gatherer. The house is a treasure trove of his assorted collections and obsessions, such as the first issues of various publications, Lake District books and Beatle memorabilia. The last has been collected over years of personal friendship after writing the Fab Four's first and still only official biography. He sets me little quizzes as we go from room to room and floor to floor. Pointing to a picture of himself and family on holiday in Portugal with Macca, Linda, little Heather and dog, he asks, 'And the name of this sheepdog is?' I pass the test. It is Martha, as immortalised in 'Martha My Dear' from the 'White Album', as all we Beatle geeks know. Later he produces in a plastic Ziploc bag from a filing cabinet a pair of McCartney's underpants.

He has the born journalist's knack of asking questions and remembering details about you – family, home town, football team, past jobs – with disarming ease. I wave these away though. Today the subject is Hunter and his time at the front line of the battle for comprehensive education. 'I'm not really a political person, Stu. I've always voted Labour, as did Margaret, and some would say we did it blindly. I used to be a school governor round here whereas Margaret did fuck all for the community. But I did because when I was at school we never met anybody who came from south of Penrith. I never met anybody who wasn't a local constable. I never met anyone who'd "made it" who came from my background, so I got involved with comprehensives. I thought they were the most wonderful idea; fair and best for everyone.'

Hunter hooked up with other like-minded and sometimes eminent local enthusiasts for comprehensives. 'I started an action

group. I organised demos. I was an activist. I held meetings at
Camden Town Hall and got my chums like Fay Weldon on board.
I had personal reasons to an extent because I actually went to a
grammar late in life having never taken an eleven-plus. But I ended
up going to one at the age of sixteen and I was horribly looked
down on. It was only at eighteen when I went to Durham Uni that
I felt I was starting from scratch and on the same footing as
everybody else.'

He hit on a winning literary formula around the early 1970s,
writing 'year in the life' books – most famously *The Glory Game*
about Tottenham Hotspur – which led him to want to write about
spending a year as a comprehensive teacher. 'I've got a diploma in
education. I can teach anywhere and they won't call the police. But
I thought, I don't want a brand-new "comp". I want an established
one, somewhere near me. Maybe Haringey. So I rang round and
people suggested the Creighton. Wrote to the headmistress,
eventually got a reply from a woman called Molly Hattersley[6] who
was taking over the school the same day as I wanted to arrive. A
brand-new head. Amazing she took that chance on a complete
outsider coming in to teach and then write about it. So I devoted
a whole year to that school. I went there every day. It was my full-
time job. I followed whole classes, went to staff meetings,
interviewed people and did some teaching, although I was useless
and scared stiff and couldn't keep control. I found six interesting
sixth-formers – one who'd come from Westminster School, one
from a mixed-race background and so on – and as time went on I
dropped the half who didn't have a "narrative" as they say today.
You have to have a drama. There was stuff I couldn't put in then,
like the head of sixth form being gay and some dodgy stuff about
saucy films being shown in the gym which I couldn't mention. But
they trusted me. I didn't stitch anybody up and Molly the head
became a good friend.'

---

[6] Wife of Labour grandee Roy Hattersley.

The Creighton Report was initially written as a series of articles for the *Sunday Times*. Hunter delivered sections of the book as pieces for the paper and the articles drew an enormous postbag. 'After I'd written the book I was very pleased and proud because, although I absolutely told it like it was, it was an unashamed hurrah for comprehensives. I came away still a huge supporter of them. But it's complicated. In Cockermouth, it's brilliant because there's only one school and the middle-class kids and the farmers' children all mix and go there. But in Birmingham or London, you'll get good comps and "sink" ones because the well-off are still shit-scared and they'll send their kids somewhere fee-paying. I'm still all for them, but until you close the grammar schools and all the fee-paying schools you won't have a level playing field.'

The final section of *The Creighton Report* is quite unlike Hunter's typically breezy, deceptively light style. It's a passionate, intellectually rigorous, detailed and analytical defence of comprehensive education that takes on, rebuts and refutes many of the myths and straw men about them. He tackles literacy, numeracy and general educational attainment and attempts to cut through the muddled and ideological objections to them while acknowledging the difficulties. In a fabulous final flourish, he leaves us in no doubt where he stood and where he still stands.

> The social class and academic attainment of comprehensive students can be measured and compared even if the experts then argue about what the results mean. But there is one aspect of a comprehensive school that can't be measured – the quality of the young people it is producing. This will be my most impressive memory of Creighton. In their concern for tolerance, equality, fairness and democracy, they are unrecognisable from the pupils of my generation. They help the less fortunate. They try to do what they say they believe. I have no proof but I am sure they will make better citizens and will strive to make the world a better place.

The bill arrives. 'Aren't you going to eat your tatties? Don't you know there's a war on!' Hunter insists on paying. 'Did I tell you I gave all the money from the book away? Gave it to the school. It's not there any more. Last year was the fortieth anniversary of the book and I was invited to a thing at the school that now exists on the site; Fortismere, now the most desirable comp in Highgate and Muswell Hill.' With a bottle of lunchtime red inside us we amble happily alongside the heath. Hunter shows me the comprehensive all his kids, made famous by his 'Father's Day' column and TV series, went to. Then he points me in the direction of the tube. 'Back to work, eh? Poor sod. I'm going to bed now for a bit.' He strolls off into the London afternoon, back to his books and collections and rich, full, late life. Truth is, I'm still a little envious.

A tube stop away, in Camden Town, lives another northern-bred doyen of the north London literary scene with the same strong views on education. I'm not going to call Alan Bennett a national treasure because that's often a way the establishment neutralise working-class writers and artists, to reduce and dilute them to their cutest, cosiest, safest dimension. Thanks to a continual lazy trope in British comedy beloved of Radio 4 particularly, Bennett has become caricatured as a fey elderly northern bachelor forever wibbling on about Thora Hird and Hobnobs. Little could be further from the truth. Over the decades of his writing life, his work has grown increasingly political and his anger at the folly of modern British governance has grown hotter. When he was asked to address an audience at Cambridge University in 2014, he chose not to eulogise the institution's illustrious history or the delights of punting on the Cam. Instead he told them some home truths about most of their backgrounds.

> Private education is not fair. Those who provide it know it. Those who pay for it know it. Those who have to sacrifice in order to purchase it know it. And those who receive it know it, or should. And if their education ends without it dawning on them, then that education has been wasted.

My objection to private education is simply put. It is
not fair. And to say that nothing is fair is not an answer.
Governments, even this one, exist to make the nation's
circumstances more fair, but no government, whatever its
complexion, has dared to tackle private education.

What Bennett is getting at is what everyone who has no
vested interest in maintaining the current rotten and unfair system
knows: the most direct and effective way of changing Britain for
the better permanently would be the immediate abolition of the
private schools. In Enver Hoxha's Albania (admittedly not always
a model of progressive thinking and sound governance) he closed
all the churches and turned them into leisure centres. Modern
professional atheists like Richard Dawkins probably think this a
splendid idea. But then Dawkins grew up on a country estate and
attended Oundle public school in leafy Northants. He seems
rather more quiet about this than he does about people's faiths.
Never mind the churches, Richard. If you want Britain to become
more just, more equitable, happier overnight, even if it does
reduce the status and power of rich white men, we should turn
Oundle into an Aldi.

For years, the public school experience had been handed down
to us as 'normal' via privately educated writers, to the extent that
the tuck shops and prep of Billy Bunter and Jennings were more
familiar to us than the Butler Act or technical schools. But then, as
the 60s gave way to the 70s, the social fact that the vast majority of
us were educated by the state became belatedly reflected. State
schooling became our most shared commonality, the root of a
shared identity and experience from *Grange Hill* to the Bash Street
Kids, from *Please Sir!* to 'Don't Stand So Close to Me'. But
behind the egalitarian façade and the chatter about a new classless
Britain, there lurked a deeper structure and a shadowy monolithic
truth. Where it mattered, a privately educated minority continued
to dominate Britain's corridors of power and spheres of influence.

*

In his book *Posh Boys: How the English Public Schools Ruin Britain*, Robert Verkaik puts it brilliantly:

> Imagine a world where leaders are able to pass power directly to their children. These children are plucked from their nurseries and sent to beautiful compounds far away from all the other children. They are provided with all the teachers they need, the best facilities, doctors and food. Every day they are told this [is] because they are the brightest and most important children in the world. Later, in the outside world, they are presented with the best jobs, the grandest houses and most of the money. Through their network of friends and family, they control the government, the army, the police and 'The City'. The leaders tell all of their people that everyone is equal and that everyone has a chance to become a leader but this isn't true because the leaders have made it impossible for the other people's children to become leaders.

In North Korea? China? Soviet Russia? Feudal Europe? No. Britain today.

The alumni of public schools make up 40 per cent of the cabinet as I write. Our last two male prime ministers were both not only privately schooled but schooled at Eton, the most exclusive and elitist of all such institutions. Fifty-nine per cent of permanent secretaries in the civil service and two-thirds of senior judges went to public school, as did most army officers. We bemoan the lack of social mobility and working-class achievement in our country but accept mutely the fact that schools that educate just 7 per cent of the country account for 74 per cent of judges, 71 per cent of generals and 29 per cent of MPs. While this is the case, all talk of increasing social mobility and greater equality is just that; talk. The inescapable fact is that the public school system as it stands blights British life immeasurably.

Sometimes, it's actually been famous old boys and products of the system who've pointed this out, especially with regard to the kind of man the elite 'top' schools have been wont to turn out. Cyril Connolly claimed that 'it results that the greater part of the ruling class remains adolescent, school-minded, self-conscious, cowardly, sentimental'. When Old Etonian George Orwell lay in hospital at the end of his life, he described the man in the next bed, an old boy of a 'good school', in a way that suggests several major players in our current politics. 'A sort of over-fedness, a fatuous self-confidence, a constant bah-bahing of laughter about nothing, above all a sort of heaviness & richness combined with a fundamental ill-will – people who, one instinctively feels, without even being able to see them, are the enemies of anything intelligent or sensitive or beautiful. No wonder everyone hates us so.'

Scandalously, private schools enjoy charitable status and are subsidised from the public purse. The state pays for teacher training and the private schools share the teachers' pension scheme. This is not a minor point: 16 per cent of teachers work in private schools and they are paid better than in state schools, so their pensions amount to more than 18 per cent of the projected payouts of the scheme – a total of £4.79 billion by 2024 – which is helping to drive the current wave of cuts in state schools. Janice Turner cited more lurid examples of this inequality in a piece called 'The 7 Per Cent Problem':

> Eton has an Olympic grade rowing lake – in fact the actual 2012 Olympics were held on it. Stowe has an equestrian centre, golf course and nightclub apparently kitted out from the remnants of Crazy Larry's in Chelsea. St Paul's Girls has a restaurant whose typical menu includes Spanish smoky samfaina with eggs and rocket. Rooms at Roedean are en suite with, according to *Tatler*, 'chic interiors, designer lighting and sea views'. Private schools in London have fifty-nine theatres compared to forty-two in the West End. (The auditorium at my sons' school, more state-of-

the-art than the Young Vic, was dark between student productions yet, astonishingly, never lent to local comps.)

That last sentence is instructive. Turner sends her son to public school. It's a weird piece of cognitive dissonance that many liberals feel, if not comfortable with, then liveable with. David Kynaston and Francis Green in their recent book *Engines of Privilege* admit that they were both privately educated (though not their kids) and, while rightly savaging the current system and the status quo, recommend not outright abolition but reforms; more places for ordinary kids, tinkering with the subsidies, quota systems for university places. As far as I see it, these are sticking plasters and deckchair rearrangements.

I like David Kynaston and Janice Turner. They are excellent writers and their hearts are in the right place. I like those very few of my friends and colleagues who send their kids to fee-paying schools. But let's be absolutely straight about this. Any opinion other than the conviction that private education should be abolished immediately is cant and bullshit. It may be tough. It may mean your kids have to work harder to get on. It may make your domestic life less smooth. But so did abolishing slavery for the comfortably off. Privilege and unfairness will never be eradicated, social justice will never be achieved while well-meaning but handwringing liberals pay for their children to go to private schools. Sorry, guys, but it's hypocrisy, and you know it. Abolish them. Turn them into Aldis, sports halls and nail bars. Today.

We have become almost inured to this absurd situation. We've taken it for granted that our top lawyers, judges, politicians, journalists, military officers will be drawn from the small and exclusive ranks of the privately schooled. But over the last few years, this has become the case even in the entertainment sphere, once seen as a route to the top for the working class. A survey of 2010 found that 60 per cent of acts in the pop charts today attended public school compared to just 1 per cent two decades ago. It's a striking list: Chris Martin, Mumford & Sons, La Roux, Florence Welch, Pixie Lott, Lily Allen, Laura Marling, Eliza Doolittle, Mark Ronson, all of the talent-school academy graduates marshalled by one Simon Cowell, old boy of the £3,995-a-term Dover College. There have always been a few posh boys in pop. But previously these were very much the exceptions. Their backgrounds made them figures of exotic curiosity. For instance, 60s hitmakers The Zombies were bright Home Counties grammar schoolboys with rafts of O levels between them, and so this 'poshness' was thrust upon them as a default gimmick in the teen press. Every early Genesis article in the rock inkies relished the fact that they formed at Charterhouse School, so outlandish was it that hirsute, touring rockers would be educated thus, though oddly not for the public schoolboys who played or put out their records such as John Peel or Jonathan King. (If he'd written for *NME*, Marx would have had a field day with this.) Even then their greatest success would come when they handed the creative reins to a savvy stage-school upstart from Chiswick called Phil Collins. Yes, Nick Drake attended the exclusive Marlborough College, whose alumni includes future queen Kate Middleton, and Radiohead formed at Abingdon, fees in excess of £10,000. But Jim Morrison claimed his parents were dead rather than admit that his dad was an admiral and Joe Strummer didn't exactly dwell, in his many interviews about street riots and wealth redistribution, on his being a diplomat's son who'd gone to an exclusive boarding school.

But once, in what some would call its Golden Age, popular music belonged to the working class. Unscientifically but persuasively, it's detectable right there in the names on the sleeves. Where have all the Erics, Joes, Bills, Georges and Brians gone that formed the rock elite of the 60s and 70s? Top indie act The Maccabees included a Hugo, an Orlando, a Felix and a Rupert. Entering Paul McCartney's childhood council-house home at 20 Forthlin Road, Allerton, Merseyside, American visitors are often visibly shocked by how tiny it is and how plain, spartan even. John Lennon's was slightly bigger and thus he's routinely and wrongly labelled as 'middle class'. But his dad was an itinerant galley hand and he was brought up by an aunt in a modest Liverpool street. Posher than Macca, maybe, but it's hardly Downton Abbey. But from these tiny, unassuming houses on drab streets, from terraced streets across the north, or unlovely boroughs of London, from mill towns and ports, factories and coalfields, were to come the working-class kids who would shake the world with every shake of their heads.

In the arts generally – music, theatre, literature certainly – it's clear that cuts to benefits, the decline of the art school (where many a luminous layabout found room to bloom), the removal of grants and the growth of intern cuture are making it increasingly a playground for the comfortably off. The relatively benign benefit system that sustained the pre-fame Jarvis Cocker or Morrissey is being dismantled daily. Maxine Peake (Bolton-raised, Salford resident and one of our finest actors currently working) told me that she could simply not afford to train for the stage now. Actor David Morrissey said recently, 'We're creating an intern culture – it's happening in journalism and politics as well – and we have to be very careful because the fight is not going to be there for people from more disadvantaged backgrounds.' In the media generally, preferment comes often through nepotism or via those internships which only the comfortably off and their families can afford. The Sutton Trust report of 2009 found that the proportion of national newspaper journalists educated privately had actually increased over twenty years. Only 14 per cent went to state school, a statistic as worrying as it is remarkable.

In 2010, the *Daily Mail* – of all publications – reported on the growing gap in music provision between the state and private school system. In the state sector local authorities are now spending less than half the amount on music teaching than they did in 1990, a figure as little as £1.15 a child per year. 'On top of this, families who can afford private school fees are often affluent enough to also pay for extra music tuition, for equipment such as drum kits, guitars, amps, and also for rehearsal space.' When the *Daily Mail*, hardly a seedbed of revolutionary fervour, notices and bemoans this trend, you know there's something rotten in the kingdom of culture.

Does it matter? Surely Noel Gallagher is no better than Nick Drake just because he went to a Burnage comp rather than Marlborough School? Of course not. But pop culture should reflect the lives of its people in all its vibrancy, challenge and hurly-burly, not the rarefied interests and experiences of a few. I think all this matters, and even through the enveloping fog of Brexit, it seems that the issue is attracting more and more attention. At the 2019 party conference, the Labour Party, after years of cringing and prevaricating, finally committed itself to the complete abolition of private education. Clem Atlee had always had too much affection for his old alma mater of Haileybury and even the more pugnacious Harold Wilson did little more than produce an ineffective Royal Commission report. But in September 2019, the party said that a future Labour government would 'integrate all private schools into the state sector' as well scrapping all subsidies and tax privileges and even selling off all assets and land and redistributing the proceeds 'democratically and fairly across all the country's educational establishments'.

About time too. This politician knows the score. 'We have one of the most stratified and segregated education systems in the developed world, perpetuating inequality and holding our nation back ... From the England cricket team to the comment pages of the *Guardian*, the BAFTAS to the BBC, the privately educated – and wealthy – dominate. Access to the best universities and the most powerful seats around boardroom tables, influence in our media and office in our politics are allocated disproportionately to the privately educated children of already wealthy parents.'

Corbyn? McDonnell? Abbott? No. Step forward and well said, former Education minister and grammar schoolboy Michael Gove. During his time at the Department of Education, he also said that children should be reading fifty books a year.

Difficult, though, when Michael's party just closed your library.

CHAPTER 4

I LEARN TO READ

'LIBRARIES GAVE US POWER'

Four moss-green cardboard tickets, somewhere between the size of a postage stamp and a playing card. Dog-eared, not glossy, not laminated, not wipe-clean, definitely not in 'stylish' credit card format. No chip, no hologram, no logo or slick promo slogan about 'believing in books' or 'opening your mind'. They were as municipal as a gas bill but as precious as a passport. Indeed, they *were* a passport – to the Centre of the Earth and Twenty Thousand Leagues under the Sea, to Elidor and Middle Earth, the Forest of Arden and Mowgli's jungle, to Treasure Island, Kirrin Island and the isle of Lyngvi where the wolf Fenrir was bound, to the Grimpen Mire and the Sea of Tranquillity, second star on the right straight through till morning.

My library tickets.

Without a library, said Ray Bradbury, we have no past and no future. According to Einstein, it's location was the only thing in life that we absolutely needed to know. Anne Herbert insisted that 'libraries will get you through times of no money better than money will get you through times of no libraries', a line which should be inscribed upon the forehead of every politician, councillor, alderman and apparatchik who ever colluded in the closure of a public library. The US writer Rita Mae Brown claimed that her life began the day that she got her library card. I know that feeling. I don't know where Rita Mae's library was (York,

Pennsylvania, I assume, after consulting Wiki) but mine was on Powell Street, Wigan, by the swimming baths, the dole office and the police station. I would come to know all these institutions as the years of childhood and youth passed, but none of them would give me as much pleasure or would feel even now as enchanted as the Children's Library.

Its proper name was the Powell Library, gifted by the local philanthropist Francis Sharp Powell, twice Tory MP for the town in the Victorian and Edwardian era before there was a Labour Party to vote for. An idea of how these stern patrician patriarchs would rule towns like fiefdoms in the days before workers got themselves organised can be seen in the fact that the library and the street it was in were both named after him (see also Jarrow, where the name of Palmer, the shipyard that made and ruined the town, is everywhere from hospitals to schools to parks). The kids of Wigan had two reasons and two artefacts to be grateful to Francis Sharp Powell for. Firstly there was the famous statue of him seated and pensive in Wigan Park. It was obligatory to rub his toe for luck as you passed and thus, polished and buffed by the shirt cuffs of several generations, this was the only part of the Powell, otherwise covered in verdigris and pigeon shit, that gleamed bronze. It was also traditional for bad lads of the town to 'goz up a green 'un' into their hand and smear it on Powell's toe and from thence on to the next passing and subsequently disgusted 'toe rubber'.

Powell's other gift to us was the 'Children's Library'. Even the phrase has something 'hauntological' about it as the fashionable description would say. Something eerie and strange glimpsed down the years from a past that may or not have existed. It conjures dust motes in the weak sun of a winter's afternoon, a creaking door, the echoing tick of a clock, a figure disappearing behind the shelves. In my mind it is forever Tuesday afternoon in November in the Children's Library. Outside the orange and white buses sploosh through the wet oncoming dusk to Scholes and Whelley and Blackrod. Inside the atmosphere is somewhere perfectly pitched and trembling between the scary and the sensual. Contributors to the Wigan World forum seem to agree.

'Every Saturday morning, after I'd had my swimming lesson at the baths across the road, I used to go to the library with my mum to get books to read for the week ahead,' recalls Catherine. 'I loved it. All the wooden shelves, the hushed atmosphere, the musty smell of the books. Fabulous place. As much as I love new libraries, you just can't beat an old library, and Wigan's children's library was one of the best.' Irene says, 'I can feel the atmosphere in the Powell library yet; it was a "proper" library in that it was hushed and peaceful and you had to be quiet. It made me want to work in a library, although I never did.'

Despite the name, there was nothing child friendly, child focused, child facing, as we would now understand it, about the Children's Library. There were no toys, no posters, no talking. It was a 'proper library' in Irene's words with all that that implies; the silence and mystery, the chilly calm, the stifling, alluring ambience that was part church, part Aladdin's cave. Upstairs there was a museum where the exhibits were most definitely non-interactive, not to be touched on pain of the librarian's icy basilisk glare. Here, no chatty descriptions or helpful audio or dressing-up box to be rummaged in. Just a series of brass plaques and weird antique objects under glass; a Civil War musket from the siege of the town, a stuffed owl, a vicious-looking mining implement of obscure function.

I loved it. I would hold the tickets in front of me as I squeaked in my 'pumps' along the waxed parquet floor, using them like a divining rod to seek out the treasure hidden on the shelves. I remember all my favourites. How they looked and smelled. The elegant calligraphy and design of the Arthur Ransomes, the cheery wartime gaiety of the Outlaws' ruddy faces in Richmal Crompton's *Just William* series which I adored. Quentin Blake's quirky, seemingly effortless scribbles for the *Agaton Sax* series, funny, odd stories about a Swedish detective which I had heard Kenneth Williams read on *Jackanory* and had become obsessed with. They

cost a packet now on eBay. I wonder where the ones from the
Powell ended up when they closed the library? In a landfill or a
jumble-sale box or in a teetering pile in a musty back room in a
second-hand bookshop. Find them, open them and you'll see the
blue smeary stamps where I took them out pretty much every week
between 1970 and 1973.

At some point in their life, every bookish child – no, make
that 'book-mad', since bookish implies a certain fragility that
some of us never had – those of us who propped our battered
Puffin paperbacks on sauce bottles at the table, then stuffed them
in our pockets before heading out for a day of football and
foraging, has wanted to be a librarian. To live among books all
day long in the enveloping calm and whispered sweet nothings of
the library. We have all fancied being a librarian and yes, if we're
honest, we've all fancied a librarian too. The owlish Larkin, our
most famous of the species, knew that well, the secret sensual
world and meanings behind the primness and spectacles and
buttoned cardigans. For all his affected misanthropy, he
surrounded himself with female staff in Hull University Library
and had affairs with at least two of them. Casanova himself ended
his days as librarian in Bavaria.

We think of libraries as being at the very heart of public
provision, the mark of an enlightened state. But their origins are
rooted in private philanthropy and individual property, the book as
collection and private treasure hoard. There is not one mention of
libraries, for instance, in the compendious fifty-page index to
Nicholas Timmins's magisterial history of the welfare state, *The
Five Giants*. In my town, as well as Powell's library, up in Pemberton
there was the beautiful Carnegie Library, one of the 2,509 around
the world built by the Scottish philanthropist Andrew Carnegie.
By the time I was using these places they had been taken under the
wing of the state, but their names reflected their origins. That
strain of individual beneficence in the provision of books and
libraries persists. Right now, a disadvantaged kid somewhere in the
world is reading one of the 100 million free books given out by

country star Dolly Parton's Imagination Library, a tribute to her illiterate father.

The great libraries of the ancient world – Alexandria, Ashurbanipal, Ephesus – were nearly always monuments to powerful men as much as they were temples of learning. It even became a fad for wealthy illiterates to build and exhibit libraries full of books they couldn't read, which oddly reminds me of the fake books you would sometimes see on shelves in restored northern pubs in the 90s. In Britain, the first libraries were very definitely not accessible to the public. They were for monks and scholars and the credentialled gentry, as in the famous Chained Library of Hereford Cathedral where the volumes are attached to the desks by hefty clanking links of metal like the cutlery in a prison or Brum's earliest Balti houses. Then came the various benefactors and the self-improvement of the workers' institutes. As Alistair Black puts it in his *A New History of the English Public Library*, 'a truly free library service did not appear overnight: they emerged on the back of a healthy tradition of independent library provision made by a diverse range of social, political and educational institutions'.

There had been libraries that graciously opened their doors to the public since the early seventeenth century: the library at the Free Grammar School in Coventry established in 1602, Norwich (1608), Bristol (1615), Leicester (1632) and the famous Chetham's Library in Manchester set up in 1653 by the wealthy Lancashire wool magnate and money-lender Humphrey Chetham. He bequeathed a sum of £1,000 to establish a library in his name. It's still there down by Victoria station and the Manchester Arena. You can visit if you turn up at the appointed hour these days, on the hour through the afternoons midweek. It isn't fully open to the public but you can take a tour and book an appointment for research. It's a beautiful building and a historic one. But it exists as an independent charity born of the gift of a wealthy benefactor rather than a right. We hadn't yet acknowledged that libraries were as essential a service as water or roads and should be similarly paid for from the public purse, not left to the whims and generosity of the rich.

For a small crowded island – perhaps *because* we are a small crowded island – Britain has achieved an extraordinary number of world firsts, and you don't have to be Nigel Farage to feel a little proud of them in all their giddy range: magnifying glasses, fixed-wing aircraft, the rules of boxing, carbon paper, the vacuum cleaner, anaesthetics, the World Wide Web. It's quite a list. The first inter-city passenger railway service in the world connected the two great cities of the industrial north-west, and both had their impressive share of other individual firsts. Liverpool brought forth the first public art gallery, the first public baths, the first prison and the first ambulance. It was home to the first public park and the first municipal golf course, as we shall see in both cases. Manchester, as it is not shy of telling you, gave the world communism, vegetarianism, feminism, the nuclear age and the computer. I have a book on my shelves titled *How Manchester Invented the Modern World* and, for once, this is not just typically 'Manc' braggadocio but a perfectly reasonable assertion. Down the road, though, it's smaller, older, tougher sibling Salford can boast some pioneering feats in the public and civic realm. Salford's streets were the first to be lit with gas, for instance. The first public bus service ran between Manchester and Salford and if you'd hopped on that bus from Chetham's Library to Market Street and along Chapel Street to Salford, you could have walked those newly gaslit streets with an entirely new and precious item under your arm: a book, not bought, but borrowed from a public library.

In 1832, Thomas Carlyle wrote, 'what a sad want I am in of libraries, of books to gather facts from? Why is there not a Majesty's library in every country town? There is a Majesty's jail and gallows in every one.' By the end of the century there would be 250 public libraries in Britain, thanks to the Public Libraries Act of 1850, a piece of law-making as important as any in the history of our legislature. Amazingly though, this Act didn't reach the statute books without a fight. Hard to credit, but there were committed opponents of public libraries, for reasons ranging from the short-sighted to the sinister. Firstly there was the usual whingeing and moaning about cost. Some opposed the Act on the grounds that the new libraries would mean increased taxes. Others worried that it would affect the profits of private booksellers. But some, especially in the Conservative Party, quite explicitly feared that free access to books and newspapers and literature would lead to greater knowledge and therefore greater agitation among the lower orders. Libraries might actually give them power, as the Manic Street Preachers were to sing a century or so later.

I think a man or woman who would close a public library is capable of anything. Sadly, there are plenty of them about. Some 130 public libraries shut in 2017 and spending on libraries by local authorities fell by £30 million to £741 million in that period. An army of thousands of volunteers props up what remains of a once vital part of our cultural and civic life. According to a chilling article in the *Guardian* by Laura Swaffield of the Libraries Campaign, 'What does emerge is a nasty secret that few people and least of all the government talk about: we no longer have a national public library service.'

We see the closures of libraries, rightly, as the work of the barbarian; a stain on any society calling itself civilised. But the left should not be complacent here. It was a 'strategic asset review' by the Labour–LibDem council that called for the closure of half of the Wirral's libraries in 2009, causing widespread anger and prompting a 55,000-signature petition. Moreover, it was a Tory turned Independent councillor, David Kirwan, who mounted a legal challenge, warning that the plan would turn the area into a 'cultural desert'. (As a result, he was banned from every library in the district; the very places he was trying to save.) Fife Council closed sixteen of its fifty-one libraries in 2015 and the executive director of education banned the children at Crail Primary from participating in a photoshoot to protest against the closure of their local one.

With so many enemies about, I decided to scout around for friends and lovers of libraries. Some were welcome and expected.

Alan Bennett had launched into the libraries debate with his usual late-period vigour. 'Libraries, like hospitals, like public transport, should come out of the rates. They are, or should be, a community service,' he told the Cheltenham Literature Festival. 'The best moments in reading are when you come across something ... a thought, a feeling, a way of looking at things, which you had thought special and particular to you. Now here it is, set down by someone else, a person you have not met, someone even who is long dead. And it is as if a hand has come out and taken yours.'

In the privacy of his diary, he was less diplomatic: '22 February. Switch on *Newsnight* to find some bright spark from, guess where, the Adam Smith Institute, proposing the privatisation of the public libraries. His name is Eamonn Butler and it's to be hoped he's no relation of the 1944 Education Act Butler. Smirking and pleased with himself as they generally are from that stable, he's pitted against a well-meaning but flustered woman who's an authority on children's books. Paxman looks on undissenting as this odious figure dismisses any defence of the tradition of free public libraries as "the usual bleating of the middle classes".' The entry, remarkably, is from 1996. Years later, he remarked, 'it's hard not to think that like other Tory policies privatising the libraries has been lying dormant for fifteen years, just waiting for a convenient crisis to smuggle it through. Libraries are, after all, as another think tank clown opined a few weeks ago, "a valuable retail outlet".'

Philip Pullman has weighed in regularly since the purge on public libraries began. In the *Guardian*, he saw the war on libraries as part of a wider, nastier assault on what were once our core values.

> Market fundamentalism, this madness that's infected the human race, is like a greedy ghost that haunts the boardrooms and council chambers and committee rooms from which the world is run these days ... I love the public library service for what it did for me as a child and as a student and as an adult. I love it because its presence

reminds us that there are things above profit, things
that profit knows nothing about … things that stand
for civic decency and public respect for imagination and
knowledge and the value of simple delight … Leave the
libraries alone. You don't know the value of what you're
looking after. It is too precious to destroy.

This presumably is what the men of the Adam Smith Institute
mean by 'middle-class bleating'. It's only books, after all. It's not
business. It's not money or finance. It doesn't actually matter, does
it? Well, it seems more thrusting and dynamic societies than our own
understand the power and value of a population who reads. When
the fantasy author Neil Gaiman attended the first party-approved
science fiction and fantasy convention in Chinese history in 2007, he
asked an official why the Chinese state, so long inimically opposed to
science fiction and fantasy – indeed anything that wasn't drearily
propagandist – had suddenly embraced it and begun producing great
writers in the genre. Gaiman went on to describe their conversation.

"'It's simple," he told me. The Chinese were brilliant at
making things if other people brought them the plans. But they
did not innovate and they did not invent. They did not imagine. So
they sent a delegation to the US, to Apple, to Microsoft, to Google,
and they asked the people there who were inventing the future
about themselves. And they found that all of them had read science
fiction when they were boys or girls.' Gaiman has also pointed out
that in America, planning for the next wave of private prison
construction takes into account levels of literacy. 'How many cells
are they going to need? How many prisoners are there going to be,
fifteen years from now? And they found they could predict it very
easily, using a pretty simple algorithm, based on asking what
percentage of ten- and eleven-year-olds couldn't read. And
certainly couldn't read for pleasure.'

I started to bring up libraries whenever I spoke to people I
met for other reasons if I could steer the conversation toward the
public good and the public realm. Interviewing Ian McEwan for

my radio show, he pointed me towards his *Desert Island Discs* appearance where he said, 'Although we were too poor for books, we had a weekly trip to the library. So there were always six books in the house, two each.' Chatting to Frank Cottrell-Boyce in the café at Whiston Hospital for the conversation that appears in the NHS chapter, we strayed happily onto libraries. 'I was such a child of libraries. When I was a little kid, me and my mum pretty much lived in our local library because our house was tiny and cramped and we weren't high enough up "the list" to get a new one. Kirkdale Library was across the road and it was a haven, as she must have been going mad in that little house. I think of my childhood in that library as magical. Opposite our house was a bombsite, but my childhood feels like *Where the Wild Things Are* because once you'd crossed that ruined bit to Kirkdale Library, you entered these amazing places. A library is a benign, truly public space. One of the few we have left. My local library closed. It was as if they'd lost confidence in what they were supposed to be. So the books go and they get a few crappy PCs in. And, like my daughter says, every house has got a computer now, but not every house has books. And the computers they've got at home are way better.'

I remember the thrill I got when my publisher told me that my book *Hope and Glory* was one of the most borrowed travel and history titles from public libraries the year it was published. It's a buzz that surely every writer except the most money-minded knows. Frank certainly does. 'As a writer, the best feeling I get is seeing my books in Liverpool Central Library. I remember going to town to the library and feeling that this is my birthright. Someone built this place and filled it with books because they thought I was worth it. The idea that this all belonged to me. It tells you how important you are. The Hornby Library upstairs had an Audubon,[7] for God's sake. I loved nature and art books and I

---

[7] James Audubon's *Birds of America*, along with the First Folio of Shakespeare, is one of the world's rarest and most prized books.

couldn't believe that I could manhandle these fabulous Taschen
art books that I could never have bought because they were fifty
quid.'

Frank knew from his and Danny Boyle's first seedling
thoughts that he wanted to include Britain's children's books and
authors in the 2012 Olympic opening ceremony. 'I wanted
Voldemort and Mary Poppins in there because we are the Brazil
of children's literature, we are to children's literature what Brazil
is to football. That had to be celebrated. The books you read
when you're eight, nine, ten ... they make you for life. If you can
get kids reading for fun by then, they'll be all right. It's like a
secret we've forgotten, that you can turbo-charge your life if you
read a bit. No one talks about it because some people don't want
you to know.'

Don't they? Doesn't every government want their people to
know more? Doesn't government of every stripe want greater
social mobility? The evidence certainly would suggest otherwise.
Why cut libraries first and hardest first when times get hard? Maybe
because, call me paranoid, there's perhaps something in those
books they don't want you to know. When Manchester Central
Library opened, children in the city were given an embroidered
handkerchief with an image of the library and the words 'Knowledge
Is Power'. If this is true, then so is the opposite. Ignorance is
impotence. Power is a dangerous thing to share if you already hold
it. Remember again the opposition to the 1850 Public Libraries
Act; an educated working class is a potentially seditious one.

In every corner of every town and city, the library was a little
citadel, a refuge, a fortress. Minds were trained here and vistas
opened. Pillgwenlly, usually shortened to 'Pill', is a formerly gritty
and industrial area of Newport, South Wales, now regenerated and
centred on the old docks. Young Nicholas Jones was a regular
library user who would raise his eyes every time he entered to a
phrase above the entrance which inspired and excited him. Later,
when he had become Nicky Wire of the rock group Manic Street

Preachers, he would turn it into the defiant, declamatory opening line of their anthem 'A Design for Life': 'Libraries gave us power, then work came and made us free …'

'That opening line was adapted from an engraving above the entrance to Pill library in Newport that read: 'Knowledge is power'. The weight of those almost Orwellian words became intertwined with an idea about what the miners had given back to society when they built municipal halls and centres across the country – beautiful-looking institutes that they proudly left for future generations. In the summer of 2009, the band were honoured to be asked to open the new Cardiff Central Library. 'For us, it seemed like a chance to give something back to Wales. Seeing one of our lyrics – "Libraries gave us power", from "A Design for Life" – inscribed on the opening plaque was in its own way as affecting as playing the Millennium Stadium.'

When I was writing for the *NME*, I sent a questionnaire to the Manics for a feature called 'The Material World of …', which was designed to give readers an insight into the lives of their favourite musicians. A few hours later, I ripped from the office fax machine the best set of answers I had ever received; each question had been answered not with a fatuous, desultory grunt but with a brilliantly apposite quote from the likes of Sylvia Plath, Dostoevsky, Flaubert, Andy Warhol, R.S. Thomas, Kierkegaard, Emily Brontë, Elvis or similar. They had clearly been waiting to be pop stars all their lives, reading, planning, absorbing, and now they were going to launch themselves on the minds of a generation. Instantly curious and a little smitten, I asked them to contribute to the next week's student special issue, an annual bore that we nonetheless felt obliged to put out yearly every Freshers' Week, asking various indie numbskulls for their advice to new students. Every year the smirking replies would come back about packing condoms and Rizlas and bog roll. The Manics simply replied, 'Don't just go to the bar. Make use of the excellent facilities of the university library. You might improve your mind and learn something.'

Naturally, a few of us fellow prole autodidacts in the music press fell instantly in love with them. We had found our band. The same reverent faces would be seen at every early gig. It's the same faces that I see still whenever the Manics play, a little family of now older but still infatuated lovers. One of them was a young girl from the Midlands with big hair and a look of permanent surprise and delight who wore floppy hats and big boots and chain-smoked and was rumoured to have written a novel at twelve and read every book in Wolverhampton Public Library. Bollocks, I thought, possibly nurturing a little prole autodidact envy. But it was true. She had. Even the geology ones.

'Especially the geology ones. Ask me anything about feldspar,' says Caitlin Moran, rolling a fag as we sit on a kerb in north London. Behind us, inside a working men's club taken over for the week, a crew of actors, technicians and directors are busy turning Caitlin's semi-autobiographical novel *How to Build a Girl* into a movie. We have just been inside watching a re-creation of the lives we lived in the early 90s; young kids up from the sticks still drunk on the thrill of being on a guest list, of getting our hands stamped and waved through to drink fizzy lager and shots and cheap vodka, looking studiedly cool while watching the fledgling Suede or Blur or Manic Street Preachers.

'I ordered Baudelaire's *Les Fleurs du Mal* from Wolverhampton Public Library because I'd heard the Manic Street Preachers talking about it in an interview. That took the longest of any of my orders to arrive. Seven months to come from Penrith or something, and after five pages I thought, right, this is not for me, and went back to Jilly Cooper and feldspar. I read literally everything. I was obsessed with the mastering of skills in preparation for future scenarios. So for instance, I went through a phase of wanting to know how to ice cakes. I studied techniques where you'd use greaseproof paper to ice the transparent outline of a dolphin or some such. It didn't matter that we couldn't afford greaseproof paper or an icing bag. When the time came I would be ready.'

There is something enormously touching about this to me, probably because it reminds me of my own obscure and outlandish enthusiasms nurtured for free in the quiet of the library. With me it was heraldry and Norse mythology. Given this, I suppose it's amazing that I have grown up (unlike Caitlin) with absolutely no interest in *Game of Thrones*. Reverse-engineered from an initial love of the rubbish versions in the Marvel comics *Thor* stories, I soon learned that the originals were far darker, wilder and more mysterious than the garish comic books. I borrowed every edition I could find. I liked Kevin Crossley-Holland's terse poetic modern versions but my absolute favourite was a battered old collection that made absolutely no concession to modern tropes or language and was all the more strange and powerful for that. I would pore over the woodcut illustrations: Yggdrasil the gnarled and curling tree of life, Baldur the bright being struck down by Blind Hodur's mistletoe dart, the one living thing in the world that had not sworn never to harm him, so innocuous did it seem. Audumbla the cow licking the world into shape from the salty rime-covered stones of Niflheim and Muspelheim. Aurgelmir the giant formed from the melting ice. The words still give me a shiver of chilly delight. Not being a twelfth-century earl, my enthusiasm for heraldry is harder to explain. But knowing my couchant from my rampant and my dexter from my sinister does stand me in good stead in pub quizzes.

There were ten of the Morans. Mum and dad and eight kids, of which Caitlin was the eldest. It was a logistical challenge rivalling the Normandy landings when the Morans went to the library. Unlike the D-Day landings, though, the Morans did it every day.

Every day. Sometimes twice a day.

'You were given an hour's notice of the library visit so we would scour the house collecting all the books because all of us would all have our cards maxed out. Even the babies would have ten board books out, covered in banana and sometimes poo. So first we'd stick back the flaps on *Spot* books where they'd been torn by pudgy toddler hands. Then you'd have to find the story books for the four-to-tens. Then we'd all get in the van in brightly coloured knitted ponchos and wellington boots bought from jumble sales and we would disembark and explode into the library in the middle of the day. This cyclone of noise and energy would arrive and because there were ten of us there would be a literal wall of books piled on the counter.'

The arrival of the Morans was not always a cause for rejoicing. 'The staff would groan and three extra would emerge from the back room where they'd been having a smoke and a cuppa. Then twenty minutes later when we'd all made our choices, the reverse enormous procedure would happen. This would happen sometimes twice a day. In my head I thought that the staff must admire my protean compulsions for language. But really I bet we were just the people who lost a lot of books. The younger members of the family really let us down. Then they started to do computer games and we'd lose them too. We were never malign. But we were a pain in the arse.'

Two years ago, Caitlin went back to Wolverhampton Library. Afterwards, she wrote one of her most devastating pieces about what had become of it after nearly a decade of cuts. 'That place was the making of me. So when I went back and saw it now I said it was like seeing a lobotomised parent or Aslan dead on a slab with its brain out. Once it had been this ugly, squat municipal building rammed with closely packed shelves of books on everything: World War Two, how to build a plane, how to be a shepherd, how to ice a cake, everything. Now there's three carousels of all the shit I hated: Mills and Boon and spy books. Andy McNab and *Fifty Shades* and rip-offs of *Fifty Shades*. One untouched shelf of classics like *Mill on the Floss*. Some homeless and mentally ill people left there by care in the community and a couple of teenagers at computer terminals. A whole network of goodness, a whole circuitry of cultural life switched off.'

Caitlin's article appeared in *The Times*, for whom she now writes. She is a writer, a brilliant one, because of Wolverhampton Library. As the cuts to library services began to switch off the circuits of learning and delight, to lobotomise every Aslan in the land, Nicky Wire wrote a similarly sadly raging piece in the *Guardian*.

Ridding our villages, towns and cities of libraries, which are essential in shaping a nation's consciousness, seems like a direct attack on the soul of the country. Libraries have always reassuringly been there when I've needed them ... One of the most amazing things about public libraries remains their utter classlessness. You don't have to have gone to Eton to make the most out of a library. They aren't inhabited by the kind of people currently damning them ... We need to cherish these things while they still exist. Seek solace, seek knowledge. Seek power.

The barbarian is not just at the gate. He's inside it now, in the parliament and the council office, closing our libraries, relishing it in some cases. It is easy to feel that all is lost or nearly lost. But there are pockets of defiance, strokes of luck, unexpected joys. One of them is the Library of Birmingham, opened in 2013 in the teeth of a world economic crisis at a cost of some £188.8 million. That sounds a lot of money. It is. But it's only about a third as much as Chris Grayling lost us for his privatised probation service catastrophe. It's not much compared to the £27 billion bailing out the banks cost the British taxpayer. You pays your money and you takes your choice. Except you and I have no choice.

Birmingham Library is also beautiful. A transparent box of glass, its delicate filigree lattice skin reflects the skilled artisan work that'd gone on for centuries in the workshops of the Jewellery Quarter down the road. Elevators and escalators criss-cross the immense airy interior, linking the eight circular spaces within the building. Rotundas echo both the city's mosques and the striking 60s brutalist tower that greets all those exiting New Street Station. The rooftop rotunda here contains the Shakespeare Memorial Room, a Victorian reading room lined with wood moved from the very first Birmingham Central Library. Here, pride of place goes to one of the world's rarest and most precious books, a First Folio of the plays of local boy made good William Shakespeare.

Architects say that a building under construction is always much more beautiful than when it is completed. The architect's intentions are present, unsullied and uncompromised, the raw materials sing of promise and the space is alive with possibilities. No one who isn't an architect though would ever say this though, as it's clearly nuts. For three years or so, the Library of Birmingham took shape under sheets of plastic and in long afternoons of rain. It was an eyesore of a building site. But the city's inconvenienced pedestrians were witnessing an extraordinary thing growing in the piazza at Centenary Square, eventually to burst from the cladding like a butterfly. Sorry, architects. It's far more beautiful now.

A proud palazzo of mesh and glass in black and gold. A postmodernist symphony of man-made materials. A dazzling cage of light made of steel and what looks to be golden barbed wire. But it's more than that. It is that rarest of things these days: a new library. A bold and brilliant new library that nearly didn't exist but does against all odds and in the teeth of cuts and critics. It is remarkable not just architecturally but culturally. It is Britain's biggest public library, moreover it is the largest regional library and public cultural space in Europe. The great and the good in the world of letters queued to sing its particular praises. Poet Laureate Andrew Motion, John Banville, Alan Ayckbourn, Ruth Rendell and Philip Pullman all said deservedly nice things. Irvine Welsh went as far as to call it, excitably but without recourse to any of his trademark sweariness, 'an audacious and compelling initiative which promises to redefine and modernise the entire notion of public library services, and in the process create the greatest public information resource in Europe ... Writers will love it, and so will readers.'

They did love it. In its first year Brummies queued around the block every day to be let inside. From further afield, two million people visited it, making it the most popular tourist attraction outside London. On 2 September 2013, after those mere three years of construction, it opened to the public in a palpable buzz from crowds more akin to a Saturday at the Villa or a gig at the

NEC than the opening of what is, essentially, a big building full of books. Lines of people waited at the door in shirt sleeves with water bottles on a baking September afternoon. For a new library. Once inside, they were like awestruck children entering Willy Wonka's factory: ten storeys, an art gallery, a children's area, a multimedia centre, two cafés, a music library, a performance space, an adjoining theatre with restaurant, terraces with herb gardens and more. That's not to mention the books.

In its opening week, I was given a tour of the library by its architect Francine Houben, founder of the Dutch collective Mecanoo. I was late getting there after a day in a Manchester radio studio but she'd waited for my train and swept me along on a giddy guided excursion made all the more exhilarating by Houben's pride in her creation and her evident love of the library and what it meant for the city. 'This is a people's palace,' she enthused. I asked whether the library expressed a striking visual statement on her part. She shrugged amiably. 'It's not about me, it's about them,' she said, indicating the throngs of people who were already flowing and eddying into every cranny and terrace; chatting, reading, writing, flirting ('Perfect for a snog,' she twinkled as we passed a little love seat arrangement by the video booths).

Walkways radiate out to the terraces and gardens. These are spaces with the kind of views – breathtaking vistas across the city to the soft green hills of Clent, the Malverns and Wales – that are usually the preserve of upscale bars and hotels where WAGS and minor celebs sip eye-wateringly pricey cocktails. Thanks to Francine and the far-sighted city council, these are here available to anyone who can get up here (and everyone can thanks to the building's exemplary accessibility). It is a genuinely democratising *coup de théâtre*, giving the city back to its residents.

Francine invited me to smell the mint and basil in the herb gardens and picked me a delicious raspberry. Later we rendezvoused with the library's director, Brian Gambles, his walkie-talkie crackling with updates, on his way to one of the two-hourly briefings the team were having to monitor progress and problems.

When he first came to work at the Brum central library in the mid-80s, one of the first tasks he oversaw was the installation of two PCs. His new library cost £189 million. Brian candidly admits that the whole project came in just 'under the wire' of the financial crisis. 'We were given the go-ahead in October 2007, just before the crash. I spent the first two years preparing cancellation reports, detailing just what the cost would be if we abandoned the project.' I got the feeling on that sultry, happy evening that a good deal of quiet steely determination and driven passion had underpinned this venture, characteristic of a great, unfashionable, vibrant city that, like Chicago or Detroit in their heyday, has always worked hard and got on with things without self-aggrandising blather.

On the day it opened to the public, the inaugural address was by an adopted Brummie, Malala Yousafzai, the teenage girl shot by the Taliban for the crime of going to school, who had recovered thanks to the care of the NHS and the geniuses at the Queen Elizabeth Hospital, another modern architectural and civic marvel of the second city, embraced and loved by all who used it. At the end of her speech, Malala placed her copy of Paolo Coelho's *The Alchemist* on the shelf, the final volume of the 400,000 on display. There are hundreds of thousands more in the archive, including two, a Shakespeare First Folio and Audubon's *Birds of America*, worth £14 million between them. Leaving that night into the Midlands dusk we passed a group of sightseers and librarians; one of the latter touched Francine's sleeve and whispered, 'This is beautiful. I love it. Thank you.'

Not all new libraries are so well received. When the new British Library opened, the usual ringleaders of the entrenched forces of conservatism got the ready-made speeches out, the tired diatribes about ugliness and soullessness. Routine, of course, but particularly rich in the case of professional naysayer Prince Charles, whose Poundbury development is both enormously ugly and horribly soulless. He said that the new British Library looked like 'the assembly hall of an academy for secret police'. This struck me as a particularly stupid remark, since if there is one thing I know about secret police HQs, it's that they're secret and also that Charles Windsor wouldn't have the first clue what they look like. They wouldn't look like the British Library, that's for sure. Another whinger said that the edifice resembled 'a Babylonian ziggurat seen through a funfair distorting mirror', which actually makes it sound brilliant if you ask me.

Some took sideswipes at the poor old, or rather poor new, British Library when they were supposed to be doing something else entirely. In an article in the *Literary Review* called 'Delights of the Public Catalogue Room' about midtown Manhattan's public library, a writer called Frances Wilson sniffed, 'The British Library is by contrast a dystopia. There is no singing or dancing or fine dining off the desks because there is nothing to celebrate. When it was housed in the British Museum it had gravitas and glamour but its current home is as bland as a high street in Bromley.' That last little detail tells you that whatever else Frances might be, she's a snob. I like the British Library, possibly out of sheer cussedness or possibly because I have had some fun nights there, such as when I drank a bottle of brandy with Johnny Rotten in front of a packed house during an event and we both wobbled back to the dressing rooms.

More to the point, as Caitlin pointed out in her piece, what was beautiful about Wolverhampton Library was not its architectural aesthetic but what it contained, whole universes of thought and experience, its value to the community it serves. Halfway between Brum and Wolves, on a bus route Caitlin would know well, if you take a little detour through Smethwick in the Black Country, you'll see a library that is both loved and lovely. Smethwick has persistent and ugly associations with Enoch Powell, the local MP who did his damnedest to sow bigotry and ignorance in the area, though he happily failed. But the little working-class multiracial suburb has two delightful buildings much better to dwell on than horrid old Enoch. Both are in a little area called, quaintly, Thimblemill. One is the baths, the first genuinely modern public baths in England, famous as a dance hall and for the visits of

the Beatles and the Rolling Stones. The other is down Wigorn
Road by the roundabout junction, its sister building, pretty as a
Poirot episode and a true People's Library. Thimblemill Library is
one of those shy treats that hides down suburban avenues in
residential England or in the squares of quiet market towns. It was
built in 1937 and is rightly a Grade II listed building, a beautiful
example of the elegant and svelte style of that decade. Its citation
in the canonical list of British Listed Buildings reads:

> Library. 1937, by the Smethwick Borough Engineer
> Roland Fletcher and the architect Chester Button.
> Monk bond with stack bonding to plinth; flat concrete
> roof. U-shaped plan, the Adult Lending Library being
> contained in a single-storey oval which projects forward
> from the concave face of a 2-storey curved block with
> stair tower to its rear elevation … A fine example of inter-
> war Moderne style, ingeniously planned by its designers
> in consultation with the librarian Mr HP Marshall.

Where are the men like Messrs Marshall and Fletcher and
Button today, men who thought nothing too good or too lovely
for 'ordinary' working people and their families? They must exist,
because they must have been there in the chamber of Birmingham
Council fighting to win their city its stunning new library. But
every day their voices are being drowned out by calls for prudence
and austerity, always demanding the tightening of workers' belts
but never the shrinking of bosses' bonuses.

It's a bitter, bright, icy winter's day and, flapping my arms and
blowing on my hands, I can only just stand around outside
Thimblemill Library for long enough to take in a fraction of the
posters and notices outside: ukulele classes, baby ballet, gigs by
various artists, UK and international, 60s discos, vinyl record
nights, Zumba and something called intriguingly *Chip Shop Chips*.
Stepping inside, you feel a warming heat that's not just the central
heating or the winter sunlight beaming into the semi-circular main

room. No, there's a warmth here to do with, and I use the word unashamedly, love; love of books, of creativity, of people, of place and community, of young and old.

For the young, there is 'Stay and Play' currently in full swing and voice in the adjoining room, a lusty arrangement of 'Old MacDonald Had a Farm' for high trebles. There's a laptop with the signage 'only children age 12 or under have access to this computer', but above it a poster reminds the mums and dads, 'an app is no substitute for your lap'. For the older visitor, there's a Recollection Chair, a comfy seat surrounded by vintage books and magazines with headphones attached on which local residents share their memories of Thimblemill days past, perhaps of Ringo or Mick Jagger or Henry Hall enjoying a saveloy in the local chip shop after their gig at the baths. More morbidly, but attracting much attention, is a flyer for a forthcoming theatre production of a one-man show about an infamous and unsolved local murder of the 1930s. Another notice tells us that Thimblemill was Britain's first ever 'Library of Sanctuary', an initiative begun here in 2017, and has 'an ongoing commitment to refugees and asylum seekers'.

There's a lovely picture of the band Buzzcocks in their central library in Manchester standing in front of a section marked 'Fiction / Romance', which devotees will know became the title of one of their finest early songs. Strolling the shelves here in Thimblemill throws up all kinds of philosophical questions and juxtapositions: 'Sport / Poetry'; 'True Crime / Maths'; 'Science / Religion'. A picture of Stephen Fry beams down from above (as in the wall above, not heaven) and bears one of his many quotable *bon mots*. 'An original idea. That can't be too hard. The library must be full of them.' Thimblemill is packed with them and they're just in the pages of the books or the hard drives of the laptops. Smethwick Library has Julie McKirdy too.

Julie, presiding spirit of this brilliant place, was there when I popped in to visit. That's not surprising really. She's hardly ever away. She has been here thirty-eight years and made a small if beautiful local library into the absolute heart of the little community. Not just a house of books, tremendous a thing though that is, but a gig venue, a theatre space, a playground, a sanctuary, a university. Even, as I'll find out, a chip shop. When I walked in off Wigorn Road, I didn't mention what I do or why I was there. This was no prearranged visit. Just came in off the roundabout one weekday afternoon and within minutes Julie was handing me her phone and inviting me to scroll through the pictures on it. 'Don't worry, it's all pictures of the library. That's my life. That's all I do! You won't see anything you shouldn't. Unless it's my bad leg when I fell off a boat in Belize.'

The sheer amount of stuff going on here is astounding. This week, there's a performance by a new young female singer-songwriter in the alt-country vein because, remarkably, Thimblemill Library has become a regular stopping-off point for touring musicians in the genre, largely down to Julie, even though her music of choice is northern soul. 'We have jazz, Americana, folk. We've had a silent disco. Next week, we've got a new theatre piece about Frank Freeman's Dancing Club in Kidderminster. It was set up by a local couple, Frank and Wynn, as a dancing school but then became a very popular venue. Victor Silvester, Joe Loss and Edmundo Ros, he had them all. Len Goodman off *Strictly* used to go there.'

Thimblemill has had its legendary gigs too. 'We had over two hundred people in here for Sally Barker of *The Voice*,' says Julie. 'She's been twice. When we have live music and theatre, it's a wonderful atmosphere. All this space' – she indicates the book-lined semicircle – 'is full. It's really marvellous. We get great audiences. It's fabulous of a night here. Fabulous.' Perhaps glancing at my finely honed physique, she says, 'You should come for a play next month called *Chip Shop Chips*. You'll love that. But you have to tell me in advance what you want – pie, sausage or fish – as there's a chippy tea included in the price. From George and Helen's in Quinton. Deadline Friday of the week before.'

Lightly salivating, I buy a ticket and promise to get my chippy order in early. It is George and Helen's, after all. As I leave, I ask

Julie whether they've felt the sting, or rather the slash, of 'austerity'. 'Cuts? We've only really felt it in our opening hours, and opening hours are a bit meaningless here as I'm here all the time, paid or unpaid. We never keep to opening hours and there's always something happening at night. It never stops, love, it never sleeps. I've been here for donkeys' years. It's my baby. I love music and I love theatre. I mean, I love books as well. But this is what the modern library has become: a creative hub.'

A colleague gently interjects, 'She's got the BEM for services to the community, you know.' Julie looks awkward and sheepish. 'I just love this library.'

I'm happy for Julie. Delighted. But mildly irritated too at the truth behind it. Why don't we reward people like Julie – and there are scores of them quietly making life better in your town right now – reward them with power and status and maybe something like the wages of hedge-fund managers and lawyers instead of relying on their huge good hearts. Julie's love of this library is evident in everything about it and that is a wonderful thing. But as those famous library lovers and users Manic Street Preachers once sang, love alone is not enough.

When the defeated fascist barbarians of ISIS were retreating from the Iraqi city of Mosul, one of their final acts of ignorant desperation was to burn the university library. UNESCO called it 'one of the most devastating acts of destruction of library collections in human history'. Thirty thousand books went up in flames. All that poetry and art and science and philosophy drifting to the sky in a shroud of black and burning paper. Maybe even the philosophy of William Heine, who once wrote, 'Wherever they burn books, they will end up burning people.' 'The smell,' remembered one heartbroken academic of Mosul, 'was like hell.' It was hell. Because hell is a place where they burn libraries. Our little hell in the UK today, the one we've stoked and let stink the place up, is where we let our barbarians close them to pay for the greed of bankers.

Once not even the most severe of market ideologues would have actually opposed public libraries. It would have been like

being against babies or fresh air or sunlight. When she opened
Keighley Public Library in 1975, the then education secretary said,
'The library service is very closely linked to education, and I say
this not as a matter of politics or local organisation, but very much
from my own experience . . . I owe a very great deal of my education
to a library being available for regular reading.' Libraries gave
Margaret Thatcher power too, it seems, a thought to be considered
by some of those who take her as their moral compass and guru.

But here's a thing. They're restocking Mosul Library. With
the help of Book Aid International and maybe you. They've got a
few thousand volumes still to go but they will do it. The academics
and students of Mosul University danced when the books started
to arrive. In vaguely related other good news, I went to see *Chip
Shop Chips*. It was ace, especially the chips and the bright-green
mushy peas. Also the curry sauce was free. Good old George and
Helen. There was one family who clearly had come just to eat, not
that they looked in any great danger of starving to death, and they
burped and smirked all the way through the earnest and heart-
warming play. But in an admirable example of how small working-
class communities have always self-policed, we glared at them and
then eventually one woman – who later turned out to have a degree
in 'experimental theatre' – turned to her mate nearby and said,
'Rachel, tell 'em to shut the fuck up.'

'Hope you enjoyed it,' says Julie as I leave. 'Come back soon.
Next week it's a lovely new singer from Austin, then it's the Eastern
European music workshop plus drop-in advice night,' she adds
matter-of-factly, as if libraries have never been anything other than
vibrant places full of singing kids, fish and chips, ukuleles, balalaikas,
plays and play groups and willowy American singer-songwriters,
here in the heart of the Black Country.

Thinking and reading and talking about libraries for this
chapter, I often encountered, even among some reasonably liberal
people, a sort of weary resignation and acceptance of the cuts that
libraries have suffered under 'austerity'. They would make
sympathetic noises, but, almost apologetically, would conclude

that councils' hands were tied and the axe of cuts had to fall somewhere, wielded by those tied hands.

I disagree. While I feel sorry for individual councils, 'austerity' was a political choice and involved a politically motivated prioritisation. Many economists, most of those in universities and academia as opposed to the more partial and vested City economists, have pointed out that the cuts could easily have been postponed until the countries wider economic fortunes had changed and the threat of recession receded. But more to the point, when Christopher Grayling can squander billions on botched privatisations and Boris Johnson waste the same on harebrained garden bridge schemes, we have to ask what kind of society we want before we decide where to cut. For me, libraries, like schools and hospitals should be the last things we should cut not the first, alongside parks and leisure centres, swimming baths and sports pitches, the great panoply of healthy – and sometimes not so healthy – organised fun that was another reason some of us grew up grateful for the nanny state. It was not just stern and pragmatic. Nanny also knew how to have a good time.

CHAPTER 5

I HAVE FUN

'NO BOMBING, NO DIVING, NO PETTING'

According to the Beatles, there are two things that money can't buy. You'll have thought of the first one right away, I bet. Yes. Love, as in 'Can't Buy Me Love', their raucous, joyous hit of March 1964.

Have you thought of the other? Bit more tricky. It's 'fun'. According to 'She's Leaving Home' from *Sgt Pepper*, fun is 'the one thing that money can't buy', as sung by Lennon in the song's Greek chorus. All right-thinking people respect and love the Beatles. Never trust anyone who doesn't. But in this they were simply dead wrong. For one thing, if fun were the one thing that money can't buy, this would rather contradict their assertion about love just a few short years before. For another, money can absolutely, 100 per cent, definitely buy you fun. People have been buying fun ever since a bored Neolithic man first offered a bit of flint axe in return for a quick campfire snog or woolly-mammoth burger.

Apparently, people used to make their own fun. I grew up being told this most days of my young life. Each time that I optimistically put down a Johnny Seven (massive plastic multi-use assault rifle with rocket launcher) or Spirograph (weird hippie fractals graphic design thing) on my Christmas list, my nana would tut disapprovingly – her default setting – and tell me that in her day, 'we made our own fun'. Generally, this seemed to involve the use of a hoop and stick, a kind of anti-toy that made time expand sideways, or at Christmas a tangerine. Both of these seemed pretty poor fare when compared to an Action Man 'with grabbing hands' or Buckaroo, the fun game of pack-animal cruelty and exploitation.

Not everything fun-related though was left to Mammon and his generals Messrs Waddington, Palitoy and Hasbro. Most evenings and holidays would be taken up with street games. These usually involved some form of pursuit and capture of opposition team members and had names such as 'Skilly', 'British Bulldog' or 'Ticky Off Ground', all of which ended in violence as a matter of course. 'Six Bricks' required the building of a teetering column of, you're ahead of me, six bricks, whose kicking over by an insurgent released all captives. The ease with which these vital bricks could be found tells you how, even as late as the mid-70s, most British residential streets and estates would contain at least one patch that still looked as if the Luftwaffe had just done their worst.

There was a third option though, to be had in a sphere that was neither feral nor fiscal, somewhere between the anarchy of the street game and the corporatism of the toy manufacturers. It was, of course, the civic. At the start of the Victorian era, the middle and upper echelons of society started to worry about what the lower orders were doing with their spare time, a window of some twenty-five minutes between emerging from below ground or the gates of a roaring foundry or clanking mill and the knocker-upper banging on the window of your hovel. What bothered them chiefly was that they would spend it drinking or in some kind of collective revelry which could lead to lawlessness and, worse, sedition.

But in 1945, the Labour Party enshrined the recreation of the people in the manifesto that would help sweep them to power: 'National and local authorities should co-operate to enable people to enjoy their leisure to the full, to have opportunities for healthy recreation. By the provision of concert halls, modern libraries, theatres and suitable civic centres, we desire to assure to our people

full access to the great heritage of culture in this nation.' Thus the
first steps were taken on the road to the joys of the verruca bath
and the asphalt tennis court, the municipal golf course and being
chased off the putting green by the 'parkie'.

We think of the state as the stern but fair provider of schools
and hospitals and roads and streetlights and such, and – back in
more enlightened times – of libraries and water and trains and the
rest. But looking back on my childhood, though a good deal of it
was spent in cinemas and football grounds and record shops and
concert halls, places built for profit that required money, I did
fabulously well out of the state. I did particularly brilliantly out of
public parks, in which I practically lived semi-feral between the
ages of ten and sixteen, at which age the interior delights of the
pub and disco became both irresistible and attainable. Before this
though, the park, especially Alexandra Park, Newtown, was my
milieu, every evening and weekend and all through the giant days
of the school holidays.

One of the mild reservations I have about the ubiquity of
'parkruns', that modern phenomenon whereby hundreds of folk in
Lycra gather soon after dawn in public parks at a weekend to
transform them into an athletics stadium, is my fond residual
memories of a youth spent dissolutely in such places. I don't mind
the odd jogger, but mass collective path-pounding by phalanxes of
fitness nuts seems to me vaguely contrary to and might even stymie
the other essential uses of the public park: teenage assignations,
furtive smoking, three-a-side re-enactments of major FA Cup
clashes, picnics, dog walking, courtship, ham-fisted playing of
musical instruments, cricket, organised brawls, etc. If a score of
ruddy, perspiring runner types had been circling the park every ten
minutes in 1976, this would have severely limited my chances of
'copping off' with Kath Roby in the wooden cage area at the top
of the big slide, and they were slim enough to begin with. Health
is all well and good. *Mens sana in corpore sano* and all that. But
recreation can take many forms. Had we, the gang of lads and girls
that congregated nightly in Alexandra Park, seen anyone dashing

past red-faced we would naturally have assumed he was being chased by coppers.

I didn't know it at the time but in our unhealthy, rambunctious colonisation of the park, we were continuing a grand old tradition of northern urban kids. University of Manchester researcher Ruth Colton looked into the history of parks in Manchester, Huddersfield and Gateshead and found that, while the establishment thought these spaces important at a time of rising concerns about children's behaviour, health and welfare, things didn't always pan out as they'd have liked. 'There was a rowdy and unpredictable side too: while parks were supposed to promote social harmony, this was often resisted and parks could be sites of conflict and contrast. Newspapers reported that children and youths were sitting on park benches shouting abuse at passers-by. Children would also illegally fish in park lakes for ornamental fish or steal fruit off the trees.' Eating food and drinking alcohol, both forbidden in the park by-laws, were rife. We certainly did our share of that, though I don't recall Kath Roby ever landing a decent tench.

I went back to Alexandra Park this summer for the first time in decades. It was a distinctly Proustian experience, not unpleasant but unsettling. The park had changed radically for one thing. In what seemed a good move, all the fencing and gates have been removed, leaving it entirely open to the surrounding streets. If the 'youth' of the surrounding streets do use the park for nocturnal revels as we once did, they won't have to risk tearing their 'keks' while effecting ingress or egress over the spiked railings. The putting green has gone, as has the steamroller – always a curious choice as a playground accessory, I felt – but the defunct water fountain was still there, still resolutely and stubbornly refusing to dispense water.

Like so much else in our public realm, 'the park' is under threat after a decade of savage cuts. In a Heritage Lottery Fund survey of 2014, 86 per cent of park managers said their budgets had been cut. When the authorities in charge of Liverpool's famed Sefton Park wanted to sell off eleven acres to housing developers, the outcry was led by Scouse-born *Sex and the City* actress Kim Cattrall. Of course, we can sympathise with the harried finance director or council chief tasked (or rather forced) to hack budgets to the bone and make grim choices. Liverpool mayor Joe Anderson fairly bristled at Cattrall's well-intentioned intervention. 'It's all very well for a Hollywood superstar to shout from the sidelines, but what does she really know of the issues that Liverpool faces? She may have played in Sefton Park when she briefly lived in the city as a girl, but she left. I am still here and having to deal with massive and savage Tory government cuts to our budget while devising ways to grow and sustain the city and protect its most vulnerable citizens.' This seems reasonable, if a little robotically Spartist, I have to say. Burnley's Towneley Park has let a hefty percentage of its managed grounds revert to wildflower meadows for reasons that are as much to do with finance as conservation.

It's a commonplace to refer to London's various parks as the 'lungs of the city'. Anyone who, like me, has worked in the capital through dirty, gritty, noisy summers in the capital will know the delight of taking time out from a busy day in the West End and dashing up Regent Street to sprawl on the grass of Regent's Park for an hour. I have conducted several interviews over cappuccinos and cakes in the café in Hyde Park and slept off many a Soho-induced hangover in a deckchair in Green Park. But all these too are feeling the pinch. Dr Andrew Smith, an urban geographer from the University of Westminster, has studied Finsbury Park, Gunnersbury Park and Brockwell Park (where I watched The Clash and Elvis Costello in a righteous teenage glow at Anti-Nazi League rallies). He found councils were increasingly and desperately over-reliant on them as commercial assets and were restricting full public access in favour of profitable corporate events like music festivals. As he told the Royal Geographical Society's annual conference, this is all part of the 'creeping privatisation' of public spaces and public life. 'It's for good reason – they're desperately trying to find ways of making revenue, but it's got to the point where we need to think about protecting parks from local authorities' exploitation. If you live next to one of those parks, you not only lose the access for several weeks of the year, but you also endure the practical inconvenience, the noise and the trucks as well. It's a double whammy.'

In my role as president of Ramblers GB, I have much to do with the Open Spaces Society, our venerable, tough, campaigning older sibling. They have bemoaned and continue to highlight the damage that the private and commercial sector is doing to London's parks. Clapham Common now holds about a hundred days of commercial events a year, much to the annoyance and dismay of locals who find their beloved green space a cordoned and muddied desert for months on end. One of the many reasons I always approach Glastonbury with a shudder is the sheer ugliness of the site in full festival swing: a churned and oozing bog, a Passchendaele with indie rock accompaniment. Clapham Common – or 'Clapham Commercial' as the locals have apparently taken to calling it – is looking like this for most of the autumn these days. As Andrew Smith rightly says, 'A festival has this sort of friendly face, people do see them as public occasions, but they're obviously only public occasions if you can afford to get in ... Parks are a great triumph of the British state that we should be looking after, because once it's gone it's gone. We've got to realise that parks are special, beyond any financial calculation of what they're worth.'

Even if it is just about counting the pennies though, parks are indubitably a good thing for the nation. Consider these amazing statistics from the Fields in Trust report called 'Revaluing Parks and Green Spaces'. The mental and physical health benefits of parks save the NHS about £111 million a year and in order to meet the same level of life satisfaction such places bring, each of us in Britain would have to spend about a grand each year. Multiply that by the adult population, and parks generate more than £34 billion of benefits. So, as with so much else done under the guise of 'austerity', one suspects something murkier than mere pragmatism is at work.

Professor Paul Elliott, an academic specialising in public parks, told the *Daily Telegraph* that these grand places are 'part of the character of Britain', adding that 'If a library closes it is immediately obvious. But if you gradually cut back a park's funding, it's harder to notice. Grass is mown less frequently, trees start to decline and die. It's incremental.' Elliott works at the University of Derby and so is particularly knowledgeable about the Derby Arboretum, whose shifting fortunes tell a very British story, from well-meant beginnings, a period of pomp, decades of decline and vandalism, the bright new morning of Heritage Lottery funding and regeneration, and now a managed and imposed purdah through cuts. The arboretum, Elliott told the *Independent* in 2015, is:

> one of the most significant public parks in the country. It has an important place in the history of landscape gardening because of its designer, John Claudius Loudon, and because of the way it was founded as an open space that could be used for free by working people. Joseph Strutt [a local mill owner and philanthropist] wanted to give something back to the workers who had helped to make his family wealthy. He donated the arboretum at a time when other parks were only open to paid subscribers. He hoped it would also bring about social improvements, develop their moral conduct, teach them about botany and also enhance their industriousness. It was the first place that they could go on a Sunday afternoon to get away from the mills and their homes.

Incredibly, the workers of Derby were given a three-day holiday to mark the park's opening in September 1840. Twenty thousand visitors assembled among the fabulous array of trees, shrubs, flowers and bushes collected there by Loudon to watch a major procession on the first day. But it was free only on Sundays and Wednesdays. For the first half-century of its existence, admission was charged for on all other days. This is what makes the arboretum's claim to be the world's first public park contentious. Like the first libraries, it was a gift from a rich benefactor, rather than paid for from the public purse, and it wasn't completely or even largely free to enter. I wanted to visit Britain's first genuinely public park, the first one built by the people for the people, and for that, I would need a ferry cross the Mersey – or at least the Merseyrail train to Birkenhead – and the services of one Nigel Blackwell. According to writer Andrew Harrison, Blackwell is 'Britain's greatest living satirist'. He is also a cult rock musician, a keen fell walker, an enthusiast for the ghost stories of M.R. James (his email address is taken from an obscure character in 'A Warning to the Curious') and, most pertinently, about as knowledgeable and entertaining a guide to Birkenhead and its history as you could wish.

'Contrary to our image, we normally rehearse on a Monday,' says the tall, skinny droll chap with the shaven head who meets me at Birkenhead Park Station on a warm autumn evening. At this, I feel an instant icy dig of anxiety that I might be, person from Porlock style, disrupting the creative flow of one of Britain's most uniquely brilliant independent post-punk bands. Assured that they were taking a break anyway tonight, we set off along the sunny street for Birkenhead Park, model for New York's Central Park and the first public park anywhere in the world. Sorry, Derby.

There is considerable erudition in the music of Half Man Half Biscuit. References to the lonely hills of Shropshire, old English hymn tune conventions, the poetry of George Crabbe and, in the song 'Malayan Jelutong', a glimpse of Nigel's love of local history (knowledge of which has brought me to the Wirral on this lovely night), in the quotation from an 1891 essay by Edward W. Cox in the *Transactions of the Historic Society of Lancashire and Cheshire*. A ferociously smart and talented autodidact educated by the BBC, the local library and a moderately benevolent benefits system, Nigel Blackwell is a testament to the brilliance of the post-war consensus and the derided nanny state, a genuine native genius without entitlement or conceit.[8]

'My dad got me into local history as a kid. And when I got into it one of the first things you learn is that Birkenhead Park was the model for Central Park in New York. Now some of my dad's generation and the old cynics of local history, they would raise their eyebrows at this. But the first time I saw Central Park – in a book, obviously – I thought, yes, it does look like Birkenhead Park. You'll notice all these grassy mounds and knolls which are identical, and the layout is the same. So I looked into it and the actual story is like something from a *Monty Python* sketch. The fellow who designed Central Park was on a tour of the north-west and he popped over here on the ferry and apparently went into a tobacconist's on Conway Street. So he got talking to the fellow behind the counter who asked him what he did and he said, well, it's a bit odd but I design parks. So the tobacconist said, we've got a brilliant one up the road. So he wanders over, has a look, is dead impressed and when he gets the commission to design Central Park, he bases it on ours. I looked into it properly and there is substance to the story, to the point that it's now all emblazoned on the noticeboard and the literature obviously. They don't miss a trick.'

But what made both the Conway Street tobacconist and Nigel so proud of their park is not any famous imitators but the fact that it was a genuine first. Birkenhead's park, the first truly public park anywhere, was the forerunner of what became a global parks movement. Its impact and influence were far-reaching both in this country and abroad. If you have eaten a baguette in the Bois de Boulogne or rented a pedalo in Parque Ibirapuera, São Paulo, you have Birkenhead's civic fathers to thank. 'This was the first park anywhere in the world by and for

---

[8] In this he has much in common with one of his heroes, the late Mark E. Smith of The Fall. When I asked him once about a particularly arcane literary allusion in a lyric, he replied, 'Yeah, I know all that stuff, Stuart. I just don't go around fucking showing off about it.'

the people. It wasn't some rich guy's private pleasure ground that we plebs were allowed to use. This has never been privately owned. It was made with public money for the people of Birkenhead and we are very proud of that.'

In 1853, the Parliamentary Select Committee on Public Walks was asked to research ways to find more open spaces in our cities and encourage exercise and recreation. It reported that:

> with a rapidly increasing population, lodged for the most part in narrow courts and confined streets, the means of occasional exercise in the fresh air are every day lessened as inclosures take place and buildings spread themselves on either side. It cannot be necessary to point out how requisite some public walks or open spaces in the neighbourhood of large towns must be to those who consider the occupation of the working classes who dwell there, confined as they are during the weekdays as mechanics and manufacturers and often shut up in heated factories ... if deprived of any such resource it is probable that their only escape from the narrow courts and allies (in which so many of the humble classes reside) will be drinking shops where in short lived excitement they may forget their toil but where they waste the means of their families and too often destroy their health.

This all sounds awfully starchy and patronising to the modern ear, of course. But look beyond that. There's also a real desire to effect change and improve the lot of others. We may mock much about the Victorians, their prudishness, their bigotry, their hats, but they put us to shame in many ways. In 1851, they were using public money to build parks for the betterment of ordinary people. Today, we close them to save money to give in bailouts and bonuses to the rich. Sorry for the repetition. But the point is worth hammering.

Joseph Paxton (later Sir Joseph) was a Liverpool landscape gardener who caught the eye of people who notice such things. He was commissioned to design Birkenhead Park in 1843 (for a fee of £800) with a brief to create an idealised version of the English countryside. Many of the town's residents were country folk who had been drawn to the booming city in search of work so Paxton was tasked with creating a little taste of home and a rural idyll, but on a site that was common land and shallow bog and 'in some parts a low swamp exhaling the most pestilent vapours'. A nearby farm under the stewardship of one Hannah Mutch was notorious for supplying illicit beer, illegal gambling, rat killing, badger baiting and dog fighting. In a letter to his wife from the Adelphi Hotel, Paxton wrote, 'I must have lost 1lb of perspiration for I must have walked 30 miles to make myself master of the locality and it is not a very good situation for a park as the land is generally poor but of course it will rebound more to my credit and honour to make something handsome and good out of poor materials.'

He certainly did that. Paxton utterly transformed this dire patch of northern quagmire. He drained it, landscaped it, put a stop to the booze and badger-baiting evenings, and a fine new public park opened in 1847 to great fanfare and immediate success. Fifty-six thousand people attended the opening festivities. We don't know if Hannah Mutch tore herself away from her busy afternoon of rat-murder but we do know Disraeli was invited, replying that 'my engagements render it quite out of my power to avail myself of this flattering mark of goodwill'. It looks as if he missed quite a bash. 'Look at this stuff about the opening day,' says Nigel as we saunter the grassy hillocks. He has brought along the commemorative booklet, which contains the order of ceremony. 'Look at these events.' They are, by any measure, remarkable: 'A Grinning Match Through Six Horse Collars'; 'A Bell Race For A Hat'; 'A Foot Race For Women Of All Ages'; 'A Blindfolded Wheelbarrow Race'; 'A Pig Chase, Value Two Pounds, With Its Tail Soaped'.

'Grinning through horse collars,' says Nigel, thrilled. 'And look at this: "Three Basins Of Hot Stirrah To Be Eaten By Lads Not Exceeding 18 Years. No Treacle." I've tried to find out what stirrah is. No one knows. I thought it might be some kind of gruel or treacle but, as you clearly see, there's no treacle allowed. But would you look at that flyer? I've always thought it would make a great Fairport Convention sleeve.' Music was provided by Horabin's Celebrated Quadrille Band, just the sort of name that would fire the imaginations of four lads from across the water in Liverpool in their late 60s phantasmagorical heyday.

A glance at the timeline of the park's history shows the narrative of a changing Britain in itself. Two Russian cannons captured in the Crimean War were displayed on a small hill for years before being melted down during the Second World War. Fourteen thousand people processed through the park to celebrate the marriage of the Prince and Princess of Wales in 1863. Unemployment relief schemes were held during periods of economic strife in the 1890s, 1920s and 1930s. A funfair was held on VE Day. Fireworks marked the optimism of the Festival of Britain in 1951. Somewhat depressingly, vandalism arrived after the war and stayed for the rest of the century.

'We wouldn't have come down here in the 1980s,' says Nigel as we skirt the edges of the ornamental boating lake. 'There would have been all sorts of stuff going on. Heroin came here first in the 1980s before it got to Liverpool. The Liverpool gangsters brought it over to try it out on us Birkenhead guinea pigs. It was a roaring success, I have to say. It took off famously. But this here, the Swiss Bridge, this is one of our big success stories. The only covered wooden bridge in the UK. Modelled on the Swiss style, obviously. It's had its ups and downs. But it's in pretty good shape right now. I mean, there's still some darker stuff going on maybe after nightfall.' He drops into *sotto voce*. 'See those lads over there, those lads fishing, well, they may be otherwise engaged as well. But at least they're out in the fresh air fishing and enjoying the park, and I'd like to think that these days, if they saw one of their mates or some kids vandalising the bridge they'd have a word.'

If Nigel ever decides to give up on hilariously critiquing contemporary social mores through angular indie rock, he would make an excellent and unique tour guide. As we meander through the park, he takes me on various detours and digressions. We push through some bracken and through pitted ruts ('Pity you've got your nice shoes on, Stu'), blithely past a sign that warns 'Do Not Enter' and emerge at the back of a large fine house. 'This house was the childhood home of one Sandy Irvine. Friend of Mallory. That could be the house of the first man who climbed Everest. [Irvine disappeared with Mallory during an attempt on the summit in 1924.] Nothing. No plaque.'

Emerging and brushing ourselves down, we pass the mound where the captured Russian cannons once stood and with a flourish Nigel indicates a stone pillar of Celtic design by the side of the Italian gates. 'My favourite place in the park. A great story. They held the 1917 Eisteddfod here. They were often held outside of Wales in the war years because a lot of Welsh people came here to work in the munitions factories. My family, for instance. And the climax of any Eisteddfod is the crowning of the bard.' Being awarded the bard's crown at an Eisteddfod is the highest honour a Welsh poet can receive, the climax of the week-long festival of song, speech and verse. That year the three learned judges, men of letters all, had decided to award the prize to a poem in strict traditional metre called 'Yr Awyr' (The Hero), submitted, as was the procedure, anonymously and in this case under the pseudonym Fleur de Lis. It had actually been written by the Welsh poet Ellis Humphrey Evans, better known by his bardic name, Hedd Wyn. 'So they read out the winning poet's name just here by this stone. And then, as was the tradition, they ask the person who'd written it to step forward and receive the acclaim of the audience and their peers and accept the chair. It's a big thing. The ultimate accolade for a Welsh poet. National fame forever. But no one answered. So they asked again. And again, nothing.'

Hedd Wyn had enlisted in the Royal Welsh Fusiliers early in 1917. He'd started 'The Hero' at his parents' farm in Trawsfynydd and refined it in army camp at Litherland near Liverpool before sailing for Flanders, where he finished it and posted it back to Wales. On his first day of action at Passchendaele, a nosecap shell exploded under him as he advanced up Pilckem Ridge. He fell dying, clutching two handfuls of Belgian soil. He was thirty years old and one of the 31,000 soldiers who died that day. ('A fine day's work,' Douglas Haig wrote in his diary.)

'Eventually someone stood up and said that he was dead in a trench or a field somewhere. It was a terrible moment. So in this incredibly emotional atmosphere, they placed a black cloak over the chair instead. Now it's known as the Eisteddfod of the Black Chair. *Cadair Ddu.* '

As Nigel walks me to the train (via the pub) on a still sunny evening, he asks me to tell him a little more about this book. I explain as best I can after several pints of Goose IPA that it's a celebration of the public, the collective, the national, the municipal, the much maligned nanny state. I'm going to argue that 1979 was a turning point but in many ways it was a backward step. He nods. 'People talk a lot of shite about the 1970s. It may have been bad for stockbrokers and such, but if you lived round here and you were a working-class family, we probably had never had it so good. We had a decent holiday in Rhyl every year and my dad had a Ford Anglia. That seems quite a healthy state of affairs to me. Personally, I had a very enjoyable 1970s.'

And with that I leave Britain's Greatest Living Satirist, lyricist of genius, dazzling autodidact product of the nanny state to his walk home through the streets he loves in an passionate but entirely unsentimental way. One day we will hear the Half Man Half Biscuit anthem 'Three Basins Of Hot Stirrah To Be Eaten By Lads Not Exceeding 18 Years. No Treacle', I feel sure. When that happens, I hope you will smile knowingly, gentle reader.

Since their range of reference is so wide, I am surprised that I can't think of a Half Man Half Biscuit song about the phenomenon of the public baths. Perhaps you can. It would seem odd if Nigel has never offered us his thoughts on the shallow verruca bath, the café staples of giant Wagon Wheels and Horlicks or the famously jokey but stern poster that warned us off in cartoon form from the various activities forbidden within the baths: diving, running, bombing, acrobatics, ducking, shouting, pushing and petting (nearly always irritatingly misquoted and misremembered as 'no heavy petting'). The first ever use of that sign was in the 1930s at Thimblemill Baths, now more properly Smethwick Swimming Centre, visited by *The One Show* for that reason in 2009 in one of those 'mirthful' items that manages to drain all humour from the subject. It has been the location for two episodes of the daytime soap *Doctors*. It's a beautiful art deco building that is civic architecture at its finest, and has played host to the Beatles, the Rolling Stones, the Kinks, the Who, Tommy Cooper and Ronnie and Reggie Kray. It's just up Wigorn Road from Smethwick's library celebrated earlier, so avid connoisseurs of public leisure can bag two prime examples before getting the No. 80 to West Bromwich and having the chilli naan and massala chips in the Vine. Just being public-spirited with a bit of local ninja knowledge.

The first baths I remember was Tyldesley in Lancashire, a gloomy Victorian edifice into whose waters I was flung as a child by my Uncle Brian for my first swimming lesson. Not only did I not drown, it seems to have worked. I'm pretty convinced it isn't a method recommended by anyone these days, least of all by FINA, the world governing body of swimming (natation being the posh word for said activity). Then, when I was about seven, Wigan International Pool opened. A new baths or leisure pool is still a big thing for the kids of a neighbourhood today, but the arrival of this huge brutalist ultra-modern leisure facility in our unassuming town centre was an event akin to a Royal Visit or a big cup tie. That word 'International', meaning that the main pool was big enough for FINA-recognised Olympic and Commonwealth events, conferred on the town a throb of glamour. None of us expected the Olympic Games to be held in Wigan any summer soon. But if the IOC came, Wigan would be ready with its arm bands and goggles.

Actually, it wouldn't. In a tale that every Wiganer knows, the pool was built to the proper Olympic dimensions. But later, when the interior tiles were put on, that extra unforeseen quarter-inch meant it was just too short to ever be used in international competition. What should have been a shining example of our council's farsightedness and vision was trotted out in every pub and playground as blackly humorous evidence of civic buffoonery, the ultimate 'facepalm' for the doughty little town.

Is this true? I've tried to get to the bottom of it. But information is scant, especially as the pool itself is gone. But it didn't stop 'Wigan Big Baths' becoming a fixture of life in the town and beyond. I grew up here in the kind of municipal bliss we once took for granted, in the echoing, chlorine-fumed, eye-stinging interior illuminated by wobbly reflected sunlight. This was where I took each of my four swimming certificates. The last was the most exacting, involving retrieving a rubber brick from the bottom of the deep end and taking off and inflating one's pyjama bottoms as a buoyancy aid. This last task I assume was in case we were ever involved in a *Titanic*-style luxury liner disaster, which seemed unlikely as I gazed at my pimply, troglodytic classmates trying to work the lockers in the garish changing rooms.

Wigan Wasps trained here under the auspices of the town's swimming legend Haydn Rigby, who competed in Melbourne and Rome in 1956 and '60, and brought forth a new generation of great local swimmers and the Olympian June Croft. It gained fame among the thousands who came to the Wigan Casino All-Nighter as a place to cool off and get clean and refreshed after a long hot night of acrobatic frugging on the sprung dance floor. On Sunday mornings, the balcony café, like Wigan railway station, would be full of kids from all over Britain, tired, buzzing and now squeaky clean and blow-dried, swapping Dena Barnes's 'If You Ever Walk Out of My Life' for Don Thomas's 'Come On Train'.

This would be the same café I would sit every Wednesday afternoon, chlorinated and damp-haired, rolled wet towel pooling water on the table, talking girls and music with Razzer and Terry

Stokes, waiting for the coach to take us back to school chaperoned loosely by long-haired maths teacher Mr Unsworth. I felt that the hair and purple-tinted specs sat uneasily with Mr Unsworth's fairly hard-line attitude to quadratic equations and such. But I liked him for the moment one silent afternoon when the class spotted some other youths leaping about oddly on the adjacent rugby field. When asked what they were doing, he had replied laconically, 'Just freaking out on the cosmos,' not a phrase often heard from the staff.

The wrecking ball came crashing through the windows of the café one Sunday lunchtime in the autumn of 2008. It took twelve days to dismantle the roof of the old place and four days to drain the huge main pool. It had entertained the town and its visitors for forty years but someone had decided it was surplus to requirements. Maybe brutalism had fallen out of style in the council offices. Its successor, Wigan Life Centre, has a gigantic 'Face of Wigan' silver sculpture outside designed by sculptor Rick Kirby and costing £80,000. It's a huge, bulging-eyed mask in what seems to be shattered tinfoil which manages to be both comic and terrifying at the same time.[9]

On the final Sunday before closure, right about when back in the day the old All-Nighter crowd would have taken a refreshing plunge before their trains back to Airdrie and Wolverhampton, Sunderland and Slough, the oil ran out and the pool was freezing. A few hardy souls shivered back to the weirdly mosaiced changing rooms at 1.15pm, part gulag, part hippie drop-in centre, among them Haydn Rigby. The new baths in the Life Centre are wider than the old (nearly Olympic) pool but only half the length and lack the infamous towering constructivist diving tower, jumping from whose upper stages was a rite of passage for all Wigan youth.

---

[9] An actually pretty funny April Fool in the local paper claimed that it would be replaced by a giant pie sculpture: 'Acclaimed Danish artist Berndt Krusst has been commissioned to build the three-ton structure at workshops in Humberside. Features will include a foil filling and rivet-enforced pastry.'

The public baths as we know them, available to all, is another north-western first. Britain's first public baths were established in Liverpool in 1828. St George's Pier Head Salt Water Baths combined the recreational with the medicinal and environmental. The earliest public swimming pools were combined with a laundry and wash house, and the bathing was as much needed for sanitary reasons as for fun. Poor people were wrongly seen by some of the upper classes as actively enjoying their squalid and mucky lifestyles. But more enlightened voices came to be heard. In 1840 a Parliamentary Select Committee reported that there were no municipally owned wash houses in the land and that the cost of private ones were prohibitive to the working classes. *The Times* rebuked those who claimed that the poor actively enjoyed their dirty lifestyle. 'Take, for example, the House of Lords, probably the cleanest assemblage of men which could be found, condemn them to cold water and no soap, and to wash all their own clothes with their own hands in their own drawing rooms for a single twelve-month, and how would they look at its termination?'

It took several decades for the idea to spread to London but when it did, public baths, like parks, were an instant hit with we plebs wherever they sprang up. In 1921, the Conservative MP Sir Herbert Nield observed that the British people 'have gone recreation mad'. At the opening of Tooting Bec lido, the *Wandsworth Borough News* reported that a crowd of hundreds of small boys 'heedless of the presence of members of the fair sex, unblushingly undressed and were sampling the quality of the water long before the "big guns" had departed.' Swimming soon became something of a craze and is still Britain's largest participant sport, even though cuts and underuse have seen many pools fall into disuse and demolition like Wigan's once cutting-edge facility, which, like many modern baths, lasted barely forty years. In his book, *Great Lengths: A History of Britain's Public Swimming Pools*, Simon Inglis calls them 'Striking modern buildings, but just far too expensive to maintain and in areas of inter-war housing developments where there wasn't a lot of money.' Inglis points out that they are especially vulnerable to changes in lifestyle and usage when compared to other publicly owned buildings. 'Some of them are very beautiful buildings and their numbers dwindle every year. Unlike libraries and schools, swimming pools, although they're public buildings, are dependent on demand and their usership.'

It'd be easier and neater, but we can't blame all of the shrinkage and decline of our public realm and our civic amenities on the cruelty and ideological enmity of uncaring governments. Sometimes the very people they are supposed to be for have turned their backs on them in favour of the delights of the commercial sector. People are fickle. Back in my asphalt tennis court days in Alexandra Park (it wasn't all love bites and cider), my pals and I would be enormously irritated that for the couple of weeks around Wimbledon, we serious types with our Head bags and towelling wristbands could never get a court because daft kids, shrieking girls and portly businessmen would pack them out, pretending to be McEnroe or Borg but in reality clearly not knowing the rules about changing ends or tie-breaks. You could tell that we were superior, proper tennis fans in our informed and unusual choice of player to emulate. I always fancied myself as Wigan's answer to Guillermo Vilas, the dashing Argentinian bombardier of the clay court.

The municipal golf course has had its day as well. As kids, we would make what turned out to be a single pilgrimage to Haigh Hall Golf Course early each summer holiday with the full intention that this would be the season we'd correct our swing, improve our short game and approach play and have a single-figure handicap by September. In reality, we would spend one sweaty, costly day dragging an overstuffed leather bag around for six hours, hacking divots out of the fairway, smoking in the bunkers and losing our knackered and peeling Titleist balls in the ornamental lake. Then we would admit defeat and go back to Alexandra Park, love bites and cider.

These may not be alternative entertainments that are luring potential municipal golfers away today, but there is no doubt that the council-run golf course is on the decline. In a 2013 article on the website 'The Golf Business', Nigel Harte took a run-up to addressing this with a hell of an opening sentence: 'In the analysis that followed the death of Margaret Thatcher in April, much was talked about to what extent the world has changed since the 1980s. Yet, while the rise in telecommunications technology and the fall of Communism may have had a bigger impact on our lives, the transformation of municipal golf courses in the last 30 years has also been a seismic shift worthy of its own write-up.' Wow. I wouldn't go quite that far. But Nigel's on the fairway, if not quite on the green. Once, municipal golf courses were as popular as the genteel private ones. Harte quoted the general manager of Saddleworth Golf Club, Alastair Griffiths, as saying: 'Local authority golf courses were where you learned the art. They thrived. Councils even made profits for the local ratepayers from the amenities. Hundreds of thousands of golfers played the council courses week in, week out, often starting out as early as 5am to get near the front of the queue on the tee.' I can clearly recall reading an earnest article in an 80s broadsheet saying that because of unemployment and long hours of enforced idleness, golf was booming among the inner-city unemployed. It confidently predicted that the Open winners of tomorrow would not be Sandy and Nick but Wayne and Darren, and the green jacket would be headed back to St Helens or Wakefield not St Andrews or Wentworth. This turned out to be almost entirely baseless.

By the start of this century municipal golf courses were becoming unprofitable. This was not the fault of the state but part of a larger image problem with the sport. Young people saw it as middle-aged, expensive and exclusive. If anything, municipal courses with their cheap prices and informal etiquette should have been encouraged for the good of British sport. But again, the thinking was short-sighted and backward. When the economic downturn came after the financial crisis, councils reluctantly forced to make budget cuts looked at loss-making golf clubs first. The golden goose of the 90s when municipal golf boomed had become a ball and chain. Roseberry Grange in Durham and Elemore in

Sunderland have both been rented out to members. Parc Garnant, built at a cost of £1 million in 1992 on a former opencast mine and named best new course of the year in 2004 by the Golf Union of Wales, was simply given away to Clay's Golf in Wrexham to stop the haemorrhaging of £150,000 a year. Harte cites scores more that have simply closed, where the greens, 'the dance floors' as golfers call them, are sprouting weeds and the bunkers are turning to mud, waiting for the developers, for the diggers and rollers that will turn them into desirable two- and three-bedroomed family homes and out-of-town superstores.

There's forbidding fencing, rolls of barbed wire and a sprinkling of 'Keep Out' signs around the perimeter when I turn up on a bone-cold Saturday morning in February at England's first and oldest municipal golf course. But that turns out to be evidence of renewal, not decline. Had I not known that I was at a place of historic significance for both golfers and we lovers of the municipal, the large noticeboard facing Junction 5 of the M62 would have told me that Bowring Park is 'Britain's First Public Municipal Golf Course'. Traffic rumbles by, but the course is serene, not a wayward thwack or shout of 'Fore!' to be heard. I head past the Portakabins and up the course from the first tee, a broad straight hole to ease you in; I reckon even I could probably get down in single figures from here. Golfers are known for their peculiar dress sense but in my overcoat and suede brogues, I probably look even weirder to the course's sole other occupant who I catch up with just as he is tipping his plastic pail of balls on to the fairway for a few tentative drives. He's already sent one sailing impressively on to the green by the time I reach him.

He isn't playing a proper round; just 'having a bit of a practice'. He's fortyish, stubbly grey beard, with that typically Scouse mix of the gruff and genial. 'I come here quite a bit. It's my local course. To tell you the truth, it's not that great, not compared to the private one I'm a member of, but then it wouldn't be, would it. But it's near and it's cheap and it's public.' From what I've seen of his driving, he looks pretty good. He laughs. 'I'm all right, yeah, took it up when I got made redundant and needed to get out from under the wife's feet. But that was years ago. Working round the clock now, so don't get down here as much. And it's been a bit weird round here. It nearly closed. They'll tell you all about it in there,' he says, gesturing with his club towards the Portakabins. 'Anyway, they're having a load of work done now. All those old stables and stuff over there, they're going to turn them into ...' He pauses and grimaces: '... offices or fucking bespoke workshops or something.' Here is a man I think who would agree with fellow Liverpudlian's Alexei Sayle's remark that 'anyone who uses the word "workshop" who's not in light engineering is a twat'. I leave him to his practice and pick my way towards the Portakabins across the squelching grass, fearing for my suede brogues and listening to the occasional swish, thwack and muttered curse behind me.

The two occupants of the Portakabin look up from their *Daily Mirrors* and chit-chat when I enter, letting the cold Lancashire morning into their toasty prefab interior: a dark-haired lady in official fleece behind the counter, and an older man who is clearly but very genially keeping her from her work, something I'll bet he does quite regularly. They are just brewing up and, frozen and parched, I look enviously but unsuccessfully at the steaming mugs (the tea not the people). Instead I ask about Bowring's status as first municipal golf course in Britain. 'Ah,' they chorus in unison, 'you want Linda for all that but she's not in today.' I often pick the day when 'Linda' isn't in. My sense for it is unerring. 'But yes, it was the first, and so it was very sad when it was going to close, but hopefully that won't happen now.'

Briskly then, as Melvyn Bragg insists on saying on *In Our Time*, the history. The course is an adjunct to Bowring Park, gifted to the people of the district by a former Lord Mayor of Liverpool, William Benjamin Bowring, in 1906. He was the senior partner in a shipping firm, the way many Liverpool men got rich. Unlike many of his peers though, Bowring had a genuine feel for the needs of the less-advantaged of his city, and this evidently stretched to the need for fresh air, exercise and recreation, even if Mark Twain

thought famously that golf was 'a good walk spoiled'. For over a
century, the park and its course have been popular fixtures of the
neighbourhood. Once they were merely tranquil, now they feel
more like stunned into silence by the dulling roar of the motorway
alongside them.

Bowring's tale was typical of the narrative above; a downturn
in fortunes as work patterns changed and other leisure activities
encroached, membership steadily dropping, dwindling to less than
seventy. Then in 2008, councils were forced to make cuts to public
services (ironically to bail out and help with the green fees of the
kind of person who uses exclusive private clubs). Municipal golf
courses, which were always going to be harder to defend than
nurseries and libraries, were in the frontline of the assault on public
services. The solution, it seemed, was to hand the course and club
over to Mack Golf, a private concern running courses across
England. It proved the same old story told throughout this book
though. Behind the talk of vigour and dynamism, the private sector
just wasn't up to it. Mack Golf's stewardship left much to be
desired, as noted in several TripAdvisor reviews.

> This was the best municipal golf course around Liverpool
> for years but, unfortunately, since the running of it was
> taken over by Mack golf it has gone seriously down. Mack
> golf have put no investment into the course but just want
> to take money out of it, they have even had the audacity
> to increase green fees as from April 2018. I have been a
> member here for 20 years but have now reluctantly
> decided to move to another local club that have invested
> heavily in the course.
> Glad I only played nine holes as a guest with the ladies
> team and didn't have to pay as I'd ask for my money back
> … Why is this mud field open? … Management problem
> I was told by four golfers who bunked on the course from
> Carr lane as the car park had too many pot holes for their
> cars to handle … Feel sorry for those paid in advance.

Then, overnight, in the autumn of 2018, Bowring was one of eight British golf courses forced to close abruptly when Mack Golf went into liquidation, ceasing trading with immediate effect due to 'unavoidable financial difficulties'. Gates were locked. Entry barred. Staff lost their jobs. For several weeks the course and club and members were in limbo, fearing the worst for a much-loved if down-at-heel local institution. But salvation was at hand and again from the nanny state, with a little help from the lottery punters of Britain. On the very same day that Mack Golf collapsed, Knowsley Council, one of the most cash-strapped and poorest in Britain, opened talks with the affected staff, the GMB union and the Heritage Lottery Fund. The latter stumped up a £2 million grant, which is paying for the course to stay open, as well as a new café, community space, meeting facilities, offices and a refurbished golf reception area, restoration of the historic gardens, a new outdoor event space and car park. Maybe even some of those bespoke workshops (adjective excluded).

The story of Bowring Park is the whole sorry mess of privatisation in microcosm. It's a narrative arc now wearily familiar. It begins with, in Chomsky's famous analysis, 'the standard technique of privatisation: defund, make sure things don't work, people get angry, you hand it over to private capital.' Then follows in short order incompetence, liquidation and a bailout at the public expense. A depressingly similar tale and refrain being repeated continually in every sphere of national life.

I reluctantly step back out into a raw winter's morning on Merseyside. This is a place that's felt the economic chill too. You might not know it from the fine, big houses that stand back grandly from the roads from Prescot station. But that's an echo of a more prosperous era, when the shipping trade had made Liverpool world renowned and the 'Liverpool Gentleman' wealthy. They built grand houses for their families in these quiet green suburbs, well away from the city's maritime bustle, the stevedores' swearing and the Chinese laundries. This is where they came to sit and luxuriate in their salty riches. But they are long gone, as are all those bright confident mornings of British capitalism.

In Prescot, just down the road from Bowring, you can read the new mood of the New Britain, shuttered, barred, sold off, repossessed. All over our country, the story is the same. When austerity came, it came first and sharpest and hardest for those who could least bear it. And it often came in nasty, secret ways that may seem trivial to Deloitte and the receivers but made daily life just that little bit less happy and productive, like an overgrown golf course or a chained park gate. In Prescot, the old library building has been sold off and refashioned into a glass-fronted luxury home, though for God knows who. The leisure centre has been razed and with it the public swimming pool. The museum and art gallery have gone. All of this was noted by the *New York Times* in one of those pieces that feel embarrassingly anthropological; a report on our own nation that reads like a critique of a failed state or a Third World country run by a corrupt despot rather than the place we love and grew up in. In the much-discussed piece, it was reported how Brown's Field, 'a lush park in the centre of town', was one of seventeen parks earmarked for sale to developers. 'Everybody uses this park,' said Jackie Lewis. 'This is probably our last piece of community space. It's been one after the other. You just end up despondent.'

Even though the article received some criticism, it was certainly right about one thing: Prescot is one of the poorest parts of Britain. More of its people are living on benefits than anywhere else in the UK. I feel a kinship with it because I was born here. Over half a century later, I'm back for the first time since I left swaddled in my mum's arms, bound for my granny's spare bedroom in Haydock. I walk away from the golf course, past the hotel with its ads for its status as a wedding venue, a smiling bride drinking Prosecco while her beau looks on admiringly, past the big houses by the station and into a different Britain. One where there are fewer smiles and not much Prosecco, unless it's coming from a food bank.

CHAPTER 6

I SIGN ON

'YOU GOT SOUL ON THE DOLE'

I first 'signed on' in the summer of 1979. I was briefly, and not entirely unhappily, unmoored between disappointing A-level results – it turned out staying out till 2am at Bluto's nightspot most nights was not the path to academic glory – subsequent re-sits and moving away to college. Most of the literature of unemployment, from Walter Greenwood to *Boys from the Blackstuff*, is steeped in the murk of despair and anger. Through it you can usually hear the plangent clang of words like 'hopelessness' and 'humiliation'. The images are of downtrodden men in silent lines, faces etched in shame and misery, the grinning spectre of poverty at their bony shoulder. I couldn't claim to know any such desperate privations at the time. Having no mortgage to find, no mouths to feed, no debts as such beyond the odd borrowed fiver, 'the dole' (or to be more accurate 'supplementary benefits', since the dole required you to have paid a National Insurance stamp for a couple of years) was just there to tide us over till the state, in its endless beneficence, gave us a small but tidy grant and packed us off to somewhere thrilling.

'Signing on' itself was even a mildly convivial communal experience for me then, even if the building where this took place, Brocol House on King Street, looked like the kind of place the Stasi would interrogate ashen-faced East Berliners. You would often meet your peers there of a midweek morning and perhaps make social arrangements to spend the twenty or so quid a week you'd receive in due course. Since most of us had parents who didn't ask much for rent or board that summer, it was enough. You could always pick up a few shifts at the GUS catalogue warehouse in Martland Mill and even come home with a 'liberated' power drill if you were of a light-fingered bent.

Truth be told, those dire tracts of the first half of the twentieth century, *The Stars Look Down* and *Love on the Dole*, *The Ragged Trousered Philanthropists* and *Road to Wigan Pier*, did not really chime with an unemployed soon-to-be undergraduate in 1979. Though she was recently installed in Downing Street and viewed with the deepest suspicion, Thatcher's new notions were yet to become policy, and those policies were yet to bite. The young men and women of my gang in 1979 were not becalmed in middle age or thrown on a scrapheap in our prime. We were poised on the lip of a great adventure and the state was seemingly prepared to stand us a few quid to finance a frugal but fun lifestyle as we prepared to take the plunge.

These days, if you're on 'the dole', Channel 4 make a disingenuous TV show about you under the guise of 'wanting to understand' but really desperate for some shots of you sitting by the bins in your dressing gown, smoking and drinking Blue WKD. Back in the early 1980s, there was little stigma about being on the dole, because pretty much everyone was. It was just before those handy middle-class euphemisms for unemployment, 'travelling' and 'gap years', were invented, so if you couldn't afford an Interrail pass (and pretend to spend the summer picking grapes and mixing with toothless locals and olive-skinned beauties from Thessalonica while actually never getting further than Antwerp where you smoked dope and watched football with some lads from Rotherham), then you signed on. It wasn't great, and if you made it to the end of each second week with any dosh left then clearly you must have been listening to a lot of John Peel and drinking bad homebrew. But you could manage, just. And just managing has always been at the heart of even our supposedly generous

benefit system ever since its beginning in a quiet corner of rural
Berkshire in 1795.

On 6 May of that year, a collection of local magistrates stabled
their horses at the Pelican Inn, Speenhamland, went indoors, lit up
their briar pipes, filled their tankards and proceeded to change the
course of history and social policy. Years of poor harvests, a booming
population and the Napoleonic Wars had made life brutally hard in
our agricultural communities. Wheat was scarce and the price of
bread prohibitive. Food riots had broken out in many English
towns, and the spectre of more and worse was haunting the upper
classes. Their fear, not without substance, was that the English
citizenry might take a cue from their French cousins and start
lopping off some rich and powerful heads. So a bunch of enlightened
(and self-preserving) landowners decided over that lunchtime pint
at the Pelican Inn that 'the present state of the poor law requires
further assistance than has generally been given them'. In what was
a truly enlightened measure for the time, the magistrates decided to
bring in a system of allowances. A labourer or agricultural worker
would have his income supplemented to subsistence level by the
parish – a 'top up' on very low wages. It was never taken up
nationally but the idea of such allowances spread rapidly across
the south of England. It's thought that it saved many families from
starvation. Interestingly, the magistrates also suggested that
employers could always pay better wages, but naturally such insane
profligacy was rejected. Always better to let the state and the parish
take the burden than lose a penny of profit. It's a notion that
underpinned 'family credit' for instance.

The Speenhamland system is one of the few things I recall
from one of those disappointing A-level passes (Social and
Economic History) along with the six demands of the Chartists,
the Anti-Corn Law League and pretty much nothing else. Those
progressive if self-interested Berkshire magistrates were widely
copied and this kind of outdoor relief became known as the
Speenhamland system. I vividly remember Mr Rogers though (tall,
kindly, grey suit, pronounced the word 'sixth' weirdly) stressing

that this was a subsistence-level benefit pegged closely to the price of bread. Speenhamland was about keeping the poor alive in order to work and to not riot.

Despite popular myth, we have never been generous with benefits or indulgent of their recipients. Beveridge himself, author of the famous report that birthed the welfare state, once asserted that the poor needed 'the whip hand of starvation' to ensure economic vitality in the land, a sentiment not even the most rabid right-winger would dare advance now. He was a keen advocate of controlling the reproductive capabilities of the poor too, and was actually on the way to deliver a speech to the Eugenics Society (of which he was a enthusiastic member) on the afternoon parliament debated his famous report.

On its publication in 1942, *Social Insurance and Allied Services*, a 300-page tome released by His Majesty's Stationer's Office, made the sixty-three-year-old civil servant the hottest name in publishing. *The Beveridge Report*, as it was soon better known, sold 100,000 copies in the month and 600,000 within a couple of years; 50,000 were sold in America and it was widely circulated among the resistance movements of occupied Europe. An annotated copy was found in Hitler's bunker in 1945 with comments like 'our enemies are taking over national-socialistic ideas' and 'superior to the current German social insurance in almost all points' in the margins. It may have had its admirers among the Nazis but it rankled with some at home. Many leading Tories were dismayed at the proposal of anything that smacked of 'mollycoddling' or socialism. There were critics on the left too. It was pointed out, then and now, that Beveridge's unemployment benefit model gave people the very minimum to live on an absolute scale, not the earnings-related system most of the rest of Europe would adopt. There was a flat rate of contributions too, so the low paid put in as much (which is to say proportionally more) in National Insurance contributions. Beveridge believed the gap between benefit and even the lowest pay should be 'as large as possible for every man'. He also thought that the young should receive no benefits but compulsory training during periods of unemployment.

Modern critics such as Susan Pedersen have taken the ghost of Beveridge and his acolytes to task over the patriarchal nature of his vision and his adherence to what she calls 'a particular model of family life'. Beveridge believed in the 1910s that 'the ideal unit is the household of man, wife and children maintained by the earnings of the first alone'. By the time of the report, his thinking was still that men's benefits should include support for their spouse, denying women agency of their own. It was 'in the national interest' that married women not be wage-earners, for 'housewives as mothers have vital work to do in ensuring the adequate continuance of the British race and of British ideals in the world'.

This all sounds pretty grim and reactionary now, of course. But without wishing to be an apologist for Beveridge's more antediluvian views, those were different times. What we'd now unhesitatingly call out as sexism was a widespread shared attitude, even among the progressive. I'm also loath to excoriate Beveridge, as Pedersen does, for his 'invincible determination to win a place in the history books. Beveridge wanted to usher in a fairer world, but he also wanted to be remembered as the man who did the ushering.' This may be true. But you'll search hard for the entirely saintly and selfless in politics, indeed in any field of human activity. He transformed British life for the many, replacing fear and anxiety with safety and security. He famously set out to slay five giants: Want, Disease, Ignorance, Squalor and Idleness. No one can blame him if we have not succeeded yet. Also, for a civil servant, he had a distinct flair for inspirational prose. Not many government reports before or since have contained passages like this:

'Freedom from want cannot be forced on a democracy or given to a democracy. It must be won by them. Winning it needs courage and faith and a sense of national unity: courage to face facts and difficulties and overcome them; faith in our future and in the ideals of fair-play and freedom for which century after century our forefathers were prepared to die; a sense of national unity overriding the interests of any class or section.'

The story of benefits and welfare since Beveridge though is haphazard and fractured. The Conservatives are still by nature suspicious, if not hostile, to the whole idea of a welfare state. The adversarial switchback of post-war British governments has meant that the system has mushroomed in complexity and cost but not in efficiency. The real losers have been claimants. Despite the rhetoric of the taboids, this complexity means recipients are denied what is rightfully theirs. This stigmatisation and scapegoating is nowhere more cruelly seen than in the application of benefit sanctions since 2008, punishing claimants for non-attendance of job interviews or 'unavailability' for work. The sanctions could be as severe as loss of all benefits for three years.

A BBC report uncovered heart-breaking personal testimonies of callousness; a man who was sanctioned when he missed a job-centre appointment three days after being taken to hospital suffering from severe epileptic seizures. A single parent named Samantha sanctioned after childcare problems meant she had to move from full-time to part-time work and whose income fell from an average of £800 per month to £300, leaving her relying on food parcels from friends. A wheelchair user who was forced to sleep in a college library for a year when her entire benefit was wrongly taken away. Over the same period, the boss of the collapsed travel giant Thomas Cook paid himself £5 million in bonuses for ruining the company. As Ross McKibbin put it, 'A dozen bankers have done more damage to the British economy than any number of benefit cheats could. And it is those who rely on welfare who are now paying the penalty for the bankers' misdeeds.'

Benefit 'reform' has been obsessing government, especially of the right, since Beveridge. The latest experiment, Universal Credit, a means-tested Speenhamland-style 'top up' that replaces six 'legacy' benefits, has been erratically rolled out, widely criticised and will be abolished by any future Labour government. But there is growing approval and interest in another 'universal' benefit. What I wonder, would the sternly moralistic Beveridge have made of a benefit system that literally and unashamedly proposes handing out money for nothing with no strings attached?

It's known as Universal Basic Income, or UBI, and is an idea gaining much traction now to the surprise of many, me included. When I was a teenage sociology student, I read a 1966 essay by Marshall McLuhan called 'Guaranteed Income in the Electric Age'. You can probably guess the gist from the title. One day fairly soon, robots would be doing all the dirty, boring, dangerous work for us and we would receive an allowance from the state in order to not work. McLuhan was deadly serious about this. I, as you might imagine of a teenager, was also very keen on this vision of the future. But it all seemed utterly fanciful when viewed from the decaying Britain of the late 70s and early 80s. The notion of the state benignly paying for us to enjoy our leisure, improve our minds, have sex, go for walks, read Proust and such, all possibly while wearing shiny silver jumpsuits and taking our hover-jet packs to Alton Towers or La Scala seemed rather a long way away while Toxteth burned and policemen were baton-charging miners at Orgreave. Norman Tebbit, remember, was telling us we should get on our bikes – not hover-jet packs, note – and find work instead of dossing about like the feckless bastards he clearly thought we were.

But belatedly and implausibly, something like McLuhan's dreamily utopian scheme may well soon come to pass, at least in some parts of the world. Before we get into that, let's define some terms. Though there are as many variants of UBI as there are incarnations of The Drifters currently touring northern clubs, Universal Basic Income is essentially that: a benefit paid by the state to all citizens regardless of their income, resources or employment status. In its purest form it should be periodic, i.e. regular, in cash not vouchers, given to each individual not a household, universal and unconditional. It's the last two criteria that seem so shocking at first. Without it though, the scheme lacks its moral and intellectual underpinning. It should be available to everyone however rich (or poor) and it should be awarded whether or not the individual works, can work or even wants to work.

When former Labour leader Ed Miliband debated the notion on his podcast, it was subtitled 'Free Money for All!' and he called it 'a trust fund for all'. Even broadly sympathetic people still find it necessary to frame the idea humorously like this as if to admit that it is essentially nuts or at least crazy, new-fangled, snowflake thinking. So when you hear that Bernie Sanders supports it, you think, 'That figures.' When you hear that Mark Zuckerberg and Elon Musk and Richard Branson support it, you wonder what's in it for those creepy rich hippies/high-minded technocrats. But when you find out that the idea begins with Thomas Paine and came very close to being implemented in 1969 as US government policy by one Richard Nixon (rich and creepy maybe, but certainly no hippie and certainly no Thomas Paine) you begin to think again. UBI has strong supporters among the more thoughtful policy makers and economists across the political spectrum. I'm neither of those things. But I like the idea of UBI very much for what seem like eminently sensible reasons.

For one, it cuts through the labyrinthine complexity of our benefit system, which is heavily policed and often punitive. Everyone gets UBI, and the same amount. How much you work or don't work, how much you have in the bank, where you live; it doesn't matter one jot. You get your money. You don't lose benefits when you work, thus avoiding the 'poverty trap', whereby low-paid workers would be better off on benefits. Starvation-level wages are abolished, since no one is forced to work, as is the ongoing gnawing fear of automation (the coming era of robot workers is the primary reason Musk et al. think UBI is inevitable). It reduces the risks of setting up one's own small business and therefore could be seen to encourage entrepreneurialism. Women will be freed from the financial obligations that keep them in abusive or unhappy relationships. Perhaps most importantly, the security and freedom UBI gives would be hugely beneficial to mental health and family relationships, reducing NHS costs. UBI acknowledges that life is to be enjoyed not endured.

Job done, take the rest of the day off, you might think. But not everyone is so keen. Critics point to various flaws. It lacks proportionality: a twenty-year-old man receives the same as a seventy-year-old woman or a single mother of three (although as long as the benefit is adequate for the worst-off's needs, this wouldn't necessarily be a problem). Also, it ignores the supposed notion that work confers status and meaning and is a good thing in and of itself, the old 'dignity of labour' notion beloved of Gandhi and others. More practically, its opponents say, it will cost too much. Then of course there are those who are simply philosophically opposed to any increase in the role of the state in people's lives. If you've got this far though, you'll know that that is not the position of this author.

But regardless of both the considered reservations of some and the belligerent blather of the ideologically opposed, it is looking more and more like UBI is an idea whose time has come. All over the world, governments of every stripe and alignment are seriously considering it. Namibia, India, Canada and Scotland have considered or are trialling it as I write. On 8 February 2019, the results of a Finnish trial of UBI were announced. Two thousand people on the dole were picked at random by researchers and for two years received 560 euros whether they sought or started work or not. After a year it was found that recipients of UBI were no less likely to be working than those on dole. On average both groups worked nearly fifty days a year, earning 4,520 euros on average. The idea that UBI will encourage everyone to stay at home watching *Bargain Hunt*, or its Finnish equivalent, exists largely in the mind of the fundamentalist opposition. The Swiss held a referendum on it in 2016. True, it was rejected, but perhaps we should remember that women didn't get the vote there till 1971, suggesting a certain conservatism. More to the point, even the gnomes of Zurich are at least thinking about it. Five Star (the Italian populist party, not the 80s Essex pop siblings) have promised a basic income of 780 euros a month should they be elected. As I write, a pilot of UBI will be promised in the next

Labour manifesto. Beveridge himself wanted something very like UBI, but Attlee and then successive governments of all persuasions have moved steadily away from this towards ever more proscribed and means-tested benefits. Maybe we will come full circle under a future Labour government.

Why the change of hearts? Call me cynical, but I find it interesting that worries about automation and a subsequent rash of new thinking about basic incomes and protecting livelihoods and indeed our essential humanity are emerging now when white-collar and middle-class occupations are under threat. As Sarah O'Connor of the *FT* has pointed out, it's easier for artificial intelligence to take over the job of an accountant than that of a care worker. It makes us think again about what exactly constitutes 'unskilled' work. We should start talking about care work and the rest as essential automation-proof jobs, because then maybe economists would give a monkey's. An algorithm can't wipe sputum from the lips of a dying old lady in a care home. But it could easily do your VAT returns. If AI makes us reconsider which jobs in our society are really worthwhile, valuable and deserving of high reward, then I for one welcome our robot overlords.

I didn't know, though looking back I think I could feel it somehow, that when I first walked into Wigan's very own 'grey Lubyanka' on King Street, Brocol House, the 'sea change' old sailor Jim Callaghan detected was happening right here on our shores in Wigan. A new mood was abroad within Toryism and it was emanating from a figure who now seems ludicrous but whose influence still lingers miasmically in the bloodstream of our system. Keith Joseph was a baronet who'd inherited his wealth and title (without lifting a finger) from his father, the head of Bovis construction. For many years under Macmillan and Heath, he had been merely a jobbing right-wing cabinet stooge. But, unfortunately for Britain, at some point in the early 1970s he read a couple of books. One was Friedrich Hayek's *Road to Serfdom*, which is, depending on point of view again, a bracing anti-socialist tract or an opiniated screed of guff masquerading as analysis. Joseph was of the former persuasion. In the cartoon version of Joseph's life (not currently in production, I imagine), after reading Hayek he'll be seen wobbling around goofily with twittering birdies and hearts circling his austere head. 'All my life, I thought I was a Conservative,' he gushed. 'Now I know that I have never been one. The scales have dropped from my eyes.'

Thus was born the 'Mad Monk', as he became scornfully but fearfully known by both left and right. His embracing of an extreme free-marketism was religious in zeal, fundamentalist and absolute. He was Thatcher's Torquemada and it was he more than any other of Thatcher's mentors who dripped this stuff into her ear; that benefits should be cut, the state rolled back, that disadvantage and its opposite, privilege, were perfectly acceptable ('the pursuit of income equality will turn this country into a totalitarian slum'), that we were growing soft and cosseted, even that selective mandatory birth control should be considered for single and working-class parents. 'The balance of our population, our human stock is threatened. A recent article in *Poverty*, published by the Child Poverty Action Group, showed that a high and rising proportion of children are being born to mothers least fitted to bring children into the world and to bring them up.'

Some would say it's a mark of the tolerance or perhaps lassitude of the English people that they are willing to let independently, indecently, unearnedly wealthy baronets push them around like this, insult them and impoverish them, and respond with a tug of the forelock rather than the swish of the guillotine. I doubt Gresham College take that view, but I would certainly agree with what they said of Joseph when they included him in a lecture series on the six post-war politicians who, while never becoming prime minister, have had the most influence. 'We still inhabit a world largely created by Keith Joseph, and we will probably continue to do so for a long time to come.'

Back in Wigan, the Mad Monk's revolutionary zeal was beginning to be felt. It was a chill in the air like a coming winter. It would take a few years for the project to fine-tune itself, for the machine to be 'run in' like a car engine, but the 'rolling back' or even dismantling of the welfare state was well under way. Even through the bonhomie of the queue, there was a surliness in the air, lurking behind the reinforced glass, simmering in the pea soup of the cigarette smoke, that would sour over the next few years. Sue Townsend was to capture that mood within 'the dole office' perfectly within a few months in the Adrian Mole books, especially in *The Growing Pains* ..., where Adrian and his mother become trapped in the Kafkaesque bureaucratic labyrinth of Leicester's benefits office. After an afternoon of disappointment and humiliation, mild-mannered Adrian comes to understand why the chairs are fixed to the floor: 'By the end of the afternoon, I felt like throwing a few around myself.'

As a young teacher in the late 80s, I used to drink in a pub in the Wigan called The Orwell. I liked it for several reasons, such as its cheapish beer and its moodily attractive canalside location, but chiefly because the clientele were not the sharpest knives in the box, to be honest. Thus the quiz machine was always stuffed to the electronic gills with money, which me and my chum Steve Pegg promptly emptied every Monday lunchtime after a weekend of drunken wobbling Wigan lads had failed to identify the opening lines of *Moby Dick* or the capital of Venezuela. It was a form of wealth redistribution that gave me, the youthful Marxist, a certain pang of remorse. But not enough to stop me doing it.

The naming of the pub had proved hugely controversial, though. Aldermen and dignitaries in variously inflated states of affront and dudgeon took turns to rail against Orwell himself. Better, they said, to have named the pub after another famous George, that cheery banjolelist son of the town and recipient of the Order of Lenin, Formby, than the Old Etonian Orwell who had done nothing but traduce the town in his dreadfully downbeat book published down in London.

Orwell, though, was not writing for the Lancashire tourist board. *The Road to Wigan Pier* is a brilliant and bitter polemic intended to waken comfortable metropolitan Britain to what was happening to some of their countrymen. It was not intended to increase bookings for mini-breaks to the town's boutique hotels, even had it possessed any. He lodged above a tripe shop where he found a full reeking chamber pot beneath the breakfast table, a detail that, granted, does seem *de trop* and comic. There are Wiganers who will tell you that he only lodged there with a family he chose because of their slovenly reputation and because his first lodgings were too clean for a good story.

Similarly, when the *New York Times* ran its controversial above-mentioned report about Prescot in 2018, opinion was divided. Even those who broadly agreed with its sympathetic thrust were conflicted. Locals were torn between wanting to lament the damage done by cuts and to 'stick up' for their town, naturally. Their response echoed some of the reaction Orwell received in the 1930s regarding Wigan. Yes, the town had had it tough, but there were good things too. Some even said the town was 'on the up'. The outcry from the right was more predictable, locally and nationally. Someone from the Institute of Economic Affairs declared it 'bullshit'. Andrew Neil, like most of the BBC's politics heavyweights, a conservative, got angry on Prescot's behalf with a bit of patriotic bluster thrown in: 'Coverage of Britain by @nytimes has become a parody of reporting. Almost as hostile to UK now as it was slavish in its support of Stalinist Russia in 1930s'.

By comparison, the response of the article's author, Peter S. Goodman, was refreshingly sensible. 'First we published a story about British austerity using Prescot as lead example,' he tweeted, continuing:

Then, an ideologue who has not visited the town in a quarter century claimed inaccuracies. Town residents debunked these claims. It became fodder for UK tabloid ... Prescot is a great town. It has challenges, like all communities, but many strengths. I don't pretend to be able to parachute into a place and understand it better than locals. Grateful for the help in figuring it out. Britain has indeed been refashioned by austerity, but it's [*sic*] history is not over: It's a wonderful country with so many strengths, and it's a thrill to get to watch it up close.

Goodman's piece, which is excellent by the way, was part of a wider series on the damage that a decade of deep cuts have done to this nation as a whole. He frames it well and shamefully (for us) when he writes:

> For a nation with a storied history of public largesse, the protracted campaign of budget cutting, started in 2010 by a government led by the Conservative Party, has delivered a monumental shift in British life. A wave of austerity has yielded a country that has grown accustomed to living with less, even as many measures of social well-being – crime rates, opioid addiction, infant mortality, childhood poverty and homelessness – point to a deteriorating quality of life.

One of his conclusions cuts through any residual cant about 'Big Societies' or us all 'being in this together': 'To a degree, a spirit of voluntarism materialized. At public libraries, volunteers now outnumber paid staff. In struggling communities, residents have formed food banks while distributing hand-me-down school uniforms. But to many in Britain, this is akin to setting your house on fire and then revelling in the community spirit as neighbours come running to help extinguish the blaze.' Brilliantly put, I think. But for the busy and time-poor bigot without space in their day for such thoughtful fare, you could always look up Rebecca Perring's rather less nuanced take on the *Daily Express* website.

REVEALED: Shocking map shows the towns GUZZLING the most benefits cash in Britain THIS shocking map uncovers where the real life Benefits Street constituencies are guzzling up the biggest chunk of the UK'S £161billion welfare bill. The nations' benefits hotspots have been revealed in jaw dropping statistics, which show how some areas of the country pocket SIX times as much in handouts as other parts of the country. Capital of the group has been named as Knowsley, in Merseyside, which received an eye-watering £149.8million last year. With a population of around 80,000 it means that on average every adult resident there gets an annual Government top up of almost £1,900.

Top Up. Handout. Pocket. Guzzling. Shocking. Jaw dropping. This kind of partial and inflammatory reporting creates a specious, dangerous perception in the minds of the public at large. A 2013 survey found that Britons overestimate the amount and cost of benefit fraud by thirty-four times. Thus I yearn without much expectation for the day when Rebecca and her colleagues publish revelatory maps of the streets in Monte Carlo, Geneva and Knightsbridge where 'real-life fat cats' are 'guzzling' the biggest chunk of UK's bailout and bonuses bill in eye-watering 'hand-outs'. Or consider how little the nation actually loses in benefit fraud as compared to tax evasion which by most estimates is considerably more damaging.[10] But I won't hold my breath while I'm waiting.

I decided, like Goodman, to see it up close, if in my case just for an afternoon. I was born here after all, even if I'd been taken down the road to my Irish granny's in nearby Haydock fairly

---

[10] According to a report in the *Independent* in 2014, for every pound lost to benefit fraud, four were stolen from the public purse in tax evasion.

sharpish. My conclusions might be less developed than Goodman's but surely better than Perring's, sitting in judgement at a PC in the *Daily Express* building in London. Despite her lurid warnings, walking through old Prescot on a winter Saturday, nothing made my 'jaw drop' or 'eyes water' and the nearest I saw to 'guzzling' was a kid wrestling with a greasy piece of chicken in a bus shelter. But I did feel the tension between the old and new, the positive and the decaying, any bright hopes for the future and the daily grind of the present.

Getting into Prescot from its railway station involves what's become a common hike and footslog. Where once towns and cities were walled and castellated, the better for outsiders to be repelled by an arrow shower or boiling oil, now we are lured by castles of commerce but must first brave the broad ring road and the vast car park before fetching up against the huge shiny bulk of the shopping centre. Cables Shopping Park is named, as much is in the town, such as the football team, for the locality's engineering heritage, one of the many places in the area where British Insulated Callender's Cables brought prosperity and even fame via the work's brass band broadcasts on the BBC. Cabling is a far from glamorous endeavour, but it was good to Prescot for most of a century until BICC was eventually swallowed up by one of its own subsidiaries, Balfour Beatty, who took their business elsewhere, a story repeated across the north-west in the years since 1979.

At time of writing, MP for Wigan Lisa Nandy is campaigning to address a social and economic problem that Prescot exemplifies; the decline of the town. Recent years have seen a drain of young and skilled people from towns towards the big cities that became transformed in the wake of the 1981 riots, often thanks to the lobbying of Michael Heseltine. Liverpool, Leeds, Bristol, Manchester, Newcastle, all across the UK cities have regenerated and boomed. Put simply, cities are getting younger while towns are getting on a bit. Those left behind in the 'left behind' towns tend to be older and less skilled and they overwhelmingly voted for

Brexit. The story's repeated across the land. Prescot is typical. Turn left at the NHS centre and fall into step with the old ladies with wheeled tartan trolleys (and, yes, some young mums with dozing toddlers) up the steep drag of Sewell Street into the old town built when this was still Lancashire and not Merseyside. Tucked away in this original Prescot, muscled out of the way by the huge and shiny Cables shopping mall, is an older, shabbier variant of the phenomenon which naturally I head for. Retail semioticians could spot that this is the less upscale sibling by the brands; Home Bargains, Farmfoods and Clintons rather than Next, M&S and Paperchase. It's pretty much deserted, just three kids on a bench shrieking loudly over something watched on a mobile phone, too loudly, as if trying to convince themselves they are having a good time, while Prefab Sprout's 'If You Don't Love Me' plays over the tinny Tannoy system. The effect is weird and depressing.

Kemble Street was one of the grimmest thoroughfare I saw anywhere while travelling for this book. To say otherwise would be lying. The Red Lion is shuttered and boarded and the Union Jack flag hanging from the window above the kebab shop is tattered and filthy. A shopping trolley has been dumped in the shabby foliage behind the railings and on a nearby lamppost someone has stapled a small pink notice that bears simply a number and the opaque phrase 'quality, discrete service assured'. Perhaps best not to ask. I walk along the street and don't pass a soul, just a silent line of sentinel wheely bins. So presumably there were people behind the flyblown curtains and grimy front doors. But who, I wonder?

Pelling of the *Express*'s motives are certainly dubious, but she'd doubtless claim that her facts were not. When she filed her story in 2016, Knowsley claimed more in benefits than anywhere else in Britain. It's a shifting picture but by any assessment Prescot jostles unenviably with Middlesbrough, Hodge Hill and Hall Green in Birmingham, Hunslet in Yorkshire and Foyle in Northern Ireland for that unwanted title. It's unarguable that around 20 per cent of working-age people receive some form of benefit here. But here's a thing. Extend that beyond 'working-age people' and guess which part of the UK is really guzzling our cash, really taking us to the cleaners in handouts and payouts and whatever other term Rebecca Perring favours?

It's the Isle of Wight. According to the *Daily Mirror* in 2015 (and, to be fair, the *Daily Mail*, who also ran the story 'against' its own core readership), the residents of that genteel isle on the Solent are Britain's real 'spongers' with a whopping benefits bill of £449 million, of which £268.2 million were state pension payments. (I don't mean that about 'spongers', by the way, but it's worth remembering that one person's fully entitled state benefit is another's handout.) Also, while we're in debunking mode, those who claim that it's immigration that is the root cause of this drain on our system (I'm looking at you, Farage, Tommy Robinson and your brethren in the media) might like to know that Knowsley is the least diverse corner of Britain: 97 per cent of its population are white; 81 per cent describe themselves as Christian.

But there is another dimension to consider here. Benefits might not only benefit the direct recipient. You might even argue that our once relatively benign benefits system has been a greater cultural boon to this country than the Arts Council. Yet successive governments have been slow to acknowledge this. From Wilson to Blair and Cameron, politicians eager to be seen as dynamic, youthful and 'trendy' have championed our brilliance at pop music, piggybacked on its global cool, given out MBEs for it and praised its contribution to our exports. But they have been strangely loath to give the dole its due, even though the meagre amounts paid in benefits have been paid back handsomely in GDP and taxes. Jon Stewart, former presenter of *The Daily Show*, could see this after speaking to J.K. Rowling about her time on the dole. 'Has a government ever gotten more back from an investment than from you?'

No, it hasn't, which goes for hundreds of wealthy, high-rate taxpayers who were once 'dolies', who learned their craft of jokes and chords and plot structure on twenty-odd quid a week. Without the dole, there would be great holes in our cultural weft and weave;

no two-tone or punk or electro, no Britpop, no alternative comedy, no Deller, Emin, Hirst or other young British artists. No UK grime, jungle, drum and bass or hip hop. No *Young Ones,* no Johnny Rotten. No *Harry Potter.* No future at all in England's dreaming. There would certainly be no John Shuttleworth, legendary and fictional comic MOR balladeer of Sheffield. Lunching once with his creator and alter ego, Graham Fellows, he told me how he had dreamed up John while on the Enterprise Allowance Scheme (enhanced supplementary benefit to encourage small business entrepreneurialism), going so far as to getting John his own credit card. 'Shall we have this one on John?' he suggested, tossing a J. Shuttleworth credit card on to the bill. I've had these conversations with scores of friends and interviewees in the arts and media over the years. The dole is the one thing we have in common; not university or public school or arts colleges or music school. No, our alma mater was the DHSS, to one degree or another.

I asked around among my friends and contacts if they had experienced the brisk comforts of the dole during their formative years. Jeremy Deller is an artist whose work often involves large-scale public art events and brilliant juxtapositions and recontextualisations such as getting a northern brass band to perform 80s acid house anthems and the Civil War re-enactors of the Sealed Knot to recreate the infamous Battle of Orgreave of the 1984/5 miners' strike. He was on the dole 'off and on from 1988 to about '95 or '96. Quite a chunk of time, really. It was very common for artists then. It was common for most people I knew, actually. I think artists saw it as a natural extension of art college.' Deller himself never went to art college (although he does have an MA in History of Art from the Courtauld) and so he incubated his talents living at home and signing on. 'The dole was definitely my version of art college. That was my artistic apprenticeship. I had time and space to think about what I wanted to do. I was trying for jobs, honest, and I did a ragbag of odd jobs,' he laughs.

'But I was unemployable in lots of ways, which I found out quite quickly. I never told them at the dole office that I wanted to be an artist. I thought that would be a really bad move, actually. But I did tell them I wanted to work in an arts and culture environment. I did art history so I could have worked in museums and stuff. But the dole weren't really equipped to deal with people like me because they had so many people to cope with. My dole office in south London was always very busy, multiple places to sign on, queues for an hour.'

Such was the demands on the system that the authorities were fairly relaxed about long-term dole recipients like Jeremy. 'I had to go on a week-long job-seekers' course at one point and towards the end of my time signing on they were getting quite annoyed with me, so I realised I had to get off it. But there was no real pressure, except my parents were bit bemused. I think you're right about it being "the other arts council". It was a kind of underground subcultural arts body. It was very important for me and lots of other artists. And in the end, you do pay it all back in taxes, which I do not mind paying at all.'

Over a couple of lunchtime pints at the BBC's MediaCity complex in Salford, musician Richard Hawley made the same point. 'Look at those bands who were sort of nurtured on the dole. Oasis, The Smiths, the Stone Roses, Pulp. All on the dole for years and then they became massive. I haven't done so bad. We lived on forty-two quid a fortnight from the government for years and now we're paying loads in taxes. What I've paid dwarfs any benefits I claimed. So in terms of a balance sheet, I think it was a pretty good investment by the government.'

Richard was on the dole in Sheffield for a decade along with his friend Jarvis Cocker from Pulp. 'That's how we met. The world of benefits and bands and tiny bedsits. I was on the dole from being sixteen to signing a record deal with my band the Longpigs when I was twenty-six. All that time on the dole apart from one stint at HMV for nine weeks over Christmas after it was discovered I'd been on the dole some considerable time. You could not do that now. And during that period of time, we learned our craft, I learned my chops. I wrote so many songs, hung out with other bands. I played my guitar twenty-four/seven. I immersed myself in music. And life on the dole gave you something to write about.'

Hawley supplemented his income with his art. 'I was playing in pub bands earning a snide tenner here and there. I owe Sheffield a fiver or two. I could sing blues and country so I'd busk, but I'd be clever. You had to be careful not to get collared by the dole, so I'd get a train, go to Chesterfield or Doncaster on a Saturday. You'd come back with fifty quid, which was twice as much as the dole. I'm not romantic about it, though. It was tough. When Jarvis bought *Scott 4* by Scott Walker out of his dole cheque, he went hungry for a few days. Same as when I bought Bob Lind's *Don't Be Concerned* from Kenny's Records. It wasn't a happy time really, because you didn't know where you were going in life. It was like holding on to existence by your fingertips and wondering how long you could hold on. I held on for ten years and then I got asked to join the Longpigs and I was parachuted out of this meagre life in a tiny bedsit and into being in London riding in taxis in a fur coat.'

Hawley has three kids and feels that young people have it much harder now. 'It was a brief window of benign neglect, I think. Our parents didn't have that option, and kids now don't. For us, it was about avoiding what our dads did and what happened to them: getting shat on after twenty-five years of hard labour in a steelworks. I wasn't going to let that happen to me. It didn't, thanks in a funny way to Her Majesty's Government's generosity.'

Richard's friend and fellow Sheffielder Jarvis Cocker, later a bona fide 90s pop star with Pulp, found the dole invaluable when early intimations of pop stardom quickly proved illusory. 'Pulp had had a Peel session when I was still a teenager at school in 1980 so I assumed it was only a matter of time before I became a fully fledged pop star. We had a mini-album called *It* on Red Rhino and we were being managed by Tony Perrin, who later went on to manage Right Said Fred. So it was clearly going to happen.

Consequently, my work at school fell off and I drifted on to the dole. I had thought all the band would do this, but they all went off to university, leaving me on the dole on my own. That's where I realised it was a lifestyle of sorts that you could sort of sustain while you dreamed of something else. Mingling with all these other scumbags. It was during the reign of David Blunkett as head of Sheffield Council, 2p bus fares to go anywhere in Sheffield. It was a very generous system. You could claim bedding allowance and everyone did, claiming they'd bought some super-new duvet when in fact they'd spent it on booze, obviously.'

Once installed in the bosom of social security, it was easy to stay there. Perhaps too easy. 'At one point I did have to apply for the Enterprise Allowance Scheme, where you had to say you were starting a small business. I think I said I wanted to make videos. But they just pretty much left you alone. You would claim that you wanted to work in the most bizarre industries or do the most implausible and ridiculous jobs so that they would never find you work. It backfired on my mate, though. He told them he wanted to be a shepherd, and a few weeks later they said, right, we've found you a job. So off he had to go to some desolate moor to herd sheep, which he had no interest in. I did end up going to St Martin's to study film, so what I said was not entirely a lie, I suppose. The thing is, I know that you're exploring this idea that the dole was a sort of alternative arts council, but the flip side of that is that it becomes very easy to get lazy and just stay in bed all day. That's what I did for a while. Pulp's music got much darker as a result. Because several years on the dole will make you darker and more alienated from the world.'

If modern British benefits literature has a laureate, it's Caitlin Moran. Her family's precarious but eventful time on the dole in Wolverhampton provides much of the rich, raw loam for her novels, her autobiography, her columns and her TV comedy series *Raised by Wolves*. It's given her a doughty, restless work ethic, deep sympathy for those in need, and a raft of hilarious, weird, bleak experiences. It felt incongruous talking to her about it in some of the places and situations we found ourselves over the time I was researching this book. We grabbed a few minutes backstage at a sold-out event in Sheffield on the hottest night of the year where I interviewed her in front of 500 acolytes (one of whom shouted out during a rare quiet moment, 'You give me fanny fireworks,' and brought the house down). We sat on the kerb outside a working men's club in Willesden. But finally, over a cup of tea in a calm north London kitchen that is nothing like the ones either of us grew up in, we had a proper chat. Her old kitchen was in Wolverhampton, a three-bedroom council house that was about six bedrooms short of their needs. Hippie mum, wannabe rock-star dad, eight kids.

'My dad would tell us that these were houses built for heroes, heroes returning from war. So using the door handle you'd think, this is the door handle meant for a hero. This is a garden for heroes to relax in. They were prefabs of steel and glass with asbestos roofs till they got rid of those in the mid-80s and then we would play with the asbestos in the garden and throw it around like lovely deathy snow, because you make your own amusements on benefits, of course.'

The humour masks a hard-headed lack of sentimentality or romance about her upbringing. Mum liked having babies but not especially children, so after a couple of years the little ones would become the charges of the elder kids. Caitlin is the eldest. Like most kids raised on benefits or on council estates or from the working classes or an unfashionable industrial part of the country, she had no idea she was different until the world told her in no uncertain terms that she was. At thirteen, she was Dillons' Young Reader of the Year (essay on 'Why I Like Books', prize £250 of book tokens) and soon after published her first novel. In her teens she was writing for *The Times* and *Melody Maker*. She was a curiosity who brought eager broadsheet writers up the West Coast main line from Euston to Wolverhampton, hungry for the exotic.

'Valerie Grove from *The Times* came to interview me when I was thirteen – which looking back is weird – and she made a big thing about me living in a council house and the family being on benefits and us going to the library every day. Next time I got interviewed was when I won the *Observer* Young Reporter of the Year at fifteen and again, it was all "she lives in a council house and she didn't go to school and she's on benefits". So it became apparent to me that as far as London media types were concerned I was an oddity, an outlier, whereas to me it was normality.

'The presumption was that it was the ghetto, that we were fighting rats with sharpened sticks in the street for meat and jumping up and down on burning mattresses. After *Shameless* it got worse. That may have been Paul Abbott's experience of life, but it wasn't mine and it wasn't for most of us. Was it yours? No, I didn't think so. The notion was, she has fought her way out of the ghetto like it was the Hunger Games and she's made it to media London so she must be so excited to see a non-municipal building.' Caitlin herself, like many young writers and artists of her background even started to frame her own experiences in this grimy light.

'So when I started to write about my experiences for the sitcom and my first book I admit it coloured it. I wrote about it like it was the ghetto: "God, I had it hard, the things I've seen, the drugs, etc." But I was writing a false borrowed narrative. I showed it to my sister Caz and she said, what are you on about, it wasn't like this at all, it was a normal, slightly boring place. When we started to make *Raised by Wolves*, well, firstly, we had real trouble finding working-class actors for the show. They're all from Harrow these days and it's very short-sighted. All those working-class actors made us a lot of money in the 60s. A lot of media companies are still living on the back catalogue of records and films made by all those working-class kids. Then when we got into production, some of the editors were saying, "Right, so is it people standing around in their pants drinking lager and having sex and crack babies?" and we had to say no, because that's not what most council estates are like. They have allotments and they clean their cars. It's really quite a lot like being middle class in smaller houses. It was quiet. If a car came down the street in the 80s we should shout "car" and stare at it. It was also the era of *Crimewatch*, which we were obsessed with, so we knew that if you ever saw a car you had to write down the registration number in case it belonged to a murderer. We had a pad by the window, a murder jotter if you will, because I became concerned that I wasn't memorising enough.'

When a car did come along her street, she would sometimes assume (or fantasise) that it was the BBC come to take her to London. 'I would think, "Yes, they've finally spotted me." I used to send jokes to *Spitting Image* and Clive Anderson. I got all these addresses of shows from *The Writers' and Artists' Yearbook*. I applied for the job of managing director of Comic Relief when I was thirteen. They obviously had a laugh in the office about it. But Lenny Henry saw it and sent back a reply on Comic Relief headed notepaper that said, "Babe, this is far too boring a job for you but I'm sure you will fly like a comet through British society." So that was a blast of the good stuff.'

My first thought at this is massive kudos to Lenny Henry (of Dudley, of course). My second is that life on my estate did seem rather rougher and wilder than that. Roaming the night-time ginnels and closes looking for kicks – cigs to cadge, love bites and cider – I might well have been one of the undesirables Caitlin would have yelled 'yobs' at from her window as she scanned the streets for potential murders in Ford Escorts. She lived very differently from my more feral outdoor existence. Maybe that was to do with me being a boy, but she has other theories.

'We didn't move around the estate and mix much and so we weren't typical. Mum and Dad were hippies who didn't really believe in society, so my house was a benign Crosby, Stills and Nash soundtracked version of Waco. People weren't really allowed to come and go. My parents were waiting for the end of the world, possibly because Dad's habits in the 1960s had made him regularly see visions of the end of said world. Our house was the last on the estate and from our garden basically it was the Wrekin and then the Black Mountains of Wales. So most days at some point my dad would stand in the bedroom window and say, "That's where we're going when the bomb drops. Load up the VW van and head there." And I remember working out that in our van, given the speed of fallout, we'd be unlikely to get much past Telford before we were all massively irradiated, since it did about 57mph top whack.'

She makes you laugh so often, so quickly and so hard that I'm not convinced I'm missing a steely glint of regret about some of this. She was 'home-schooled' or rather schooled by Wolverhampton Public Library, as we have seen. Wouldn't she have liked to go to real school, or experience the heady thrill of university life? 'The only thing I think I missed about uni was going to parties and sleeping with sensitive young men who read poetry. Wolves library had no philosophy section, so I missed all that stuff about language, the language of parliament and *Newsnight* and the public schools. I had no idea what a Socratic argument was. They know all that stuff from their schools. But they don't know anything really. They don't know about art or rock, or rock and roll. They don't know about anxiety or council housing. They don't know the value of love. They don't teach you that at their schools. So I have given myself the job of putting all that stuff into their world. In between doing knob gags.'

The Morans' insular guarded life was not just about impending Armageddon. In among that fear of 'the man' was the anxiousness that comes from being daily reliant on the generosity of the state and its gatekeepers. 'Dad was disabled and on disability benefits, so he was assessed twice a year. He really did have crippling osteo-arthritis so he would spend half of every month in bed on what I now suspect were illegal painkillers, these opioids that would totally knock him out. If you're poor, that's probably when you have to take the clutch out of your car on the driveway. But if you are seen to be doing it, you can be shopped. So Dad said we must never tell anyone we were on benefits. We had to tell them he was a jobbing musician so the busybodies couldn't shop us. That meant we lived in a sense of continual peril. Meanwhile, Dad would practise his limp. The DHSS in Wolves is across a large plaza from the car park.

Dad suspected this was deliberate so someone on the third floor could watch you through binoculars and see if you were really disabled or in pain. So we'd sometimes go and support him, and he would do his limp straight away from the car.'

Sometimes low-level anxiety would blossom into terror, which only served to strengthen the youthful Moran's resolve. 'There was a nice lady at the bottom of her road who had kittens and biscuits and one day leaving her house I mentioned that Dad was disabled and on benefits just before noticing a copy of the *Daily Mail* in her hallway. And with all the unshakable knowledge of a thirteen-year-old I was sure I would be responsible for ruining our lives and getting our benefits stopped and us thrown out of our house. It was a summer of fear spent sitting on the doorstep waiting for the post and the terrible letter. I made a pact with God that I would never masturbate again, which was something I'd recently discovered to my great delight. Anyway, it was a long hot summer so that lasted about a month. I then went to plan B. I would earn enough to support the family when our benefits were taken away. So I wrote a book and entered competitions. And I can still tell kids raised on benefits: the fear rewires your brain. You are never as blithe as the middle-class kids, that downy unconcerned blitheness that David Cameron is the par excellence of. They cannot conceive of a life where you might not know how the week will end, where one phone call or letter can change everything. If you've known that fear, you'll never be blithe again.'

We've lost much to those blithe and airy boys whose passage to the top has been as easy, swift and smooth as a salmon taken from a stretch of expensive private Scottish river. Caitlin was a ward of the state and a recipient of its undramatic but unfailing support. 'What I noticed when I went back to do promo stuff for *Raised by Wolves* and we were being driven around Wolverhampton was, here's the bus stop where we went into town, and here's the school I didn't go to, and here's the library where I educated myself and here's the DHSS office where my dad would "limp" to get his disability benefit and here's the clinic where we'd get our vitamin

C drops. It just struck me how well cared for we were, how remarkably well provisioned we were by the state. I yearned for the bright lights and the big city and I was bored. But I was allowed to be bored, kept safe and provided for and given opportunities for adventure and betterment. Now I wouldn't be yearning for the bright lights and the big city, I'd be fighting for my fucking life.

'Jess Phillips [Labour MP] said to me recently, "Your family now would not be in that house. A family your size would have been broken up and put in B&Bs and temporary accommodation somewhere on the far side of the motorway. You wouldn't have been able to educate yourself at the library because they're all closed. Your life would be ruined." Mine was the last generation to have the things that we accepted just like breathing the air. You would have a house. Yes, it might be small, but it would be OK. Maybe you couldn't paint it any colour you wanted, which apparently annoyed some people. But it seems an awfully big price to pay, the dismantling of an entire caring and efficient system just to have your door a different shade of moss green. In the end, the nanny state is love. For all its faults, it's about looking after and looking out for other people. The invention of the welfare state is love in action. It is the most astonishing thing this country ever did. To do that as well as winning a war is incredible. That's the people we were.'

CHAPTER 7

I GET A ROOM OF MY OWN

'LITTLE BOXES' or 'A NEW CAREER IN A NEW TOWN'

I grew up among poets.

Keats Avenue, Eliot Drive, Blake Close, Milton Grove.

I was raised among the warm, electrically alive, rough, ready, uncertain, swaggering swarm of kids who lived alongside their elders, a separate though connected tribe, on the huge Worsley Mesnes council estate in Wigan. The names of those great men of poetry (they were all men too; no Dickinson Avenue or Plath Place.) were not to me a litany of English verse, but simply the rugged, dependable furniture of young life.

I navigated by these mysterious, seductive names as if they were stars. Keith Clegg, who gave me all his Beatles singles in a black leatherette wallet, lived in Dryden House flats. The ridiculously fanciable Anne Thomas could be 'bumped into' (if you were very lucky) between Browning Avenue and Coleridge Place. Gary Mason had half his face melted off one icy bonfire night down Masefield Drive when kids from a rival estate threw a can full of red-hot ash at him. He'd worn a balaclava every day, summer and winter, since.

We lived among poets. We fought, played, drank and snogged among literary giants. Later I would learn that some poets themselves, a few Mitchells and McGoughs, had actually come from streets like ours, would have felt a kinship with us. Even the Betjemans and Larkins envied us our easy sensuality and natural vigour while sneering at our houses and our jobs and loathing our politics and our power. For we were powerful then; vast, grey, regimented council-house estates like mine were the citadels of ordinary men and women whose work conferred prestige and influence, the last of their kind to wield that kind of industrial muscle (though they would go on to wield it at the ballot box). Posh men in blue suits, clipped of voice, plump of lip, would tell me nightly on the news that we were 'holding the country to ransom', we recalcitrant, treacherous workers. If so, it was ransom money that paid for my school blazer and Vesta chow mein and football boots. It seemed entirely reasonable to me, then and now.

His habit of pairing an aggressively puce sports jacket with acid-lemon trousers aside, my animosity towards Michael Portillo has these days become largely containable. (Once, alongside his friend and front-bench colleague Peter Lilley, the smug, emollient face of the fag-end of Thatcherism, their appearances on TV and at the Tory party conference would leave me as apoplectic as that middle-aged lorry driver who kicked his television in watching the Sex Pistols on Bill Grundy.)

Portillo's defeat at the 1997 election, turfed out on live TV in the small hours, warmed many British hearts like nothing since the 1966 World Cup win or a *Morecambe and Wise Christmas Special* circa 1974. As his unseating was announced at the count in Enfield, he smiled thinly. At the time, we wondered what he had to look so pleased about. Now we know. Relieved (albeit briefly) of the burden of office and with time on his soft hands, he could now really make a killing as the most gallingly ubiquitous man on British television.

But when I saw a trailer for Channel 5's *Our Housing Crisis – Who's to Blame?* presented by one Michael Portillo, my mixed feelings became a heady cocktail of annoyance and awe with perhaps a dash of admiration at his chutzpah. Of the many reasons, some sartorial, that I am loath to warm to Mr Portillo in the way softer hearts have, foremost is that I remember him for what he once was, one of the most viciously relishing of the young Thatcherites, the man who opined in 1993 that we should forensically examine health, education and social security (in other words, the heart of the welfare state) 'from which the public sector could withdraw altogether'. So for him now to wonder aloud, on TV and for handsome recompense, who might be to blame for the demise of that state, was an impressively infuriating trick. He was a major public player in a party that killed off our national commitment to decent social housing, acolyte of an ideologue who laid waste the council-house sector and created a ghastly, unhealthy superheated market unique in modern Europe where houses are assets for speculators rather than homes for families. To do all this smiling, then make a good living fronting documentaries about the mess you created takes some nerve.

The story of British social housing begins in a sketchy pre-history of alms houses, tied cottages and workhouses. The Inclosure Acts from the 1750s onwards, whereby common land was annexed from the people, led to a huge increase in destitution and the consequent need for some system of rudimentary support and shelter of which workhouses were the most famous and grimmest. With industrialisation and mass movement to cities, more enlightened employers, like Titus Salt in Saltaire and the Cadburys of Bournville, provided actual villages for their workers. But large-scale social housing is a product of the twentieth century, 1900 in fact, in a corner of east London that this non East Ender knows a little.

The first time I took a cab from Euston to the new offices of an independent production company called Somethin' Else, who produce one my radio shows, the silver-haired, sixty-something cabbie turned around and asked me quite earnestly and with definite concern, 'Old Nichol Street? You sure? The Old Nichol? Why would you want to go there?' When I told him that I was headed to a glacially fashionable media company, he shook his head and smiled. 'How things change, eh? You wouldn't have gone there back in the day, mate. It was like a rats' nest of every criminal and ne'er-do-well in London. It was a real den of iniquity, a maze of low life. I wouldn't have taken you then for all the money in the Bank of England.'

He was right. But what he really meant was that the 'old Nichol' was poor. To alleviate that grim poverty, and an associated swamp of crime and disease that 'decent people' feared to enter, they built the world's first council estate here back in 1900, after much campaigning by the Fabian Sidney Webb, liberals like John Benn (Tony's grandfather) and two leaders of the London dockers' union. Its design, still attractive, was influenced by John Ruskin and William Morris. A flat in the Boundary Estate now ('perfect for a professional looking to be close to the City' says one estate agent's blurb) will set you back about two and a half grand a month. As John Boughton says, 'It remains a small working-class redoubt but around 40 per cent of its homes were purchased under Right to Buy and most of these later sold on. The defences of this little island of social housing have been breached, firstly by gentrification and more recently by corporate money.'

Graphic designers outnumber market traders now and the only cutpurses here these days work in the Square Mile and wear Hugo Boss. But on my occasional visits, it's heartening to see its alleyways and cut-throughs busy with street kids on bikes as well as web designers on tiny scooters. The area has kept a vibrancy that a lot of gentrified council estates have lost. You can still smell cooking here, see washing on the lines on the balconies. Plus you can pop out at lunchtime for a great salt-beef bagel and a 160gm vinyl edition of *A Love Supreme*.

Not long after the building of the Boundary Estate came 'the war to end all wars', as it was inaccurately billed. By throwing together people of different, previously alien, classes, war has often been an agent of social change. In the early years of that conflict, the brass hats and officer class were shocked and dismayed by the poor physical condition of recruits from overcrowded, squalid urban areas. The 'Homes Fit for Heroes' policy compelled councils to build decent, or at least adequate, homes for working-class people, but such initiatives were always a kind of drip tray; rental housing was still dominated by private landlords and was always merely a distraction from the proper business of home ownership. This boomed in the 1920s and 30s, bringing Tudorbethan suburbs and Betjeman's beloved and mocked Metroland. But cometh the hour, cometh the Welshman. And another war.

The greatest British casualty of the Second World War may well have been its housing stock. Four million homes were destroyed in the bombing. The East End of London was flattened. Whole city centres were razed: Cardiff, Bristol, Liverpool, Manchester. In Coventry a third of the city's houses were made uninhabitable and 35 per cent of its shops destroyed, leading the Germans to coin a new verb, to 'coventrate', meaning to destroy utterly. The Blitz, then, made the situation considerably more pressing but decades of neglect had left British housing a national disgrace before the Luftwaffe did their worst. In 1945, 100,000 families lived in houses officially condemned as 'unfit', with a further 200,000 in houses that would have been condemned had war not broken out. Two and a half million people resided precariously in houses deemed 'unsafe'. Millions more lived, almost secretly, in inadequate, overcrowded properties dependent on the generosity of relatives or friends. Of the Five Giants that Beveridge identified in his famous report and that the incoming 1945 Labour government were pledged to defeat, none was more immediately grave than 'squalor'. Now the situation was even more dire. 'Winning the peace' meant building a great many more 'homes for heroes'. Tellingly, in the post-war Labour administration, the departments for housing and health were combined; decent housing was not just a matter of 'lifestyle', it was a crucial battleground for public health.

Nye Bevan, the most voluble and charismatic member of the Attlee cabinet, was Minister for Health and Housing and a commitment to social housing was as much a part of his crusading zeal as the fledgling health service. He felt that council accommodation should be so good that people of all incomes would want to live in it and the very need for private housing would melt away. Speaking to the Commons in 1949, he said, 'These new estates should not just be for the poor. It is entirely undesirable that on modern housing estates only one type of citizen should live. If we are to enable citizens to lead a full life, if they are each to be aware of the problems of their neighbours, then they should be drawn from all sections of the community. We should try to introduce what was always the lovely feature of English and Welsh villages, where the doctor, the grocer, the butcher and the farm labourer all lived in the same street.' This was how he remembered the Tredegar of his youth. He unashamedly, passionately, romantically even, wanted to 'Tredegarise' the nation.

Had he not been so committed to these new houses being of good enough quality for doctors and managers as well as miners and labourers, according to Lynsey Hanley, the whole shape of British life in the twentieth century would have been different. Lynsey, in addition to broadcasting and carrying out academic research at the University of Liverpool, has written two brilliant studies of social housing, class and community in Britain: *Respectable* and *Estates*. Like me, her experience of and interest in council housing are more than merely academic.

'Bevan didn't think that working-class people should have to put up with the dregs of the housing stock,' says Lynsey when we meet on a glorious summer morning in Salford. 'The council houses Bevan built were big: three or four bedrooms, two toilets, not for luxury but because with multi-generational living it was important to have a downstairs loo for sick or elderly relatives. Big gardens for kids to play in and grow vegetables in, and for privacy. He didn't believe in that patronising notion some in politics had that the working classes live on the street, so they don't need gardens and their own spaces.'

We are sitting in the sunny, busy, classless environs of the Pret A Manger branch at MediaCity UK, the BBC and ITV's glittering new hi-tech 'hub' in the north of England, risen phoenix-like from the ashes of the old abandoned docks of the Manchester Ship Canal, where I make radio and TV programmes and where Lynsey has just finished making a documentary on public transport for Radio 4. Growing up on our respective council estates, me in the north, she in the Midlands, in our little bedrooms with our Smiths and Pet Shop Boys records, this was a destination we'd have hoped for in our own municipal dreams, but never have dared to think a real possibility. Over our emblematic aspirational lattes and Mediterranean wraps, Lynsey tells me more about Bevan's vision for Britain.

'Because of that commitment to quality, he couldn't build fast enough. The Conservatives probably won the election in 1951 because of impatience over new housing. Macmillan promised quantity. He built 800,000 houses in three years by drastically reducing quality and building flats rather than substantial properties. Tories subsidised building above the fourth floor, so the higher you built, the more money the building companies received. Blocks of flats began to dominate the landscape. The ethos that "nothing is too good for the workers" is replaced by "the workers should be grateful for whatever they get".'

Lynsey and I both grew up on big council estates, me in Worsley Mesnes, Wigan, she in the vast Chelmsley Wood estate on the outskirts of Birmingham. 'They called it the Town of Strangers when it was built as it was this huge community filled with people relocated from all over Birmingham. It's enormous. My primary school was on it, and my secondary school was on it, so for most of my childhood I never left it. It was the world to me, sort of hermetically sealed. I was vaguely aware when I was about eight of someone asking me whether I lived in a "bought house" or a "council house". But I had no idea what that meant. I said I just lived in a house. And I probably never thought of it again until I was fifteen or sixteen and went to sixth form, and it was only then that I was aware that I was different from the kids from Solihull School and King Edward's. Up until then it had just been the place where I lived. But then after that I realised it was somewhere to be giggled at, or at least mentioned in an exotic way. "Do you know you live on the biggest council estate in Europe?"'

This is a notion that occurs again in both the real-life histories and the artistic creations surrounding working-class kids who 'escape' into the world of middle-class culture and education; a subsequent queasy cocktail of guilt, pride, shame and confusion. It was an *idée fixe* in 60s literature, the burning core of plays like David Storey's *In Celebration* and the novels of John Braine and Stan Barstow. Its most serious and enduring exploration came in Richard Hoggart's landmark work *The Uses of Literacy*, for which Lynsey has written a foreword to the latest edition. In her own book *Estates*, Lynsey neatly evokes this inner conflict as 'The Wall in the Head', a cultural barrier every bit as difficult to scale as the concrete borders of the huge brutalist estates. I don't remember quite the same confusions that Lynsey felt. But I still recall flickers and shudders of unease and awkwardness as I entered the bourgeois world of further education and realised how other people lived and how their world looked. Like the day in General Studies class when the teacher asked what papers we 'took' on Sundays and when, among the *Telegraphs* and *Observers*, my answer of 'The *Sunday Mirror*' was met with 'No, I mean, do you get a "proper" paper?' in a haughty and amused tone.

In a podcast interview with Lynsey, journalist and ex-council-house kid Dawn Foster talked of how the privately educated students she met at Warwick University – largely making the best of not having got into Oxford or Cambridge – would enjoy the exotic nature of working-class culture ironically, with trips to Greggs and Wetherspoon's regarded as 'wild safaris'. This of course is the scenario that informs Pulp's brilliant 'Common People', a song that wears its righteous anger lightly and attractively. The posh kids who want to taste the full salty flavour of lower-class life will never have to live on it as a diet. They will never really know what it's like to live like common people, either the joys or the privations.

'My complex,' Lynsey continues, 'it was about continually having to keep saying "We're not all like that" to people who assumed essentially that we were all scum. I got into that rough/ respectable dichotomy, I bought into that stuff about myself. I believed that I "did well" because I worked hard. But at sixth form it dawned on me that loads of the people around me were only doing well because their middle-class lives had primed them for it. Comfortable homes, selective schools, private tutors, visits to art galleries. I began to reflect on the lives of my peers on these estates. They had economic stresses of course, but the expectations of them were low. If you did want to go to college, it was hairdressing and nursery nursing for the girls and car mechanics for the boys ... It was about how class functions. And in terms of housing, class is reflected in the landscape through physically distinguishable types of housing.'

Lynsey cites the great radical geographer Doreen Massey, who herself grew up on the huge Wythenshawe council estate in Manchester. 'She said that the way that most people live, waiting at bus stops in places like Harlesden or West Bromwich for a bus that might not come, is never reflected in films or TV or in "elite culture". Or if it is, it's about comedy or criminality.' Massey herself said that in later life, travelling on the 'smooth roads, and lanes, and through small contented villages' of middle England, 'The landscape of these villages is supposed to stand for me, in the classic iconography of the nation. Yet I feel utterly and totally – and both wilfully and not – excluded from it.'

But the way that Doreen, Lynsey and I grew up – on big council estates in conurbations – was the way most people lived. Not in leafy hamlets or suburban avenues, but Wythenshawe, Worsley Mesnes and Chelmsley Wood. I was once driven in a car full of writers from the airport to downtown Kiev. The main drag into town passed whole streets of tower blocks, giant skyscraper flats disappearing into the distance. I realised that some of my companions were watching this scenario with a kind of dread. But I thought it looked amazing. I realised that I felt more comfortable here than I would ever in a Somerset village or behind the leylandii of suburbia. It felt like home.

In 1979 (that date again) more than 40 per cent of people in the UK lived in council housing; the figure is now just 12 per cent, with another 6 per cent renting from housing associations. In 1980 12 per cent of people rented from private landlords; now the figure is 18 per cent and rising. Worst of all, a third of former council houses are now owned by buy-to-let landlords. The decent, affordable housing bedrock for half the population has been gifted to the rapacious, precarious rentier economy. Yet we still don't seem to want to get our collective heads around the idea that there could be another way. Indeed, it's the way we used to do it back in the days when housing was regarded as a basic social necessity rather than a speculative investment asset. Decent, affordable, rented social housing for life. As I was writing this chapter, one Sunday morning, *Pienaar's Politics* on Radio 5 Live began with luxuriantly moustachioed presenter John Pienaar asking, 'Are you listening to this in bed, or in the bath? ... then you are lucky. Fewer and fewer Britons own their own home.' The bizarre assumption here is that if you don't own your own home, you are therefore and by definition homeless, or some kind of couch-surfing oddity. No other country in Europe, possibly the world, has become so obsessed with home ownership, so fixated on house prices and 'getting on the ladder'. It isn't healthy. Indeed, it's making us sick.

'We're stuck with this obsession about being a property-owning democracy,' says Lynsey Hanley regretfully, 'this notion that full citizenship only goes with owning property, even to the extent that you couldn't vote once if you didn't own property. So now for the first time in fifty years, there are more and more people at the mercy of private landlords, without rent controls by and large, than in social housing. The government subsidises these landlords and the banks make it easier to get buy-for-rent mortgages. OK, both the Labour and Tory 2017 election manifestos promised that large numbers of council housing must and would be built. But they still said the priority is to build affordable housing to buy. They both think they have to keep alive that distant dream for people.'

In Scotland, until the Right to Buy was forced on them, over 70 per cent of people lived in council housing. More than half of Wales did. But in spite of the best efforts of Bevan, and despite it becoming a large part of the housing sector, Bevan never succeeded with the popular image and perception of social housing as he did with the NHS. 'Council housing always remained the "wobbly pillar" of the welfare state,' says Lynsey. 'People, people like you or I, who would not dream of sending their kids to a fee-paying school or using private healthcare, still think we need to get a mortgage and own our own homes.'

The paradigm shift, the seismic break with the certainties and securities of the past, came with the Right to Buy legislation, forced through by Thatcher and her generals with a zeal that far outweighed and outstripped any public desire for it. Like rail privatisation, like the NHS free-market 'advances', there was no great appetite among British people for these hacks and slashes to the social and economic fabric. Just long-nurtured grudges and obsessions masquerading as essential reforms, simmering hatreds that were purely partisan and bred in a kind of curtain-twitching fear and suspicion of one's fellow Britons.

Why did Mrs Thatcher and her allies hate the idea of council housing so much? I think there were two dimensions to it. Firstly, there's no profit in council housing and, by its very nature, capitalism desires profit above all else. The bottom line is the bottom line. But there's something more. Perhaps they saw something innately worrying and distasteful, communistic even, in people living together in a communal experience and a kind of happy uniformity, of architecture, of income, of culture. Writer Stephen Moss put this well when he recalled his childhood on ...

a large council estate in Newport in south Wales. Back in the mid-1960s, more than 65% of the population in the town was housed in council-owned properties ...

the estate, which would these days be labelled 'sink', was stable and generally content (almost everyone had a decent job in the local steelworks, which helped); the large greens in front of each block were communal, well-tended and great for games of football, rugby and cricket, often involving 20 children or more. The smell of new-mown grass after the council gardeners had come round to mow the lawns lives with me still. Looking back, it seems idyllic.

Keats Avenue, Eliot Drive, Blake Close, Milton Grove.

I can see that there's a certain irony in adorning council estates like Worsley Mesnes with the names of the grand versifiers of our mother tongue. The juxtaposition is too keen, too absurd surely, between the heady grandeur of *Paradise Lost* and the proletarian homeliness of Milton Grove. But compared to the first houses I had known – my two grannies' little terraces and cottages in Haydock and Poolstock, full of love and shadow, heavy with the relics of dead granddads and antimacassars and the occasional puff of soot – this new brutalist estate, thrown up on the last great wave of 1960s expansive council-house development, was gorgeous. In his book *Raw Concrete*, Barnabas Calder said of brutalism – stark, tough, primitive – that it was 'widely seen as the architectural style of the welfare state – a cheap way of building quickly, on a large scale, for housing, hospitals, comprehensive schools and massive university expansion'. This implies the cost-conscious, the purpose-built, the merely functional. But to me, who'd come as a baby into a world of coal fires and larders and houses built in the Edwardian era, my new home was not a bit brutal. It was stark, elegant, the future. I hadn't a clue who Le Corbusier or Ernő Goldfinger were, but they had an unknowing fan and architectural ally in the ten-year-old me who loved having his own room and squares of grass to play 'three and in' and head-tennis on, and underpasses and arcades and balconies to run free on. I didn't regard Eliot Drive as a wasteland. I didn't think Milton Grove was paradise lost. I thought it was paradise.

In the photographic archive of the Wigan World website, there's a picture taken in 1985 by one Alan Dalgleish from the fifteenth floor of Masefield House. This was the tower block we lived in briefly before moving to a more 'normal' life in the sprawling estate below. Among the more homely, touching pics of long-dead darts teams from the Bold Hotel and old 'Walking Day' parades, this image is straight from a Joy Division album sleeve or a Factory Records poster: streaks of light from cars below smudge and blur along bleak nocturnal '*Strasse*' that look more like East Germany than West Lancashire. Alan clearly saw the artistic potential in this moody study of alienation by night (photographed using a ten-second exposure from a 35mm Nikon SLR camera fixed on a tripod, notes Alan). I can see too the chilly dystopian vibe the shot intends to evoke. But looking at it now, I also think, 'There's the Fine Fare minimart with "Apocalypse Now!" painted in disturbingly huge letters on the wall and there's the house where Brownie got off with the girl from the chip shop and Quinny set fire to his pubic hair.' It works well as a symbol of a depersonalised urban aesthetic. But it was also home. It was my domain, from the giant substation at Westwood to the slag heaps of Goose Green. They were good times to be working class. We had jobs, we had power. We had joy, we had fun, we had seasons in the sun … in Blackpool and Butlin's Skegness, in Torremolinos and Famagusta if you'd put in the overtime.

Worsley Mesnes. The second word is pronounced in a curious francophone way ('Manes'), making it sound like the fiefdom of a feudal lord in the Domesday Book or a Norman baronetcy rather than a big council-built Radburn-style concrete estate, named after Radburn New Jersey where the pioneering architectural style was invented. It's a beautiful May evening and I'm sitting in the front room of my mum and dad's flat. I'm tucking into home-made chips with her slow-cooked steak and onions from a tray on my lap and we are watching a teatime TV quiz show. (There is no point telling working-class mums that you 'had a big lunch' or 'will grab something light' later. They will not let you sit in the house without eating; food equals love in houses where hugs and kisses are still awkward currency.) The TV show is *Pointless* rather than *Blockbusters* but otherwise this is a scenario you could have found me very much part of most teatimes in the mid-1980s. *Plus ça change, plus c'est la même chose.*

But they do change. My Auntie Mollie has just died in a home for dementia patients and the family is phoning around trying to establish funeral arrangements. I end up chatting with my Uncle John and Auntie Kathleen, the Westhoughton branch of the family. Westhoughton is about four miles from Wigan but when I was a child, this staggering relocation was debated as if they had moved to Anchorage or Ulan Bator. Kathleen, now in her early eighties, has had a fall and broken her hip. She says that she's 'been a bit low but your Uncle John's been marvellous'. They praise a snazzy overcoat I wore on a recent TV show and before I go Uncle John says, 'Don't forget to send me tha' new book, lad.' Because of all this, I feel oddly emotional even before I set out to tour the estate I grew up in, this time for a new book ('Not another!') and my loins are girded against the tidal Proustian rush that I am fully expecting to knock me off my feet this golden evening.

A broad, grey river of Tarmac winds like an asphalt Amazon through my old urban jungle. Long and winding, it curves from west to east, and throughout the 1970s I navigated it daily. It was the limits of the known world and I was Magellan in shorts and a snake belt. You could take it and follow it from its source in Poolstock to where it met the sea at Newtown, as long as by 'sea' you mean the A49, Warrington Road. The poetry falls down quickly here, and the road is called, prosaically, Worsley Mesnes Drive. But it is not long before things become more high falutin, more literary, as I stroll down Eliot Drive and Huxley Close (T.H. or Aldous, I'm not sure, more likely the latter as it was a Brave New World here in 1965).

Shakespeare Grove, Blake Close, Longfellow Close. Here is where the tower blocks, Dryden, Thackeray and Masefield, once loomed like concrete colossi until they were pulled down in a wave of demolition and 'improvement' in the early 80s. This is when that Alan Dalgleish picture was taken, back when the area was semi-affectionately nicknamed Beirut. Now there are small, neat houses. Each has a car and rather smart cars in a few cases. It isn't St Albans or Wells. But neither is it the feral swamp of underprivilege and neglect that you might fear and that the TV commissioning editors love to demonise. On its nicer, newer fringe, now tower-less, it is essentially a homely suburban estate, with Previas and Focuses and satellite dishes tilted to catch the warm golden syrup of the evening sun.

I have never been to Radburn, New Jersey. But if I did, I'd feel at home. It was designed and built in 1929 as 'a town for the motor age'; cars were kept away from the house fronts of the tidy, squat breeze-block houses which face each other across shared spaces and communal areas. The style became hugely influential across certain areas of the world, especially Canada, which is why I now realise my part of Worsley Mesnes was sometimes referred to as 'the Canadian Houses', which again made me feel pioneering and exotic. There were Dutch houses too, characterised by their flat roofs, perhaps the better for clog dancing or the rolling of cheeses.

There was an idealistic impulse to the Radburn idea: Walt Disney was a big fan, modelling much of EPCOT and Disneyland along Radburn lines. 'Children going to and from schools and playgrounds will use these paths, always completely safe and separated from the automobile' was a stated aim of the Radburn ideal that was exported to the world. Clusters of houses in Closes and Groves were linked by pedestrianised zones, grassed areas, walkways and entries. The result, in a sense, albeit in a fairly odd sense, is reminiscent of Venice without the canals and palazzos. Like Venice too, it was an easy place to get lost unless you were a denizen of its ginnels, corners and walkways. Far away from passing traffic and cop cars, the labyrinthine interior of my estate was also ideal for various illicit and nefarious activities, some more innocent than others. Unlike its more famed counterparts in Hull, and the Meadows in Nottingham, Worsley Mesnes doesn't get into many of the histories of planning or the architectural treatises. But it is classic Radburn. The original 1920s poster for Radburn shows smiling kids on bikes or clutching football helmets with the slogan 'Radburn; Safe for Children'. I don't know about safe, but what with Anne Thomas, nocturnal street football on electric-lit concourses and all the cans of red-hot ash being lobbed around, it was certainly thrilling.

Even after all these decades, I still know where to turn, guided by old desire lines grooved into the heart. I turn at where the Crooked Wheel once stood, a purpose-built estate pub that geometrically resembled its picturesque Constable-ish name but only when seen from the highest storeys of Thackeray, Dryden or Masefield Houses and even then only with keen eyes and a dreamy imagination that could overlook the pigeon shit and security rows of jagged bottles. It's gone now, swept away when 'Beirut' began to smarten up – which it definitely did – in the 80s.

So the Crooked Wheel has gone, but one of the two chip shops on the estate is still there. A few customers are queuing for their 'chippy teas', still perhaps the ultimate working-class comfort food despite the arrival of Nando's and 'Maccy D's'. I remember that when I was a very small boy, some people would arrive with bowls from home to collect their chips in, thus ensuring a larger portion. We never did this, as it was thought slightly common and needy, but even the detail feels more reminiscent of wartime than the era of *Blake's 7* and Brian Clough. The old world gave way to the new slowly, and old habits die hard, and maybe somewhere in the north right now, someone is standing in a chippy queue with a white porcelain mixing bowl in one hand and an iPhone 9 hooked up to the Cloud in the other.

I stroll down Eliot Drive hoping that the other chip shop is still there. This was the one I'd walk to from my nana's in Poolstock during the school holidays, fetching chips, steak pudding and curry sauce ('small fish, little batter' for Nana) to eat in front of *Crown Court* or *The Sullivans*. The woman who would serve these to me had green eyes, freckles and red hair and was, I guess, about thirty. I confess now that she engendered the same slightly painful, confused feelings in me that Agnetha from Abba did. I wonder if she noticed. Maybe all eleven-year-old boys look that tense and awkward, especially when being asked if they 'want a mambo with that, sweetheart?' But not only is she gone, so is the chip shop, which makes me a little sad, even though I'm not hungry.

'What are you looking for, love?'

The voice comes from a woman of indeterminate age leaning in her doorway. She is chatting to her neighbour, of equally mysterious age, who leans on his. They are both tattooed but whereas once that would have been the mark of the ageing Teddy Boy, the ex-squaddie or naval rating, now it means nothing. I imagine the Duchess of Cambridge has a tattoo, and possibly the Archbishop of Canterbury. It is as classless and empty of significance as *Strictly* or Primark or curry or football.

'Shops went years ago,' he says, in a voice like sandpaper on raw brick, when I tell him my business. 'I used to live here,' I say. They look me up and down sceptically and I become very aware of my brogues and man-bag.

I move into the heart of the estate, headed for my old house. It looks smart and fresh and not at all dilapidated. The grass has just been cut, perhaps by the council, although it occurs to me that many of these houses now will be owner-occupied, bought under Thatcher's relentless drive to privatise the country, starting with its housing stock. Toddlers on bikes wobble around the grassy squares. The designers of Radburn had their heart in the right place when they put kids first rather than cars. There are grannies and their infant charges swinging on gates and girls still in their ties and blue pleated skirts from school, skipping and chatting. Two young couples are making plans. 'We'll sithee at weekend and go and have some food.' In contrast to the typical image of a council estate, that of a cacophony of screaming kids and red-faced shouting adults and the squealing tyres of hotwired cars, there is birdsong and the musical tinkle of children's laughter. It is just like where the nice ordinary people live. Because these are nice, ordinary people.

I know these streets, I know where to turn. I get a weird emotional charge when I round the corner into Fisher Close. There is my old house. The house where my Uncle Cliff passed out behind the front door one Christmas Day in the late 1970s and I couldn't get back in after skulking out with some mates to escape the trifle and relatives and depressing late period *Morecambe and Wise*. There is the little patch of grass where I slipped in the cold wet mud and sprained my wrist dashing away from an errant Jumping Jack one bonfire night. There is the little visitors' car park where we re-played every game of the 1974 World Cup, me always Johnny Rep, my new dashing hero from the swashbuckling Dutch national team. Here's where I first heard 'Floy Joy' by the Supremes on Mike Tyrer's transistor radio in the company of Brownie and Nidge and Clegg, Gary with his burned face and my next-door neighbours Richard and George.

I walk away past a children's playground that was full and noisy at 7pm and I remember the deserted, forlorn one I saw in Poundbury, Prince Charles's model village in Dorset, a lifeless experiment in ersatz architecture and fake community. I feel happier here, and the kids do too, as I walk from the streets named after poets, to ones commemorating those long-dead civic busybodies, to one that brings me up short, there by the playground, the slides and the 'Witch's Hat', the satellite dishes and the Kias and Focuses and Clios.

Grenfell Close.

Field Marshal Francis Wallace Grenfell was a senior British Army officer who fought in the 9th Xhosa War, the Anglo-Zulu War and later the Anglo-Egyptian War. He later became Sirdar (Commander-in-Chief) of the Egyptian Army and commanded those forces at the Battle of Suakin in December 1888 and at the Battle of Toski in August 1889 during the Mahdist War. Eventually he became Governor of Malta and Commander in-Chief of Ireland. A dead white male of the military variety, he is commemorated in much council (and private) housing nomenclature. The electricity substation wall that backed on to Grenfell Close on my estate was the venue for many a marathon game of 'wallie'. And of course there was a tower in west London. I say 'of course' because everyone knows that tower now. I knew it slightly once myself, having worked a little at another independent TV company based nearby.

I would make the trip to Watchmaker's west London offices twice a week or so, taking the Hammersmith and Circle line to Latimer Road and then navigating my way through the mazy mix of streets around Westbourne Grove. I would pass through a section of council housing dominated by a cluster of high-rise blocks. Work colleagues would sometimes look askance at me for taking the short cut through 'a rough bit' but, maybe because it looked very like where I'd grown up, it seemed perfectly, boringly normal and safe to me – there was recognisably a community here, a vibrant one. Up in the windows of the tower block, there were pictures, ornaments and vases of flowers. On the balconies and walkways, the happy ramshackle clutter of urban proletarian life; kids' trikes, drying football jerseys, skateboard.

Originally I'd included here a few paragraphs of what was, on reflection, pretty lurid and disrespectful stuff about how that tower was now a Dark Tower comparable to Tolkien's Barad-dûr: 'crucible of evil, a pitted, smoking thing of nightmare' and 'a hellish monolith that stands above the streets of the fabulously rich and the desperately poor alike'. I include those few quotes in the interests of honesty, but I've deleted all the rest as they make me queasy. They feel like a kind of grief porn or disaster tourism, the kind that rightly angered locals when, in the months after 14 June 2017 and the dreadful fire that claimed 72 lives, with the ruined tower still smouldering above, busloads of tourists or curious groups of sightseers would pause and gather to take selfies, smiling in front of the charred bulk where seventy-two people lost their lives and many more their homes. It was this that made me awkward when I went back to the area about a year after the fire, when the handmade signs reading 'please don't take selfies' were still there in the window of the kebab shop and the community centre. I felt shameful muttering notes and thoughts into my phone – I was ready with an explanation about how well intentioned I was in my prurience.

All that said, some points beyond a reading of Grenfell as simply a terrible accident and a human tragedy are worth bearing in mind. If you want to experience the most unequal place on earth, see where squalor sits cheek by jowl with unimaginable wealth and power, the rankest of poverty and the excesses of luxury side by side, you do not need to fly to the barrios of Latin America or the slums of the fetid and crowded African cities. You do not need to visit those backstreets that lie in the uneasy shadow of condominiums and presidential palaces. You do not need a subscription to *National Geographic* or the Discovery channel. You do not even need to watch a Ross Kemp or Reggie Yates documentary on the no-go areas of Miami or Brazzaville. All you need do is get the 295 or 316 bus or the Circle or Hammersmith and City line to Latimer Road tube station and simply take a little stroll around. Because the most unequal place on earth, the most divided, the most extreme in its unfairness, is the Royal London Borough of Kensington and Chelsea.

In a lecture at the LSE, Danny Dorling gave a trenchant analysis of inequality and its roots in the areas of west London around Grenfell. The Luftwaffe bombed the working classes out of the East End (areas like the Old Nichol) and drove them here out west. The new and deadly V-2s pushed those who could afford it away, never to return, so these streets became a solely working-class and later ethnic enclave, hence the Notting Hill Carnival and the council estates. Yet these same streets fall, awkwardly and embarrassingly, within the richest borough in England, Kensington and Chelsea, home of the headquarters of the emblematically middle-class Cath Kidston design empire. Dorling points out that in the area that Grenfell Tower is in the majority of the schools and hospitals are privately owned. Big business runs this district of London and it forces some to live – and die – in rooms in the sky. Kensington and Chelsea borough is so rich that, when the axe of cuts began to swing after the banking crisis, the council really didn't need to make any at all. It did though, big cuts to the usual suspects and soft targets of education, welfare and leisure, for largely political reasons. As Lynsey Hanley puts it, 'It wanted to be seen to "be doing austerity" and getting with the programme.' The £167 million in lost revenue and slashed spending mostly impacted on people like the 5,263 homeless people here, one in every twenty-nine in the borough. In some ways though, they are the lucky ones. Better to live on the streets than to be living in Grenfell Tower on the night of 14 June 2017.

The streets around the Tower on the late afternoon I visit, for the first time in nearly two decades, are illustrative of a different, no less attractive Britain than cupcakes and Cath Kidston. In the shadow (literally) of tragedy, in this funky maze of streets where the hipster and the hoodie co-exist edgily, life goes on in all its rough, engaging vigour. Two Rastas are having a loud, cod-aggressive argument over a bottle of alcoholic ginger hooch. A gaggle of girls in dramatically piled headscarves are laughing in that way that girls do, not because anything is that funny, indeed nothing could be, but because simply, here they are laughing and young and alive. From the gates of the Kensington Aldridge Academy hangs a large bright professionally produced banner which reads, 'Ofsted has found this school outstanding in all categories. People use words like "inclusive", "family" and "community" to describe the school and students have hugely positive attitudes to learning.' Around the corner, a mural proclaims that 'The children of Kensington are the future of Ladbroke Grove'. This is the west London of Damon Albarn and The Clash (whose Mick Jones once said he 'never lived below twelve storeys up', though not in Grenfell), of the Westway, Jamaican sound systems and 'carnival', of squats and trustafarians in Puffa jackets and white jeans and Portuguese natas in the cafés. Down the road is Richard Curtis, here there's a room to let above the chip shop. There is bustle and life of the kind that London is rightly proud of, even if they do never stop going on about it.

As the Book of Common Prayer has it though, in the midst of life we are in death. Everywhere there are reminders of June 2017. The steps of the community centre are still festooned with bouquets of flowers, some newly placed, a year on. There are more bouquets and homilies and heartbreaking handmade cards at the Notting Hill Methodist church as well as, more bluntly, a 'Justice for Grenfell' poster. But more than any of these, the real reminder is there, around the corner from the Westway Sports and Fitness Centre, where the eye is drawn upwards, to the sky, to the tower.

When I visit, a white plastic shroud rises to half Grenfell Tower's considerable height, about twelve of the twenty-four storeys. Above now are the black eyeless sockets of the upper windows. On this afternoon, nearly a year on, just as the public inquiry is about to begin, the charred upper storeys are now a forbidding cage of metal. Around this, a hundred feet up, hard-hatted workmen move gingerly about the structure. What do these men feel as they negotiate this place? Are they local? Is this just another job or do they feel some heavy significance on their shoulders as they expose the interiors, unstrip the tape, unfold the sheeting and presumably ready the whole edifice for demolition. However determined you are not to exploit the moment, not to speculate or fantasise, it's impossible not to wonder what it must have been like to be up there on that June night.

A tube train rattles by to bring back the now. Below, in the smaller houses, and in the doorways of the maisonettes, a few pairs of suspicious and searching eyes follow me, justifiably. They've had their share of attention, good and bad, serious and lurid. They've had slur stories from the right-wing press about overcrowding, subletting and looting. Then demagoguery of a different kind from their left-wing counterparts and editorials about 'murder' and 'class war'. Former local Will Self wrote an essay in which he said, more suavely and prolix than most of course, that 'Grenfell Tower may prove to be a climacteric for our social housing ideals – but the change occurring is simply the burning of whatever illusion we once had that under conditions of centralised and neoliberal governance it was still possible to provide decent homes for working people on low incomes.'

Almost as quickly as the shock came the anger, especially from those who had survived the blaze. Michael Paramasivan was asleep on the seventh floor and woken by smoke and cries. 'We've been told by the people who run the building that if there's a fire, put a wet towel under the door and wait an hour before doing anything. But the fire was so aggressive, if we had done that we would be dead. I was not waiting for an hour ... There is cladding from the building everywhere. It just went up. It's like wrapping a human in cotton wool and throwing them on a fire.' Ed Daffarn lived on thirteenth floor of Grenfell Tower and the reasons his words carry such weight is they were written in a blog piece seven months before the disaster. 'It is a truly terrifying thought but ... only a catastrophic event will expose the ineptitude and incompetence of our landlord ... and bring an end to the dangerous living conditions and neglect of health and safety legislation that they inflict upon their tenants and leaseholders.'

From outside the community itself, the most exhaustive and controversial of all the responses to the Grenfell fire was a special edition of the *London Review of Books* entitled 'The Tower'; 60,000 words, a monograph the size of a small book, arrived at after more than ten months' research and one million words of notes based on interviews with victims, council workers, firefighters, people inside the cabinet and the council, put together by a team based in an office on the estate and written by respected author Andrew O'Hagan. But O'Hagan's conclusions dismayed many and surprised even the author himself. 'I felt I knew what was at stake in the story. I came with my agenda and I wrote to everyone and I briefed my colleagues – "let's get the bastards who did this" – and I felt enthused by the general outrage, and by the people on the ground who appeared to be saying the right thing. And then I listened more, and I began to notice the inventions …'

Essentially, O'Hagan bucked the dominant trend among the liberal press of singling out for blame the council for neglecting the tower by also acknowledging the failures of the fire service's response, and when the initial inquiry reports did just this too, there was much consternation that the fire service was being scapegoated. However, the council's deficiencies can't go unacknowledged. Much research had pointed to the coating of the building in a cheap and unsafe cladding for cosmetic purposes and ignoring residents' long-term complaints and grievances. The public inquiry heard reports from several experts that were very critical of the council and their contractors, hearing that during the refurbishment of Grenfell Tower between 2012 and 2016, the contract was switched from Leadbitter to Rydon, a cheaper bidder whose rainscreen contained polyethylene, which can 'provide a fuel source for a growing, spreading fire'. Dr Barbara Lane said there was a 'culture of non-compliance' over fire safety measures, adding that the building's cladding resulted in a 'disproportionately high probability of fire spread'.

It's undeniable that there was a litany of failures, but O'Hagan also pointed to the area's rampant inequality and its prioritising of Kensington's wealthy community over its social tenants, reminding us all of the real responsibility for Grenfell's tragedy. 'What if the cause of those deaths wasn't a few conveniently posh people, but our whole culture and everybody in it, the culture that benefited some but not others, and supported cuts and deregulation everywhere?'

What O'Hagan seems to be saying is that no man is an island, that the notion of communities supported by local government is vital to maintaining the wellbeing of people. As this is a Christian notion, it is possibly enormously and embarrassingly unfashionable.

But make no mistake, we need to get back to it. Not just in the sphere of housing, but across the span of our national life. To stay with social housing for now, the conclusions Danny Dorling put in his lecture to the LSE seem cogent and powerful to me. The answer to our housing crisis is in a massive programme of social housing building, the removal of all the financial incentives of Right to Buy, the removal of attractive financial incentives to become a private landlord, proper rent regulation, short-hold tenancies to be made illegal, and furthermore the compulsory purchase of buildings left unoccupied for more than a reasonable time. As Dorling concludes, 'We should live in a country where you have a choice whether to rent or buy and it doesn't make much odds either way. Basically, you buy a house if you like DIY.' As for me, I have often expressed an admiration for the late Jeremy Hardy's view that DIY is a form of blacklegging that takes work away from skilled men. This is perceptive and thought-provoking, and it means I'll never have to faff about up a stepladder again.

Back in Fisher Close, the sun is dipping behind the still-crowded playground, and walking these streets again I was mulling a passage in Lynsey Hanley's *Estates* that chimed perfectly with how I felt. 'Even though I have lived away from home for a third of my life now, it continues to shape the way I think about the world outside it. Rather like rappers who continue to talk about the ghetto experience long after they have moved up and out to their country ranches, it's a lifelong state of mind.'

I know these streets, I know where to turn. Walking through them again, I realise that these little houses are in my blood. These streets made me. And I turn up the main road towards Wigan as I have a thousand times before, to the Latics ground, to the Wigan Casino, to school, to the John Bull, to get the coach to London or the Free Trade Hall. The cliché that leapt to mind was that growing up here didn't do me any harm. Except that viewed objectively it did, when you compare the life chances of the kids who grow up on these estates, compared to those who go to Eton or live in the

Home Counties. But I don't feel that way, and even framing that thought seems mean and disloyal and treacherous.

Because I'd rather have grown up pretending to be Johnny Rep with a plastic football, drinking illicit Pernod with Anne Thomas and listening to 'Floy Joy' in a car park than to have ever set foot in the dining room of the Bullingdon Club or worn an Eton collar. You had to watch out for the odd flying can of hot ash. But it was worth it.

In 1985 I walked out of a job I hated and into a new career in a new town, just as David Bowie once sang. Well actually, he didn't. It's an instrumental. But the comparison works well and literally. I left the sales office of a Courtaulds mill in Bolton, defiant but nervous, for a new career in Skelmersdale New Town. It had been built in 1965 to offer a clean fresh start to families from dilapidated and crowded inner-city Liverpool. Now it was offering a lifeline to a confused, desperately unhappy young man with no aptitude for the buying and selling of yarn.

I got a job teaching at the new town's squat jutting college – brutalist, of course – and every day I would walk through Alexandra Park to the bus stop outside Greasy Lil's chippy to wait for the red single-decker 395 to hove into view. The journey to 'Skem' took about half an hour but culturally the dimension of the trip was epic: from flat-vowelled, simple-souled Lancashire into sharp, savvy, scally Scouse, from a horrible office of moustaches and car talk and the casual bigotries of middle-class mortgage-belt tedium to a classroom bursting with ungovernable working-class energy and wit and flair, from the private hell of commerce to public salvation with the state. It's not too much of an exaggeration to say that Skem and some of its people saved my life. I still feel fiercely loyal to it.

As Rodgers and Hammerstein noted in *South Pacific*, prejudice is something 'you have to be carefully taught'. Racism, sexism, anti-Semitism ... all the big nasty isms. No one's born with this stuff. You need to put in the hours. You have to pick it up as you go along, even the mild varieties like snobbery. I had no idea that the streets where I grew up on a vast new estate were depressing and soul-destroying because I just hadn't learned it yet. This was my world. It was the world of everyone I knew.

My estate was great. But new towns like Skelmersdale just up the road were even better. New towns, which I learned about in Miss Hart's primary geography class, were indisputably a good thing. I had done a project on them, crayoned a Harlow skyline, reproduced stats on Peterlee. They were my home estate writ large, with even more walkways and underpasses and bridges and towers, even more futuristic and streamlined, even more like something in a sci-fi movie or a cool model kit. I hadn't learned yet that new towns and new architecture were not in actuality modern, sexy and thrilling but in fact brutalising, ugly and sterile. I had yet to learn that the correct response to them was not excitement but horror, that they weren't fit for humans actually, as John Betjeman had once pointed out in his famous poem about Slough, and the only reasonable thing to do was to bomb them (and presumably their inhabitants) flat.

Three years after Betjeman's poem, in 1940, a little Pelican paperback called *Town Planning* was to prove a far more healthy influence, with a huge shaping effect on modern Britain. In it the planner and academic Thomas Sharp, an implacable enemy of both Betjeman's beloved suburbs and the ravaged, rundown towns and cities, argued that 'it is essential that we should get our minds clear now as to what is to be done when the war is over. We can continue to live in shameful slum towns. Or in sterile and disorderly suburbs. Or we can build clean proud towns of living and light.' Elite snobbery from the old and rich persisted. One Winston Churchill railed against the burgeoning new towns movement. 'All this stuff about planning and compensation and betterment. Broad vistas and all that. But give me the eighteenth-century alley where footpads lurk and the harlot plies her trade and none of this new-fangled planning doctrine.' Like Betjeman in his genteel Georgian parsonage, it is difficult to conceive how much experience Winston, born in Blenheim Palace, resident of Chequers and Chartwell, had of harlots and footpads in dark alleys. But in any event, this kind of humbug had had its day. A country emerging from the bomb shelters and the fog of war into a ruined Britain was hungry for change.

The 'New Town' was a very specific innovation of the 1945 Labour government, and the charge was led by the redoubtable Nye Bevan. Faced with the task of rebuilding a war-ravaged nation and a booming population, they rolled up their sleeves and rolled out the maps. In a sense, the towns planned and created under the powers of the New Towns Act 1946 were all the Luftwaffe's children. Similar notions had been tried previously; garden cities such as Welwyn and Letchworth, places whose townsfolk were railed against by Orwell as orange-juice drinkers, sandal wearers and sex pests in his mad closing rant to *The Road to Wigan Pier*. But the new towns were the first proper and widespread projects along these lines coming from the hand of the state. They were not mildly eccentric arts and crafts ventures but huge public building and planning initiatives.

'New Towns' was chosen as a term for these 1946 developments in order to avoid them being known as 'satellite towns'. 'This term has been used in different senses and we purposely avoid it.' All were keen that these bold new towns were not merely seen as drip trays for urban overspill. Most were centred largely around London's green belt. There was Harlow, Hemel Hempstead, Basildon and Bracknell as well as Corby in Northamptonshire (which rapidly filled up with Scots migrants coming to the steelworks) and Newton Aycliffe in County Durham. Previous books have taken me to several of these early new towns. I went to Basildon to investigate the phenomenon of Basildon Man, the psephological concept supposedly responsible for the rise of both Thatcherism and New Labour; upper working class, family- rather than class-oriented, blandly aspirational. I didn't find him, but I could see maybe a little of him in Depeche Mode, who grew up here – the early upbeat stuff rather than the heroin, BDSM and cross-dressing years though, obviously.

Walking from Jarrow to London recreating the famous unemployed men's crusade of the 1930s, I stopped off in Newton Aycliffe. At the risk of sounding like John Betjeman, I found it hard to love, as I sat and ate my prepacked ham salad baguette on a breeze-block planter in the desolate town centre, essentially a pedestrianised concrete strip between the bookies and the discount shops. Mark Gatiss went to the comprehensive here and lived opposite the Victorian psychiatric hospital his parents worked in. This may explain a deal about *The League of Gentlemen*. 'I hated it. I used to wish I had been brought up in Oxford or somewhere pretty. I retreated into Sherlock Holmes. I wanted to live like an 1895 detective, not in a grim post-industrial town.'

In the second wave came Redditch, Runcorn, my old stamping ground Skelmersdale and what was originally called Dawley New Town in Shropshire until an unnamed public employee – these were the days before expensive branding consultants took 250 grand for telling you to put an exclamation mark after something – thought the new town should have a name more reflective of the area's proud history as a cradle of industry and engineering. The industrial era was birthed in nearby towns and villages such as Coalbrookdale and Ironbridge and so it was fitting that the new town took the name of a Scot who had honed his game in rural Shropshire, the Colossus of Roads himself, Thomas Telford.

Telford New Town, thirty miles north-west of Birmingham, twenty-five miles from the Welsh border, is one of the fastest growing towns in Britain and its population is significantly younger – average age thirty-nine – than the rest of the country. Back in the late 70s, the kids here might well have read the infamous local punk 'zine *Guttersnipe*, on which subject a correspondent called Anthony Goodwin alerted me to a YouTube documentary. This is an absolute sociological gold mine for insights into kids and the state in Thatcher's new Britain. Local lads and girls make angry, sweary samizdat mag, council and schools ban it, graffiti appears all over Telford supporting it, local aldermen make fabulously barmy and antediluvian comments. ('Utter filth ... decadent ... next we'll have the destitute and the prostitute coming with their begging bowl.')

Nadia Shireen was too young for *Guttersnipe*. In fact she wasn't even born when its last issue came out. She grew up on *Smash Hits* (which she later ended up working for) and Pet Shop Boys and a lasting obsession with Paul McCartney to the extent that she can and will offer a spirited defence of the *Spies Like Us* soundtrack. Now a successful children's author and illustrator, she grew up in Wellington, one of the small market towns that has now become largely absorbed into Telford. Her family came here from Pakistan in the 80s and her dad became the local GP. Compared with the West Midlands conurbation as a whole, Telford is overwhelmingly white, at some 93 per cent of population with only around 3 per cent of Asian descent. 'As a kid, your view of things is quite strange and I suppose distorted. I remember small horrible incidents quite clearly. A girl at school pushed me in some dog shit because "that was what I was". Some bloke was horrible to my mum in the shopping centre and I could see she was upset.'

Some of Telford's other aspects impacted across racial divisions. 'The main problem I had when I was here is that it wasn't really built for walking about. You either have to have someone drive you in a car or it was all traipsing through underpasses and stuff which isn't great if you're ten. It didn't have a high street, not when I was there. It had a shopping centre, which I thought was a town centre for years. I thought town centres were just big shipping malls, till I saw a normal one. None of this is great if you're a teenager. So we'd sit on the grass verges of the retails park dreaming of life going on somewhere else like a lot of new-town kids. There was one nightclub called Cascades which I only knew to look at and laugh cos it was townie and we thought we were cool. Too cool for Telford anyway.'

*

The town took shape in the late 60s and early 70s, created from a cluster of smaller towns and villages. Dawley, Wellington, Madeley and Oakengates were all fused together around the central hub of the new development. Most of the influx of new residents came from inner-city Birmingham and Wolverhampton; sons and daughters of the smoky Black Country forges and Brummagem's workshops and factories now transplanted to the green pastures of middle England. Back then we were happy to use terms like 'overspill', but it's fallen out of fashion and favour now to describe towns and their people in this mildly demeaning and negative way. Then, as now, Telford preferred to accentuate the positive (as seen in a couple of fabulous promotional films available online). The first, dating from the 70s and in the British Film Institute archive, is heavily front-loaded with footage of the towns mini dry ski-slope being used by athletic flaxen-haired youth, a kind of Kitzbühel of the Welsh Marches as framed by BBC Shropshire's own Leni Riefenstahl. But it does have some amazing footage of the shopping centre – rows of men's slacks being flicked through desultorily to a mournful Herb Alpert ballad – and some salient gen about the town's design rationale. Tower blocks were eschewed in favour of rows of new houses with gardens and nice views of the nearby hills. Now here comes the science bit. Telford has 1,007 kilometres of road, 212 kilometres of cycleways, 135 bridges, 80 underpasses, 16,000 signs, 60 pedestrian crossings and 1,100 bus shelters. It has one of the nation's paltry 57 ice rinks, and on a clear day you can see 17 counties from the top of the Wrekin.

The second film dates from the 1980s. The vintage is gloriously apparent in every frame of *Telford! A Great Day Out!* from the shots of the bar staff mixing pina coladas in Quenchers cocktail bar to the actually pretty decent Level 42-style jazz-funk workout. 'Great shops! Yes, it's true what they say! There's all you want at Telford!' The enthusiasm is easy to mock. But I find it charming. I also like the mildly wry quality of the films of one quirky local history YouTuber. Over shots of fresh-faced kids in peardrop-collared shirts and feather cuts kicking a ball around, he intones in Eeyorish Midlands tones, 'Here their kids were going to grow up healthy, happy and well paid, making car door seals for British Leyland.' Things didn't pan out quite as well as they'd hoped, although that was not Telford's fault. When British manufacturing was choked, Telford struggled for breath. Even now, 15 per cent of its residents live in low-income households. But in other ways Telford has weathered that economic storm. It is even economically resurgent. Telford is one of the cheapest places to buy a house in Britain and there is still a decent social housing stock. New towns may still evince a certain scorn among the Betjemans. But they offered and offer decent, affordable housing and lives for ordinary people; at best and in intention a respite from the exploitative precarious life under private landlords in the inner cities, the dark England of *Kathy Come Home* and Peter Rachman.

Telford is one of the top ten happiest places to live in the UK according to Rightmove in 2014. It has a fantastic hill to climb in the Wrekin and the best park I have ever visited (sorry Birkenhead). Its McDonald's is still in the same location as in the groovy 'Club Tropicana' style film though sadly Quenchers has gone. Shame. I quite fancy a pina colada. I make my way to Telford the way that a lot of the New Telfordians did, from Brum on a train bound for the heart of Wales. Arriving in the town by rail is a disorienting business as the station is essentially on a tiny island surrounded by three major roads: the M54, the A5 and the A442 Queensway. The cars and lorries roar by beneath as you cross the Queensway by a hi-tech bridge shaped like a giant dorsal fin. I don't know what state of the art is in the world of bridges but this certainly looks like it, an elegant parabola of glass and steel thrown over the lanes of traffic and with electronic displays and video screens alerting you to the very many good things about the town you're approaching. There is nothing akin to a town centre. New towns lack the landmarks a traveller can navigate by and gravitate towards; the spire of a church, the floodlights of a football ground or some obscure but tall Victorian monument. After a moment or two of mutely gazing into space frowning, a nice young woman passing by on her way home takes out her headphones and asks me gently, 'Are you lost? Lots of people do get lost here.' I'm pretty sure that she's added this last bit to make me feel less decrepit and inept but I thank her as she points me onward up the hill, up a huge curious bank of steps like an old-fashioned football ground terrace, over another road and towards a thrillingly familiar sight.

Great shops! Yes, it's true what they say! There's all you want at Telford! The shopping centre looks to have changed little since the heady days of the promotional film. Fewer butchers and bakers and more vape shops and barbers, I guess. The C&A will doubtless be a Primark now and I bet you couldn't get a stuffed paratha from a street vendor back in 1973 like you can today. But the principle is the same, shopping as mass recreation, and the accents heard are that same rich, unusual mixture of Brummie drone and *Archers* burr. On this warm, balmy afternoon much of Telford has decided that the best way to spend it is indoors engaged in retail therapy with the listless ennui of the flâneur rather than the dedication and purpose of the bargain hunter or housewife. And we have become obsessed with slogans and messages on our clothes, bodies and accessories. Men of fifty who would once have sported a uniform of dark suits, sports jackets or cardigan now wear baggy shorts and shirts imploring me to Just Do It or reminding me that You Only Live Once (YOLO). Some go beyond mere meaning; a thin man with a wispy beard is apparently an Arch Enemy. Elsewhere I learn that Mermaids Do It Better.

I'm assailed by the heat even in the air-conditioned interior. Also smells: the pear-drop acetone of the nail bars, the reek of hot pasties, the cloying heaviness of cosmetics. Reeling a little, I emerge by a Greek restaurant named Odyssey which seems apt for my confused wanderings. I take a muck-streaked pedestrian walkway that looks like a drainage culvert in an abattoir and end up back in exactly the same place. Odyssey again. By a blown-up picture of some dolmades, a man in an England shirt with 'No. 8 Lampard' on the back is telling someone at the end of his Samsung that he is lost. Finely tuned to augury and symbol, the Greeks would know that this is not a good omen.

There are so many signs to Telford's Town Park that I decide it must be worth a look. To get to it, I stride up Telford's Walkway of Achievement, which is actually just a slope with some placards but splendidly details in pictures on a timeline the many memorable feats and occasions of the town's half-century of life. Here's some New Telfordian families skiing on the Wrekin the year after the town was built. There's Telford United winning the FA Challenge Trophy in 1971. Welcome the coming of the Ever Ready batteries factory in '75 and Prime Minister 'Sunny' Jim Callaghan in '77. Admire Reverend Awdry of *Thomas the Tank Engine* fame opening the tramway in 1980. In '81, when even leafy Wellington rioted, the Queen came to spread harmony and visited the shopping centre, possibly in her Just Do It T-shirt. In '84, her daughter opened the ice rink. In '89, they won the FA Trophy again and in 1991 the Thomas Telford School opened, one of the best comprehensives in Britain. They got their own radio station in 1998 and in 2014, both the mysterious epicentre of fun Southwater and the Town Park opened.

Telford's Town Park won the Best Park in Britain in 2015. Frankly, I'm surprised it doesn't win every year. Only the fact that I spent a deal of time in a previous chapter eulogising the joys of the public park prevents me singing its praises at fulsome length here. Suffice to say it is the nonpareil and the *ne plus ultra*, the Beethoven's Ninth, the *Sgt Pepper*, the *Pet Sounds*, the Messi, the Shakespeare, the Bach of parks. It can hold its head up proudly with the Bois de Boulogne and Hyde Park, with Tokyo's Hibiya and Bangkok's Lumpini and Barcelona's Güell. Perhaps even higher, because Telford's has a massive water play area and a giant metal tube slide and a sand pit as vast as the Kalahari. Flowers and stuff too, if you're into that kind of thing. And who provided it? Not some beneficent rich guy or multinational conglomerate but the boring old council and the ordinary ratepayers of Telford, which makes it even better in my book. And this after all *is* my book, celebrating just such things. In elevated mood, I pass three kids screaming as they dash in and out of the water jets and get mildly soaked in the crossfire, then past two African guys with pushchairs earnestly discussing football and into the information booth.

There are four staff: a smiley and enthusiastic lady called Jackie who asks if she can help the second I'm through the door, flanked by three tough-looking but amiable middle-aged dudes in shades and council polo shirts. All have either Brummie twangs or Black Country accents as thick and warm as faggots and peas or balti and bhuna. All came to Telford from 'Wolves' or 'Brum' in the 70s or 80s. They unfold the maps and leaflets and gather round, like generals in a wartime campaign.

'Fifty years ago when they decided to build Telford, all this was pit spoils and farmland. But then they built the town and all the houses all around this area here,' Jackie points to the green splurge of the park on the map, 'around all the old pits and pools and slag heaps and they decided to do it up and leave it as a park.' Her colleague, an older man with a salt-and-pepper beard, chips in, 'Back then they thought all we needed was a shopping centre.' He grimaces. 'That was all we were going to do with our time. But thank God they decided we needed a park too. So here it is, all three hundred acres.'

Later, I sit in a stone chair in the park and write all of the above up. The table I sit at is actually an engraved stone chessboard. Next to me there's a stone ping-pong table too. Two young grandparents are teasing their tiny charge who is muttering sternly, 'I'm very, very angry,' over and over again at some unknown slight, which just makes Granny and Granddad tease him more. Sitting back, I take it all in. From the rear, Southwater reveals even more: a large, pretty lake ringed with picnickers, wobbling toddlers followed by nervous dads and exuberant youths, a pub called the Wrekin Giant doing quite nicely this Maundy Thursday afternoon. The buildings look elegant and attractive to me but as they speak of the present and the future rather than some idealist, fictive past, they'd have the Betjemans and Prince Charleses of this world reaching for 'soulless' and 'inhuman' and calling for wrecking balls and bombs.

So let me give my two penn'orth in praise of Telford. Lovely as those places might be, not everywhere is Bath or Rome or Venice. Not every building is a fading wedding cake of a palazzo or a Georgian parsonage or a Dorset farmhand's cottage. Not everywhere should be either. In the right light and in the right frame of mind, Southwater Lake and Telford Town Park are beautiful because they do what they are here to do – make a happy, useful space for the people of this new town. While the pubs and pizzerias are doing OK, most Telfordians have made for this outdoor civic, public space, a place for toddling and snogging, football and play fighting, the lazy throwing of Frisbees, the unscrewing of flasks in October and the wafting out of blankets in July. So let's remember those words of John Updike about giving 'the mundane its beautiful due'. Well done and happy birthday, Telford, and your ace town park. I'll come back with a toddler or two and bring a picnic.

A new career in a new town. Having walked out of Courtaulds on a nervy whim, I was left with a year to kill before taking up the teaching job in Greece that my friend Vitty had got me. I managed to get a part-time job teaching English and sociology at Skelmersdale College. Back in the mid-80s, A-level teaching paid twelve quid an hour so a perfectly happy, if not quite Grecian, lifestyle could be afforded by a young man with no dependants. Though it will seem unbelievable, I ended up loving Skem so much that I quite forgot about the olive-skinned beauties and fishermen and Retsina that Vitty had promised and stayed among the walkways and bridges and pubs and flats and parties of the new town for four years.

Now I'm making the trip again on a bright May Saturday morning, through Alexandra Park to Warrington Road for the 395 to Skem. Greasy Lil's, named for a particularly fun-loving and attractive staff member but never really actually called that, is still there and now bears the much more sober moniker of Allan's Quality Fish and Chips. The Plessey engineering and electronics workshop is gone, replaced by a snack bar and a beauty parlour. These are small telling signifiers of how we have changed these last four decades, from a country that makes things to one that sells each other baguettes and hairspray.

The bus ride is predictably Proustian, once again. Through Pemberton and Orrell, past the old motorbike shop at Orrell Post above which the Verve's Richard Ashcroft held famously dissolute parties. Onward past Up Holland seminary, alma mater of Johnny Vegas and Paddy McAloon, now a spooky ruin. Finally to the tangle of roads and roundabouts that mark the end of smoky old Wigan and the beginning of what we used to call 'the People's Republic of Skelmersdale'; part Liverpool, part purpose-built Ukrainian Workers' City, a kind of Hughesovka in West Lancashire. When the new towns were mooted after the war, the Labour government was keen that they follow Bevan's dream for social housing; that it would be fluid, mixed and, if not classless, then class blind. The words of the Minister for Town and Country Planning, Lewis Silkin, now sound touchingly naive.

> The towns will be divided into neighbourhood units, each unit with its own shops, schools, open spaces, community halls and other amenities. [I] am most anxious that the planning should be such that the different income groups living in the new towns will not be segregated. No doubt they may enjoy common recreational facilities, and take part in amateur theatricals, or each play their part in a health centre or a community centre. But when they leave to go home I do not want the better-off people to go to the right, and the less-well-off to go to the left. I want them to ask each other, 'Are you going my way?'

In truth, new towns like Skem quickly became single class, that is to say working class. So when that class was declared war upon in the 1980s, they suffered more than leafier brethren in Bracknell and Stevenage new towns. When I worked here, Skem was having it tough. Indeed, it was the reason I was there. With no jobs around, everyone from sixteen to sixty, 'schoolies', 'dolies', single mums and redundant car workers, came to the college. They were hard times. But for me they were very good times. Skem had the raw, hedonistic, alive feel that places at war often do.

One of the reasons I loved working in 'Skem' – and there were many – was that on hungover mornings at the bus station and in vermilion twilights by the Nye Bevan International Pool, I could convince myself that I was in a) *Gregory's Girl* or b) a video for an early Aztec Camera single. Both these obsessions of mine had their roots in Scottish new towns. Six of these had been designated between 1947 and 1973, mostly to relieve the pressure on a bursting Glasgow. Glenrothes became famous for its whisky and Livingston for its infamous UFO incident of 1979 when a council employee was knocked unconscious by aliens (the only UFO sighting that's been the subject of a criminal investigation). Irvine was built on Robbie Burns's old stomping ground. Mysteriously, Stonehouse was never built. Maybe the aliens got there first. But none of this was as romantic or alluring to me as East Kilbride (where Roddy Frame of Aztec Camera came from and whom I slavishly modelled myself on for an embarrassingly long section of my early twenties) and Cumbernauld where my favourite film *Gregory's Girl* was based. Looking back, all of this seems very odd but, hey, a guy's got to have a hobby. Some men make matchstick models of the *Ark Royal*, some run long distances in unflattering Lycra for no discernible purpose. I was intoxicated by two Scottish new towns for what seemed to me entirely sensible reasons.

East Kilbride sits between the White Cart Water and the Rotten Calder Water some eight miles from Glasgow. Alex Ferguson and Lorraine Kelly lived here (not together) but it's in the field of pop that the South Lanarkshire town has punched above its weight, with the Reid brothers from the Jesus and Mary Chain growing up here and the aforementioned Roddy Frame. At the close of the first Aztec Camera album, Roddy sings of going down the 'Dip', a reference to East Kilbride's very own flat-roofed estate pub The Diplomat, near Roddy's school Duncanrig. The Belhaven pub chain owns it now and has renamed it the much less cool Gardenhall Inn, thus eliminating its one claim to fame, although one doubts it attracted many coach parties – not everyone's as 'sad' as me.

Every Scottish person of a certain vintage knows the slogan by which Cumbernauld was promoted in the 1970s. Over shots of various bridges, golf courses and shopping arcades, luminaries such as Simon Bates and David 'Kid' Jensen would join in a chorus of 'What's it called? Cumbernauld?' The town had been on the map before Radio 1's finest championed it though. It was known to the Romans, designated a new town in 1955 but not known to me until 1981 when it became Climackston New Town, 'twenty miles from Glasgow, twenty-five miles from Edinburgh and nine thousand miles from Caracas', in *Gregory's Girl*. It would be wearisome to detail again here my love for this sweet, hilarious coming-of-age movie. I have done it many times in many media. Suffice to say that I like to do something special with my body on a Saturday night, here's 50p, you can get plenty of chips with that and off you go, you small boys. Arrivederci, Gordon, hurry back.

In the same way that *A Kind of Loving* is a hauntingly lyrical visual love poem to the north of England, *Gregory's Girl* makes the estates and parks of a Scottish new town on a long summer's evening seem a vision of paradise, luminous and enchanted. Both films reject the usual depictions of these places as forbidding and impoverished and celebrate their life and light and magic. Give me Schlesinger's foggy, rain-jewelled Leeds dusk and Bill Forsyth's endless golden twilight on the housing estate and the golf course rather than Merchant Ivory any day. Of course, I am biased, hardwired maybe to love these films from my upbringing. These are worlds and evenings and nights I know and love.

Which is why I hate this from Andrew McKie writing in Scotland's *Herald* in 2014. Here he describes Cumbernauld as ...

> like something out of Moisei Ginzburg's Narkomfin building in Moscow ... Intoxicated by their brilliant separation of pedestrians from motor cars, it does not occur to the planners that the underpasses scattered around the town will become the natural habitat of drug dealers, muggers and rapists. As they plan the luxury penthouses which will rise above the shopping centre, they do not pause to ask whether anyone will dream of living in them. Or whether, like the characters in *Gregory's Girl* (filmed in Cumbernauld) they might instead fantasise about emigrating to Caracas. Dazzled by the nakedly socialist principles of brutalism, the planners and architects of post-war Britain merrily bulldozed tenements and terraces (the natural, human-scale, form of urban architecture), ran motorways through city centres and shoved arthritic pensioners and young mothers with prams up to the 28th floor.

Some of McKie's criticisms may have weight, the ones about high-rises, for instance. But you can hear a deep bottom note of loathing for the state, community and a planned environment. You can hear it in the stock references to Moscow, brutalism, the 'nakedly socialist' and 'drug dealers, muggers and rapists'. This is the fearful litany of the curtain-twitcher. It's a riff on the tired bleatings of Churchill and Betjeman, privilege masquerading as perspicacity, a nostalgic longing for tenements expressed by someone who will never have to live in one. It's a desire to see the worst in places and maybe even to want the worst. What's it called? Schadenfreude. Of a sort.

Many were keen to leap to the new town's defence and skewer McKie's assessment. Professor Robert A. Davis wrote in a letter to the *Herald*:

Residents of Cumbernauld are well used to the *de haut en bas* sneering of the Scottish commentariat typified by Andrew McKie's selective account of the town in which they live. Setting aside his wrong-headed understanding of *Gregory's Girl* (in fact a love letter to the things that create home, wherever we are), Andrew McKie will, I trust, forgive those of us who view with some scepticism the romance of incremental urban development against which he contrasts the fortunes of Cumbernauld. It was precisely from these spontaneous and unplanned urban histories, with their overcrowding, squalor and rat-infestations, that our parents fled some 50 years ago, seeking a better place to live and raise their families.

I love this, not least because I'm now au fait with '*de haut en bas*'. Fergus Murray was prompted to a spirited general defence, also in the *Herald*:

The UK new towns were a product of their time that responded effectively to the pressing issues of the day, including the desperate requirement to replace private sector slums with houses fit for human habitation, coupled with an urgent need to stop the deaths of thousands from the likes of tuberculosis and polio. Life was generally much tougher and shorter in the slums of post-war Britain than for any of our current batch of new town residents and without state intervention these slums would still be with us today. As for the new towns' current problems I am not about to defend the highly dubious aesthetic appeal of Cumbernauld town centre. However, I am also not about to apologise for the good intentions of the people employed at that time to make ordinary people's lives better.

Making ordinary people's lives better. It could be a mission statement for the nanny state itself. It did not seem such a crazy notion once, not that long ago. Making ordinary people's lives better, rather than a few, untypical, isolated people richer, should be a shared national endeavour.

I would rather have grown up amidst the streets in the sky and windy concrete piazzas of Tanhouse and West Bank in 'Skem', the green, crowded civic spaces of Telford or Stevenage, the towers and castellations, bridges and roundabouts of Cumbernauld and East Kilbride than a draughty Surrey vicarage whatever grade its listing and whatever the Betjemans and Mackies may contend.

Come friendly bombs and maybe fall on shabby private Britain now, on its tired and huddled masses struggling to get from precariously rented flat or excruciatingly mortgaged house to work or school or the shops, on a chaos of deregulated buses, on rattling stock, down closing lines, on costly and confusing tickets, headlong in the wrong direction for forty years.

CHAPTER 8

I TRAVEL

'A TICKET TO RIDE'

I was too early for the 'school run'. Too early by about twenty years. For me, that phrase always suggests something less ergonomically upholstered and temperature controlled, less drivetime and yummy mummy, than it does for others today. It brings back the unpleasant feel of red shivering gooseflesh, chapped and mud-spattered legs, raw, aching lungs. It makes me think, not of SUVs in Fulham, but of *Kes* or Tom Courtenay in *The Loneliness of the Long Distance Runner*. Damp northern winters filmed in black-and-white. Frozen cross-country quagmire slogs in the foggy November dusk. Being yelled at by grimacing PT teacher Alec Hurst, hands on hips in a black tracksuit at the top of Gathurst Hill.

'School run', in its (hardly more) pleasant modern associations of traffic jams, exhaust fumes, harassed 'helicopter' parents and impractical four-wheeled drive monstrosities in tiny suburban streets, is a term largely unheard until the 1990s. During my 70s schooldays, no one was driven to school except perhaps Jacob Rees-Mogg and the cast of *Grange Hill* at the height of their fame. Even as late as the 90s, 61 per cent of kids in Britain walked to school. It's now less than half. It's not just tiny tots with *Paw Patrol* lunchboxes being chauffeured thus, but strapping, gangling six-foot youths who look like Olympic rowers. I would no more have allowed myself to be seen being taken to school in my dad's 1600 GT Ford Capri (cool though it was) than I would have skipped to the school gates holding my mum's hand or been carried by a uniformed flunkey. It would have been an emasculating social suicide that ensured I'd never get a snog from Pauline Johnson again.

The buses of my youth were firstly bright cherry and white like Wigan rugby's famous strip, proudly emblematic of a tough town. But around 1974, everything changed. Overnight, and in a largely unwelcome *Anschluss*, Wigan became subsumed into Greater Manchester from the much more potent and romantic Lancashire. Our addresses changed, our official forms came from somewhere new, our gravitational pull shifted. Even our buses had new livery, that of GMPTE (Greater Manchester Passenger Transport Executive). Our new buses, were orange and white like a freshly fried egg, which was apt as that's how they would appear, sunny-side up at breakfast time, out of the murk on Poolstock Lane to take us yawning to the bus stop outside Wigan Casino and thence to Orrell and school.

Nowadays when I take the bus, making use of the free Wi-Fi, the USB charging ports, the complimentary newspapers and reclining padded seats, checking our progress on the automated digital ticker, paying with a tap of my contactless card on a sleek console, I remember what bus travel used to be like. 'Ou Sont Les Neiges D'Antan?' Or rather, 'Ou Sont Les Brouillards D'Antan?' Where are the fogs of yesterday? The thick, eye-watering, rolling, choking murk of the top deck where smoking was not only allowed but practically compulsory and where the creased-faced addicts swore quietly among themselves. The top deck was really a kind of filthy, penumbral speakeasy, dangerous and secret, the air blue with Player's smoke and obscenities which stung your eyes and throat and made your hair and school blazer reek. Up there, in a queer reversal of the natural world, the air was dirtier and thicker and you could see less clearly, which was a mercy given what was going on. Some would be fighting. Some would be kissing. Some would be altering the injunctions on the seat back to read 'Fleas Keep Your Feet Off The Seat'. Most would be swearing. But all would be smoking. This is where McCartney, having made the bus in seconds flat, made his way upstairs and had a smoke and somebody spoke and he went into a dream, a detail in 'A Day in the Life' that shows his genius for finding the surreal in the everyday and the curious in the commonplace. Everyone knew that the top deck was for smokers and loners and lovers and fighters while the hurly-burly of downstairs was for old ladies, men in flat caps, mums and dads and those laden with kids and shopping.

There were experiences we all knew and shared. We knew the drivers. Always men. Usually a crabby, ageing Teddy Boy with a lustrous, brilliantine quiff, a skull ring and home-made LOVE and HATE tattoos on his knuckles. Their default setting was 'surly' and even when they were jovial there was something of the fragile good humour of the violent drunk about them, the shark-like menace flickering just below the bright surface. You would not have been surprised to learn that there was a flick-knife in his lunchbox.

The 'clippies' were often female, sometime young women who seemed wildly glamorous to me as a boy with their trim uniforms and make-up and that heavy bag of rattling, shifting change. They wore sidearms of ticket machine and leather satchel and kept a mascaraed eye on that angled circular fish-eye mirror at the foot of the stairs to watch for wrongdoings upstairs. There was always someone snogging on the back of the top deck and always tickets folded into tiny fan-like sticks and shoved beneath the metal trim at the back of the seat in front, there to be stored for the terrifying moment when the inspector got on, and panic would spread like wildfire along the aisles. As Travis Elborough wrote in his history of London's Routemaster buses, 'We enjoyed the everyday human interaction the conductors provided, the familiarity of their faces, their flip remarks (the miserable sods). We enjoyed the rituals of paying the fare, the chunter of the ticket machine, the torn strips of paper that made instant bookmarks, that cord, that bell ...' The world of the bus was wild and primal but it was our world. It belonged to us. But not for long.

Every kid knew about these things because every kid, every adult, every toddler and OAP, everyone travelled by bus. They were regular, they were cheap and they were plentiful. They went to the places you wanted and needed to go affordably and often. Once upon a time, this seemed not a far-fetched pipedream, not an insanely unworkable and paradisiacal state of affairs, but the very least one might expect from a First World country's public transport system. We had not yet been convinced against our common sense that, as Margaret Thatcher supposedly had it, 'any man who after the age of twenty-six finds himself on public transport can count himself a failure'.

It may seem trivial compared to the sell-off of the NHS, but in my view one of the most crackpot and vindictive false moves of privatisation has been the deregulation of buses. Like most of these wilful and reckless changes, no one actually wanted it apart from twitching fundamentalist free-marketeers and major shareholders in the private transport companies. None of these would dream of taking a bus anyway, even at the point of a pitchfork, a fantasy some of us have indulged in. Unlike the ruination of the railways – which we'll get to later – there is no obvious and easily demonised bogeyman to blame à la Dr Beeching for this national disgrace. But its effects have been just as profound in our towns and cities and especially the countryside. I spend much of my time when writing in a log-cabin bolthole in Cumbria. Though remote by urban standards, there are several villages nearby with pubs and houses and the big market town of Penrith is just a few miles away on a decent road. Should I want to pop into town for a new pen, however, or some batteries or even, in a mood of wild extravagance before a party maybe, a potato, I need to plan my shopping trip with military precision and forethought. This is because the only bus service passes once a week on Tuesday morning at 10am. It doesn't come back, of course. A healthy free market? Don't make me laugh.

The students, scallies and shoppers on Manchester's Oxford Road have quite the opposite problem. They have not too few buses but too many. This is one of the busiest bus thoroughfares in Europe, but as Andy Burnham, Mayor of Greater Manchester, is spelling out to me, busier doesn't always mean better. 'Count 'em,' he says as we look out on the midweek twilit rush-hour street scene in downtown Manchester. He gestures through exhaust fumes and drizzle to the snaking chain of honking, jostling, swaying, brake-slamming buses that make Oxford Road a sluggish river of polluting engines and a potent symbol of crappy, shallow thinking. The buses crawl, nose to tail, like chained elephants up this clogged major Mancunian thoroughfare, home of a thousand landmarks from the Whitworth Gallery to Emmeline Pankhurst's old house to the Church of the Holy Name where Morrissey stole lead from the roof in 'Vicar in a Tutu'. 'Five, six, seven ... different colours, different companies, no integration, no planning, no common sense, no joined-up thinking. Welcome to the joys of the deregulated bus market.'

Andy Burnham held several high-ranking cabinet positions and twice stood to become Labour Party leader. The fact that in 2017 he chose to quit as MP for Leigh (astonishingly, to go Tory at the 2019 election) was an ominous portent for the Labour Party and Westminster, but great news for the people of Greater Manchester. Despite being born in Liverpool, he's been warmly accepted by the locals as their mayor. 'It helps that I support the acceptable face of Merseyside football, Everton. I did ask the Mayor of Barcelona, would she ever have been elected if she'd been born in Madrid and she said "no way".' Andy was elected by a thumping majority and since then he has embarked with vigour on several crusades in the region, chiefly homelessness and public transport.

'Yes. You're right. It is a crusade. Not because I'm a train spotter or a bus geek or anything. Just because, a year into this job, I know transport is what will hold this place back, this city, this region. We are nowhere near where we should be and the system we have got is not capable of supporting the ambition of the north-west and its people.'

How did we arrive at the confusing and inefficient shambles that you see on Oxford Road or the wasteland of rural bus networks? I'm afraid we're going to have to round up the usual suspects. In 1986, Mrs Thatcher cast her baleful eye across the land and wondered what she might privatise next. After a rushed white paper and cosy consultations with big players in the private transport lobby, the avaricious gaze of the market fell on the poor old British bus. These homely steeds had long been a gentle, charming fixture of British life. Buses were redolent of Norman Wisdom, Reg Varney, clippies, the *Double Deckers* TV show, Cliff and the Shads going on a summer holiday. We loved them. In 1973, the *Holiday on the Buses* spin-off movie of that dire sitcom trounced the latest Bond instalment *Live and Let Die* at the British box office. 'There is almost no experience in life that makes you look and feel more suave than jumping on or off a moving London bus,' Bill Bryson said. They weren't always perfect. But they were quaint, they were sweet, they were safe, they were ours. Soon they seemed to belong to everyone but us.

Almost immediately upon deregulation, the world of bus transport became the Wild West and the cowboys rode in from everywhere. The National Bus Company was divided into seventy separate entities and sold off hastily and gleefully. A few franchises were bought out by employee and management collectives from National Bus, but they were quickly eaten up by other transport giants: National Express, Stagecoach, Arriva, First, Go-Ahead. Soon most bus services were run by four enormous companies who in turn were owned by even bigger, unknowable companies on the other side of the world.

The dismaying chaos in the wake of all this is yet another inconvenient truth that rabid free-marketeers choose to overlook. Across the country, 'Bus Wars' broke out, often nasty and sordid, never in the public interest. The result was inefficiency, passenger dissatisfaction and worse: glaring safety violations that endangered staff and customers; working regulations flouted and guidelines ignored. Many Twitter correspondents told me horror stories. Paul Haitch said, 'My home town was awash with buses in the 90s, competition got really cut-throat, and people actually came to visit Darlington just to take it all in!' Doncaster's bus war resulted in the collapse of the local transport authority after most of its drivers were poached and a halving of the number of journeys made over the next two decades. Marti told me he 'remembered when a new bus company started in Barnsley. The new buses would race the old red ones to get to the bus stop first to nick the passengers. It was hair-raising stuff as a passenger and a wonder that no one got killed really.'

In 1988, Southern Vectis were the first of many companies to be investigated by the regulators for unscrupulously damaging and baulking its competitors' services. Since then Cardiff Bus has been accused of engaging in 'predatory behaviour' by the Office of Fair Trading. Stagecoach Manchester was found guilty of using dirty tricks against rival companies in Manchester's own infamous bus war, such as parking its vehicles on the bus stops of other operators, blocking their access, then using their inspectors to obstruct doors and herd passengers to their buses. In the mid-noughties, they and UK North fought a protracted battle of this dismal war along the Wilmslow Road route that caused traffic misery and ended with two managers of the latter jailed for unsafe working practices that resulted in the death of a crane operator.

Stagecoach provide many of the bewildering array of buses crawling past Andy Burnham and me on Oxford Road. There are a variety of garish and diverse liveries, all with posters of Adam Sandler films and toothsome students clutching weekly passes, all part of a confusing and muddled range of fares and tickets that have only one thing in common – they are far too high. 'My daughter Rose is sixteen,' says Andy. 'A trip to Wigan costs her four pounds. In London that trip would be one pound fifty. Ridiculous. We are in a good place to have this discussion, here on Oxford Road. That's the mess you get when you privatise something that was doing perfectly well before. You and I remember the old orange and white buses of our youth. Getting the number twenty-six from Leigh bus station into Manchester to see bands or watch football.' He pauses and smiles. 'OK ... it took three hours,' he laughs (it didn't), 'but it was a good, reliable service. Have a look at Manchester bus market for a microcosm of the total dysfunctionality of privatisation mania. It was sold to people with promises that there'd be more routes and cheaper fares. But what we got was the exact opposite. So there's loads of buses here on a busy route full of students and office workers ... too many, if anything. But fuck all in Higher Fold [a council estate in Burnham's old Leigh constituency] because they are not lucrative routes and so the companies are not interested. They drive competitors out of business and then they put their own prices up. They are not working in the public interest. If you want a microcosm of the disaster of privatisation –' and he points to a fuming snarl-up of buses and queues of confused passengers shuffling between them '– there it is.'

If you think Inspector 'Blakey' saying 'I'll get you, Butler' to Reg Varney every week wasn't really all that funny, there is still some black humour to be found in our deregulated bus mess. Here for instance is the penetrating insight offered by the Competition Commission's 2011 report into local bus services: 'Head to head competition between bus operators is uncommon ... because of customer conduct.' Customers (that's you) were refusing to behave like proper commercial consumers and, instead of spending time reviewing the various companies' performance and availability vis à vis routes, cross referencing and comparing the differing ticket types and fare structures before arriving at a purchase decision, they were simply 'boarding the first bus to their destination that arrives at their bus stop'. With this kind of conduct, how can Arriva and Stagecoach bosses and shareholders expect a decent dividend? You ought to be ashamed of yourselves, bus users of Britain. It's almost as if bus transport in a small country can't ever be genuinely a truly competitive market, that it's a natural monopoly that should never have been deregulated in the first place.

No, it's exactly that. The Competition Commission also found that there is no real competition in local bus services and that there probably never can be because that's not how people use buses or want to use them. Since 1986, the year after deregulation, bus use across the UK has fallen by 32.5 per cent while fares have increased by 35 per cent above inflation. Again, so much for the market's ability to provide better, cheaper essential services. Want to know what Britain's favourite bus company is? Take a bow, Nottingham City Transport, the largest local-authority-owned operator in England, with the highest customer satisfaction of any bus operator in the UK. This century, Nottingham has grown its bus lanes from 200 metres at first to 24 kilometres today. It was the first city in the UK to have smart passes, three years before London's swanky and lauded Oyster card. A public body beats the private sector again for innovation and customer service.

A couple of junctions south down the M1 in Leicester (same size, same population, same kind of city and people from my experience) Leicester City Council pays £467,000 a year to subsidise a private operator. The good citizens I spoke to when I walked through Leicester on the way from Jarrow to London in 2016 were uniformly and vocally uncomplimentary about their buses. So how come more cities don't follow the Nottingham model? Because they're not allowed to. The Department of Transport won't let them. The Bus Services Act introduced by our old friend, the apocalyptically untogether Transport Secretary Chris Grayling in 2017, barred local authorities from establishing their own municipally owned providers. As Mark Fowles, managing director of Nottingham City Transport sees it, the reasons are ideological. 'Municipal bus companies run against the ethos of the ruling party.'

Let's head north. I'm afraid we can only manage a quick admiring passing glance at perhaps the one bright and beautiful place on the bus map of Britain. Next time you're in Preston, pop into the bus station. It's a Grade II listed building which has amused and annoyed some traditionalists who think such status is for vicarages and palaces. Preston bus station is a people's palace. A spare and minimal brutalist construction that wouldn't look out of place in Oslo or Tampere, which is praise indeed in my book. Pop in next time your train to London or Glasgow terminates unexpectedly at Preston. For that day will come, traveller.

And so up to Cumbria, where I don't get the one bus a week that passes somewhere near me. In fact, I'm not sure it even runs any more. In 2014, Cumbria County Council, faced with the kind of budget cuts we've become sadly used to, knew that something had to give. What they chose was buses. The private sector could not truthfully give a monkey's for Cumbrian bus routes. The county is big, empty and hard to navigate quickly, being full of hills and mountains and lakes. Lovely of course. But it makes bus timetables a headache, an unprofitable headache furthermore, the businessman's most hated kind. So the council have always had to subsidise the buses for the good of Cumbrians. Until 2014, that is, when with a stroke of what was probably a borrowed and leaky pen in an unheated office, they reduced the subsidy to zero, nada, zilch, nowt. Cumbria's buses would have to survive on their own or die. As a result, communities and tourism suffer. The economy suffers because people can't get to work or go to the shops. Life becomes harder and more boring. Meanwhile the private companies are playing the world's smallest violin. The public good is not their concern. The personal dividend and bonus are. Sorry, Cumbria. You're going to have to stay at home or walk.

We still do have a substantially government-owned bus network: it's just that it's other countries' governments who run them. In Chris Grayling's own constituency of Epsom and Ewell, most of the buses are run by the French or German government. As Jonny Ball (not that one) in the *New Statesman* pointed out. 'Most of the profits from bus fares in the Transport Secretary's constituency, then, are reinvested in French and German public services.' The fact that Grayling was an ardent Brexiteer makes the irony both delicious and bitter simultaneously.

There is one noble exception to all of this misery and decline though. London. The streets may not be paved with gold but they are certainly filled with buses, and more to the point with people happily, easily and cheaply riding them. Cathal Coughlan of the excellent bands Microdisney and Fatima Mansions had a song called 'Only Losers Take the Bus', based on an overheard scream of abuse from a braying City boy at a bus queue. But he was wrong, at least about the capital city. As Andy Burnham points out, 'In London, everyone gets the bus: City traders, bankers, teachers, students, kids, mums, tourists, workers ... all kinds of people, a real mix. Not here. Over the last thirty years, bus use here has halved, while in London, it's boomed.' Boomed is putting it mildly, actually. While in Britain at large, bus use has almost halved since 1986, in the capital it has risen by a staggering 98 per cent.

Why? Because London's buses are regulated, subsidised and integrated. The political power of the Greater London Council and its successors (and a healthy dose of self-interest) meant that Londoners were never thrown to the dogs and scavengers of the private bus sector as the rest of us were when the Conservative government deregulated the bus industry everywhere across Britain ... except London.

In London, value has actually improved. A single zone-one fare for Oyster card users in 2005 was £1. Today, fourteen years later, it has rocketed to ... £1.50. That's to travel anywhere in the whole of the huge city. Protected and privileged, as with so many elements of life in the capital, London's buses are a state-owned success. For the rest of us, abandoned by people who live, you've guessed it, in London, bus transport has come to occupy a place in a societal space similar to council housing: remedial, a poor substitute for private commercial alternatives, a last resort. The 262 night bus from Stratford to Beckton may never be as attractive as the Vaporetto Number 1 from the Venice Rialto but it gets you home. Right now, in towns all over Britain, tired, hungry, anxious people are standing with their shopping in the rain, waiting for a bus that, like Godot, will never turn up.

Not far from the bus-clogged artery of Oxford Road is a happier transport landmark, the first commercial passenger railway station in the world. The old station buildings on Liverpool Road are now home to one of Manchester's biggest civic attractions. Manchester is never shy of singing its own praises. It is a bragging, swaggering city and that is part of its bullish, cocky and considerable charm. But it's a matter of fact and not puffed-up opinion that Britain's Science and Industry Museum could not have a better or more appropriate home than here in the world's first industrial city, the mighty 'Cottonopolis'.

Manchester first got rich weaving cotton. After that, it just couldn't stop reimagining the world, bringing forth feminism, communism, vegetarianism, building a ship canal that stole Liverpool's sea trade from under its noses, splitting the atom, inventing the computer and then, this century, developing graphene. The museum closes to the public at 5pm but at 6.30 on a brisk autumn evening I'm one of an excitable throng of Mancunians queuing at the doors of the museum to be patted down and ticked off lists and handed a canapé. It's a reception to welcome back a handsome, dashing homecoming celebrity and I'm chuffed to have been invited. It's been too long. One hundred and eighty years, in fact. Flashbulbs pop, men stand around, women clink glasses and whisper admiration, pointing out the star's most attractive features: its broad muscular shoulders, its fine black flanks and pistons, its massive wheels and frankly priapic chimney. Stephenson's *Rocket* left town nearly two centuries ago bound for Liverpool on the opening journey of the world's first inter-city passenger railway. It hasn't been back since 1834. But now transport's coming home and we can only hope the party doesn't end the way the last one did. Because this beauty is also a beast. The first time it was here, it was a killer too. It ran down William Huskisson MP on its maiden voyage, taking a man's life while bunting flapped and corks popped.

Purists think the romance went out of the railways with the end of steam. Others with the coming of BR. Or perhaps with Jimmy Savile telling us that this was the age of the train in his uniquely chilling way. But all over Britain, and especially across the north these last few summers of rage and tears, you could sense that the love affair was over, just like Celia Johnson and Trevor Howard's in *Brief Encounter*. With every day, the idiotic, knotted cat's cradle of our privatised rail network began to finally unravel. I travel by train a great deal and on almost every trip these days, there's some small but acute reminder of the disaster that was rail privatisation. It's been a different kind of disaster than the one which happened 'on the buses' but just as damaging for our national life. For instance, the other day I took a train from Salford to Wigan, which I often do, back to my home town from the BBC's new northern base at MediaCity. Arriving at the station, I was dismayed though not surprised to see my train cancelled 'due to staff shortages'. 'Oh, it's not really shortages,' said an employee who I shall not name or describe. 'It never runs. But if they said that, it wouldn't be fulfilling its timetable and they could get fined, even lose the franchise. So it's cancelled every week for the same reason, as if it's an unforeseen problem.' I thought about this as we rattled along and I remembered a trip I had once taken on a Swiss train while working for the *NME*. A trip to the Alps with the then all conquering Stone Roses to shoot the Xmas cover somewhere suitably snowy.

To get to the Eiger, we took a train from Zurich to Interlaken and thence to Grindelwald. Excitable and little concerned with Swiss social niceties, the band (and possibly an accompanying young writer) smoked spliffs and swigged from a bottle of cognac in the first-class carriage. A smartly dressed Swiss captain of industry was clearly not entirely happy with this but a bad scene was narrowly averted by the sheer exuberant charm and smart good humour of the band (and by the offer of a glass of rather good cognac). We soon fell into conversation as snowy peaks passed by in the glittering winter dusk.

'Nice train,' said genial Manc bass player Mani. Our new friend smiled. 'Swiss Federal Railways. The best railways in the world. Owned by the Swiss people. Once all the railways in Switzerland were privately owned but this was a mess. The people voted for the government to take them and now we are the pride of the world. Safe, quick, easy, comfortable. Look at this.' He stroked the padded headrests and reclining seats of turquoise leather, the TV information screens, the smoked glass. 'Of course, you invented the railways, you know. That is why I cannot believe what you are planning to do.' The band looked a little bemused. I guessed they may not have been following parliamentary debates and white papers on transport policy very closely in the last few months. He looked at us with a smile of what seemed a lot like pity, and not just for our haircuts and baggy flares. 'You are planning to sell off your trains to the private franchises. That is ... insane. Switzerland is a byword for capitalism. We worship business and money and profit. But we know that no sensible country sells off its railway!'

I often think about that Swiss businessman these days. Perhaps as my train fails to arrive, or is so cramped and hot that someone faints, or a young mum struggles with a fractious hungry child because the buffet car has closed due to a faulty microwave, or a disoriented elderly person has to leave the train at Crewe in the rain of a winter evening or pay for another ticket because they can't understand why the enormously expensive ticket they bought to travel from Glasgow to Birmingham isn't actually valid on this train from Glasgow to Birmingham thanks to an opaque system that Franz Kafka would have rejected as the basis for a short story on the grounds that it was too nightmarishly complex and unfeasible to believe.

I was still mulling this as the train reached Hindley. This being a Saturday I had managed to get a seat. During the week, especially at rush hour, if the train is actually running, it will certainly be full and you will spend the whole journey with your face in someone's armpit or crotch. Faintings, panic attacks and other medical emergencies are becoming increasingly common. As we passed through Hindley station though, my mood brightened. It's a charming little halt with gorgeous floral displays and hanging baskets, paintings and murals by local children: a windmill, a smiley scarecrow, a flowerpot man and model houses. It's also immaculately clean and welcoming. Googling on my phone as we idled there in the sun at this little Lancashire Adlestrop, I discovered that all this is the handiwork and efforts of the Friends of Hindley Station, a group of local volunteers who formed in 2007 and have rejuvenated and beautified the place. They've been garlanded with awards for this, and all absolutely deserved.

Then I looked around my carriage. It was squalid and dirty. Being early spring, it was unpleasantly hot, but I knew from experience that by September it would be colder and less hospitable than the tundra of Greenland. The seats were filthy and uncomfortable and arranged in rows in bench form like a knackered old-fashioned bus. That's because it literally is a knackered old-fashioned bus. Northern England's uniquely crap 'Pacer' trains were possibly named after the weird and unsuccessful rebranding of Opal Mints in the 1980s before that pungent chew's eventual mysterious disappearance. Sadly, at the moment, the trains seem to be showing no signs of going the same way. Intended as a stop-gap to make up for a shortage of rolling stock in the 80s, these clanking, wheezing, rattling Frankenstein monster relics are literally an old Leyland Motors bus frame stuck on train wheels. The rudimentary suspension has been making even the shortest journey bone-shakingly unpleasant for thirty years now. Passing through Hindley station on a Northern train offers a powerful if painful allegory for the whole sorry mess of rail privatisation and the selling off of Britain more generally. One is a shining, heartening example of what happens when people work together collectively for the common good, the other the dirty, crappy, unloved, cheapskate excuse for service that occurs when only profit matters.

On 1 January 1948, the Transport Act took nearly all mass-transit systems in Britain into public ownership. The overwhelming feeling of rail passengers, unless you were a major shareholder in one of the big four private train companies, was relief. Decades of tired jokes about British Rail sandwiches and points failures at Bristol Temple Meads may have obscured the fact that creepy old Jimmy S might have been right. The post-war, pre-80s period may

well have been the age of the train. Again, we've been drip-fed a
received wisdom that BR, the state rail company that ran our trains
from 1948 to 1997, was some dire, mismanaged, inefficient
monolith. This is simply not true, as someone who knows will soon
tell us. But the lie's been so often and so successfully repeated by
enemies of the public sector that it's taken as fact now. So please
challenge it whenever it gets trotted out. By the standards of
today's elite trains running on profitable lines, the trains of the 50s
may look grim and functional. But they were frequent, cheap and
went to the places ordinary people wanted them to go. Despite
chronic underfunding and government weakness, they did their
job. They didn't have reclining seats and Wi-Fi. But then Wi-Fi
hadn't been invented and to a generation that still had ration
books, reclining seats would have been rightly seen as a nation
going effetely to the dogs.

Waft away some of that romantic but misleading coal smoke
and steam from the pre-British Rail era and you will find that, *pace*
all that evocative stuff about *Bradshaw's* and *Brief Encounters*, the
private railways pre-1948 were a mess and a mess used only by a
few. Forget the gilded liveries, stovepipe hats and impressive
viaducts; when the Attlee government took the railways into public
ownership, for ordinary people who'd previously only used trains
to go on rare holidays, the real Golden Age of Rail began and
lasted for a couple of decades. The first signs it might be over came
in 1963 when the reviled Dr Beeching closed a third of our rail
routes on highly spurious and debatable grounds at the behest of a
Conservative Transport Minister in the pocket of the road-haulage
industry. Still, our railways were in a pretty good if butchered state
until the late 1990s when, under John Major, along came another
privatisation that no one other than vultures and ideologues
wanted, the destruction of British Rail and the coming of the age
of franchises and chaos.

'Oh, it was a purely ideological act by the Conservatives,'
Christian Wolmar, Britain's most eminent writer on transport, tells
me. 'They won the 1992 election by surprise really and so they

plunged into these new ideas like rail privatisation. Except they didn't really know what they wanted to do, and they certainly didn't know how to do it. They came up with a white paper very quickly with a massive contradiction at its heart: it's not real competition because there's only one track. Genuine competition is actually far, far too complicated for a railway network, as every other country in Europe knows.'

The government of the UK either didn't know this, or chose to ignore it for their own political ends. In Wolmar's words 'we came up with this totally flawed, uniquely half-baked model and we're still paying for that and living with the consequences. I'm a social democrat. I understand how our system works. Capitalism works by offering a rate of return on investment or risk. Take risks and if it comes off, you deserve a reward. I'm happy with that. But there's none of that happening on our railways. There's no risk at all. Get a railway franchise, screw it up, go bust … You just lose your franchise and get another.'

For a forensically detailed account of the dismal and depressing farrago that was the botched 90s sell-off of our railways, I can recommend (as well as Wolmar's writing) the chapter on trains in James Meek's *Private Island*. It tells a tale of rank arrogance hand-in-hand with quite startling incompetence; of how unqualified but pliant assassins like John Edmonds and the late Robert Horton of Railtrack hubristically dispensed with qualified expert engineers, switched to an untried signalling system the rest of Europe had rejected, and were motivated by self-interest and the profit of a few rather than any sense of national good. Former Network South East and Virgin Trains boss Chris Green ('a fantastically capable guy', according to Wolmar) has stated: 'What Railtrack did in 1996 was quite exceptional, which was to take a really high-calibre engineering team on the BR system and destroy it.' Meek's own summation is even more damning: 'a tale of incompetence, greed and delusion'.

In the case of the trains, the fat-cat controllers really took control. Moneymen from the world of corporate finance and the new boardrooms began to replace directors steeped in the oily, sooty culture of railways. Men who knew their way around a footplate or a signal box, men with engineering qualifications or years of technical experience, were replaced by layers of managers with MBAs and smart suits, whose primary focus of attention was not safety or efficiency or public comfort but the company's share price. James Hamilton-Paterson wrote of Network Rail's disastrous, expensive electrification of Great Western, rising in cost in just two years from £874 million to £2.8 billion and quoting the response of Tony Benn to one of the many failed attempts at solving the intractable chaos at British Leyland in the 1970s. 'You bring in managers from a business studies course who'd got a degree in business management but who couldn't mend a puncture in a motor tyre – and you speak about the people who made the cars as the problem?'

BR operated 6,600 stations on 15,000 miles of route. Today, National Rail manages just 2,200 over 10,000 miles. British Rail had straightforward and affordable ticketing. UK rail fares today are the highest in Europe and you pay through the nose to travel on the oldest rolling stock on the entire continent. It costs £480 to get a return at peak times from London to Manchester. You can get from Manchester to New York more cheaply and to Australia for less than double. There has been a 300 per cent growth in public subsidy since we flogged our railways to the highest bidder or to someone's dodgy mate. British Rail took half the subsidies that the private companies of today receive. They in turn give nearly all the operating profits as dividends to the shareholders of their parent companies. Over 90 per cent of new investment in the railways in recent years has been financed by the public sector in the form of taxpayer funding or government-underwritten borrowing. The top five franchises receiving public subsidy pocketed almost £3 billion in taxpayer support between 2007 and 2011. This helped them make profits of £504 million, over 90 per cent of which was paid to their shareholders. UK trains are slower, dirtier and more overcrowded than the publicly owned rail services in Germany, France, Italy and Spain.

But in a supreme irony, mark this. Arriva is part of Deutsche Bahn Group, the German state railway. Abellio (East Anglia, London) is owned by Nederlandse Spoorwegen, the Dutch National Railway. Arriva and Abellio's profits from their overpriced journeys on UK railways go to subsidise the excellent nationally owned railways of Holland and Germany. So our railways do help the national interest. Sadly, it's not ours though, but that of the citizens of Amsterdam and Potsdam, Leiden and Leipzig, Brabant and Berlin. Just the same as our buses.

Christian Wolmar is 'broadly in favour of re-nationalisation', but acknowledges it's not a panacea. 'We definitely need to get back to having one organisation, one body for strategy and planning. There is no Fat Controller right now. No one is in charge. The idea that re-nationalisation will cure everything, slash ticket prices and save money is fanciful, but it would mean a more efficient system and stop the culture of overpayment to bosses and shareholders and massive consultancy fees.'

Some go further. Who's this Trotskyist hothead for instance? 'I am struggling to see why the government does not ... admit what is obvious to the overwhelming majority of the population, that rail privatisation has been a disaster and announce that as rail franchises run out they will all be combined into one state-owned company. What are the Conservatives waiting for? Pragmatism would conclude that in the case of the railways privatisation has been a failure. Continuing to defend it is beginning to look like an ideology of its own.'

That was from a blog by Ross Clark in the *Spectator*, home to the most immoderately right-wing opinions in the British press. When even the *Spectator* starts to talk this way, you know that the current system is a mess.

The dismal story of our modern railways hurts because, as our Swiss friend reminded us over those in-carriage cognacs, we invented them. They are woven into our cultural weft and warp, even our hearts. On the maiden journey of the world's first ever passenger train link between Liverpool and Manchester, the unfortunate Huskisson ended up under the wheels of the train. But while he was bleeding to death on a kitchen table in Eccles having emergency surgery, that train rolled into Manchester accompanied by brass bands, bunting and general hoopla. Britain wasn't going to let a little thing like a top politician's grisly and tragic death spoilt our nascent love affair with this sexy new technology.

You can feel all that love at the National Railway Museum in York. Nearly a hundred years after that fateful, lethal, celebratory day in Lancashire, York played host to the centenary celebrations for the slightly earlier Stockton–Darlington industrial railway, which were such a hoot and a hit that it was decided to open a railway museum. Since then, the museum's grown to become a national bank-holiday fixture beloved of young nuclear families, exhausted grandparents lifting toddlers on and off footplates, backpacking Spanish teens, self-identifying geeks, notepad-clutching train spotters (metaphorical and actual) and school parties running quietly riot. When I visited, all the above were present and correct and all were wowed upon entering the great hall. There's such a catwalk array of railway-engine glamour and pulchritude on display here that even I, whose love affair with engineering peaked with my 17 out of 20 metalwork exam test score of Christmas 1975, found my chest thumping a little. Behold the giant beasts of all the ages of the train; steam, diesel and electricity. Behold great engines of lore and fable now at rest like thoroughbreds at stud. Take the GWR railcar model 4WW: sleek, elegant and curvy, a vision in chocolate-brown and yellow. It was nicknamed the Flying Banana but in reality it looks like a luscious, seductive art deco version of the classic banana toffee chew, less celebrated sibling of the Black Jack and Refresher. Then there's the LNER Class A4 4468, whose dry and technocratic name gives no hint of its ageless majesty.

For this is the *Mallard*, a train to make schoolboys gasp and grown men weep. Designed by Sir Nigel Gresley, a great Brit of the old school, upright, moustachioed and prone to whimsy. It's said that his love of feeding the ducks on his country estate inspired the design of his most famous creation. It's now to be found on a million pub table mats and lounge-bar walls, tea towels, fridge magnets and even the sleeve of Blur's take on contemporary Britain, *Modern Life Is Rubbish*. Its use as cover image there – knowing, celebratory but ironic – clearly posits the *Mallard* as a representative of a vanished, glorious and above all manly Britain; huge, virile, thrusting its way through the tunnels of the land to its orgasmic final shunt into King's Cross. It is also a private Britain. *Mallard*, the *Flying Scotsman*, *Puffing Billy*, the *Rocket*, all those glamorous icons of the Golden Age of British railways were also very much the property of LNER, GWR, LMS and SR. They were built for shareholders as much as passengers and were swept away by the vastly improved nationalised system of British Rail after 1948. But old romantic notions die hard, and love affairs are never logical, and the National Rail Museum does celebrate the real Golden Age of trains too, the well-run national network of the 1950s onwards. It's absolutely worth a trip, even if its just for the retro ad campaigns. Savile has gone of course, but you can have a more edifying time watching Abba in their yellow T-shirts and flared jeans urge you to keep your station tidy.

Once every city and town had them. Now in Britain, ten have them again now or will do so soon: Birmingham, Manchester, Sheffield, Newcastle, Nottingham, Blackpool, Croydon and London's Docklands, with south London and Edinburgh to follow. Leeds, Liverpool, Bristol and Portsmouth would too if the government hadn't abandoned the funding. What? Why? Perhaps there's a clue in the title of another book by Christian Wolmar: *Are Trams Socialist?*

In it, Wolmar restates a famous and revealing statement by the gruff chain-smoker and rail privatisation disciple Nicholas Ridley: ' The private motorist ... wants the chance to live a life that gives him [*sic*] a new dimension of freedom – freedom to go where he wants, when he wants, and for as long as he wants.' Here is the right's hardwired, soul-deep antipathy to public transport laid bare. Forget the environment, to hell with sustainability, who cares about traffic jams and polluted cities, about social equality and responsibility; no, say the Nicholases of this world, I want to drive my motor car where I like when I like and for as long as I like, and with whom I like, though preferably no one. At least not another difficult, complicated other human being, just me and a Ginster's pasty and the *Eagles Greatest Hits*, living the *Top Gear* 'petrolhead' dream.

If trams are socialist, it's surprising that red-blooded Glasgow isn't one of those ten places that have welcomed them back into their civic fabric. But it might explain why Glasgow, in the face of the invasion of our city streets by the internal combustion engine, did cling so ardently to its trams when others abandoned them. London killed off its tram system in 1952 but they were still a fixture of Glasgow's lively street life a decade later. Wandering around the Glasgow Transport Museum, now located on the banks of the shining Clyde – essentially a temple to the tram and the trolleybus – you can see why. Glasgow's trams were not just clean, efficient and affordable. They were also ravishing.

I wonder what the men who used to work the Clyde shipyards think of its Govan stretches now. Before the crash of 2008 curtailed such optimism, twenty kilometres of the riverside were revived and beautified in the first decade of the twenty-first century. As they did at Salford's dormant docks, the BBC came with their lattes and laminates, along with the SSE Hydro concert hall and the Glasgow Transport Museum. The latter was my destination on this fresh spring morning, sun burning in white wobbling sheets on the Clyde, the dark cranes a guard of honour but oddly out of place now, like shipyard workers at a hipster wedding, awkward in their ancient dark suits of riveted metal. The old distillery is now a craft micro-brewery and, naturally, there's an animation studios where the shipyard was. Where once the soundtrack of this waterside was the clang of riveting, now it's the tip-tap of MacBook Airs.

The previous night, after one of my favourite train journeys, up the green spine of England's finest hills and across the sensuous, gentle, empty border country, I'd checked into my hotel late and asked about room service. The pale, thin, beautiful lad and girl in their branded red Radisson hoodies and Converses looked at me as if I'd asked for an antimacassar or an elephant gun. 'We don't do room service,' they explained. 'Everyone uses Just Eat and Deliveroo ... on their phones, y'know ...' The information was relayed in the same hesitant tone of voice they might employ to explain Bitcoin to a hundred-year-old Bolivian villager. This morning, I left my room to head to the museum, having with some awkwardness hung a sign on the doorknob featuring a pouting young woman in John Lennon glasses bearing the legend: 'Shh! Don't tell my Mum but please tidy my room.' This without any apparent irony. In some people's grumpy early-morning eyes, it might as well have read: 'An Infantilised Snowflake Stayed Here Last Night. They Probably Left Their Charger.'

On the way along the Clyde I met the new Govanites and I liked them, actually. A boy with a skateboard and a Bluetooth headset chatting happily to himself (once the mark of the weird, now the signifier of the wired), a perspiring, pony-tailed girl in lime-green Lycra, a man with gigantic turn-ups and fulsome beard with a tiny parlour guitar. Modern. Modern girls, modern boys, as they said approvingly in *Gregory's Girl*, filmed just a bus ride away in Cumbernauld. In keeping with all this sexy newness is the Museum of Transport itself, posing madly on the banks of the old river. Designed by the late British-Iraqi architectural genius Zaha Hadid, its dramatic frontage seemingly modelled on the jagged life-systems monitor graph at the beginning of *Casualty* or the outline of a fabulous, imaginary mountain range. It's the first days of the Easter holidays and every student in Europe has apparently arrived by coach, each, I can only assume, carrying their boyfriends and girlfriends in those giant backpacks.

Whether trams are socialist or not is more than I can get my head around. But, before the coming of buses in many towns and cities, they definitely embodied an attitude to transport that was (and is) more communitarian than now, one that didn't assume the ideal way to get workers and shoppers and citizens around their community was singly in private cars. The return of the tram is one of the few incontrovertibly 'good news' stories in British transport in recent years. They're quick, they're clean, they move through traffic smoothly and quietly and directly through the hearts of our cities. They're fully accessible and environmentally sound (Melbourne hopes to run its trams entirely on solar power soon). Studies have actually shown that confirmed car drivers are more likely to switch to a tram than a bus. This intrigues me. Commenting on these findings on the Bath and Bristol tram website, David Holt thought that while it was down to comfort, ease of routes, cleanliness, safety, etc., 'I feel that something more intangible needs to be taken into account. It's related to the "image/identity" benefits of trams, evidenced by their frequent appearance in documentaries, travel shows, magazine articles, posters, etc. This I'm sure is reflected in people's travel preferences, in that they have pride in their tramway system and therefore feel attracted to it.'

In other words, they're just cooler and better-looking than most things you'll see on a British street today, even if it's an Alfa Romeo. The ones in the Glasgow Transport Museum certainly are. An expert would tell you about their gauges and liveries in detail but I can only tell you that the Cunarder tram is a real looker. Glasgow Corporation Tramways was the pride of our public transport system and the envy of Europe. At its peak, it ran a thousand handsome vehicles across a hundred miles of the city. Glasgow still had those trams when the Beatles cut their first record and when the Stones played the Marquee. You could have taken one of these sexy beasts into town to see the first James Bond movie or *Lawrence of Arabia*. Glasgow was the last city to give up its trams in September 1962, and a quarter of a million people took to the streets to see the last one leave the depot. This is a city that loved its trams, and would love them back.

*

Maryhill Normal School, Mosspark, Linthouse, Pollokshields; even the names of the stops have a foggy, sulphurous romance. These are the routes the ordinary men and women of Glasgow would have ridden every day to work and pub and shop, the Clyde riveters and the weavers of Bridgeton. Maybe they were off to see local hero Kenneth McKellar at the Alhambra in *Five Past Eight* (as advertised on the top deck of the Cunarder) or to drink in a pub like the Mitre, recreated here in all its dark and sooty glory. This was a typical Glasgow ale house of the tram heyday; a place where hard men drank 'eighty shilling' with grim dedication and purpose, where artisan cuisine was a Scotch pie retrieved from the dark beneath the counter and where women and children were never seen, except to drag a recalcitrant dad home through streets that were 'going round and round', as Will Fyffe's anthem to the town had it. If that seems a bit downbeat, I found it a brisk and unsentimental picture of Glasgow pub culture in the 1930s. The information boards bid you 'Welcome to the Mitre. No women or children allowed. No tables. No chairs. No lounging about. Want a soft drink. Don't even ask. And don't get too comfortable. Last orders is half past nine. But that should give you plenty of time to enjoy the atmosphere, have a drink among friends and still catch the last tram home.' Outside the 'pub', three olive-skinned Spanish student girls in designer leisurewear and shades are grouped for a picture, smiling dazzlingly, each giving that weird sideways peace sign that the continental kids do that makes me feel as ancient and uncomprehending as a nonagenarian High Court judge.

Outside the day is as dazzling as their smiles and I sit by the catering van watching the sun on the Clyde and eavesdropping the chit-chat of the van girls as my breakfast takes shape with much sizzling. 'I wanted to go and teach for a while in Turkey, as they pay you full whack on your probation year, but the problem is the dog. Turkish Airlines will let him fly but he's so big he'd have to go in the hold with the suitcases. And I can't leave him with Ally. Not after that terrible weekend on the houseboat.' I would love to know what dread events unfolded but by now my breakfast bap is ready and arrives hand delivered. 'Enjoy,' says the blonde girl in the apron with the inconvenient dog. I do. Oh, lorne sausage, great flat square chieftain of the piggy breakfast clan. Is there a man in Europe breakfasting more splendidly? I doubt it.

CHAPTER 9

I TURN ON, TUNE IN AND LOG ON

THE ANTI-SOCIAL MEDIA

I was a child of the state. But I was never much tied to the apron strings of the BBC. Like us all, I watched with mother. Except in my case, and maybe your case, watched with nana actually since my mum was out on the day shift at Eckersley's mill. At home on Poolstock Lane, I sat before my nana's unreliable little black-and-white telly and watched, with a Jammie Dodger or egg chopped up in a cup, the sundry delights of 60s and 70s children's TV as provided by 'the state'. Countless reductive nostalgia shows have not completely normalised their preternatural strangeness; the curious, cross species ménage à trois that was *Hector's House*, the old weird folk hauntology of *Pogles' Wood*, the Lewis chessmen come to storm-lit life in *Noggin the Nog*, the knowingly psychedelic *Banana Splits*, garish and disorienting, even though the only acid I knew about came in sour face-twisting drops from the sweetshop.

As we all did, I watched those big beasts of the corporation's children's output, *Blue Peter* and *Doctor Who*; the comforting and scary, the practical and the fantastic. The self-evident death-trap that was the *Blue Peter* advent crown, a mobile fashioned of twisted wire coat hangers on which lighted candles flickered precariously, looked far more terrifying to me than the Daleks. I watched those sinister, barking robots nonetheless and their villainous peers: the

Cybermen and the other baddies, the one with the lisp and the one who looked like the rollers from the car wash gone to seed (apologies, Whovians, for these terribly approximate descriptions). I watched them all, not behind the settee but on it with a packet of Opal Fruits in the smoky winter dusk.

I gorged on commercial TV too, though. It could be just as wholesome a diet. *Rainbow* and *How* were sensible and nutritious. It could even be a little organic, as in *Blue Peter*'s untucked, hempy, braless commercial counterpart *Magpie*. For escapism, ITV also boasted Gerry Anderson's eerie marionette ranks of spies, spacemen and supervillains. Chief among them were the supremely if pointlessly altruistic Tracy brothers in their variously useful colour-coded craft, forever rescuing some prototype advanced drilling engine from the earth's molten core, and the Hollywood submariners of *Stingray*; heart-throb pilot Troy Tempest, redneck comms operative Phones and undersea temptress the gorgeous but mute (some unreconstructed male wish-fulfilment there) Marina.

In 2012, just before the BBC's new northern base in Salford opened, the then Director of BBC North (a position now axed, dispiritingly) Peter Salmon asked me if I'd talk to some large groups of anxious staff about to make the move north to reassure them that they were not headed for the frozen tundra where the wild things are. My job was partly to explain and celebrate our queer northern ways but largely to reassure them that they would indeed be able to get Wi-Fi, pizza deliveries and the *Guardian* (no, really). Part of the concern emanating from the top brass was that research had shown that the north-west was more immune to the charms of the BBC than any other UK region. This worried London. But Peter (from Burnley) and I could have told them immediately why this was. In one word in fact. Granada.

When Essex entrepreneur Sidney Bernstein of Ilford set up one of ITV's first regional franchises in Manchester he did so because 'the North is a closely knit, indigenous, industrial society; a homogeneous cultural group with a good record for music, theatre, literature and newspapers, not found elsewhere in this island ... Compare this with London and its suburbs – full of displaced persons.' He loved the area because of what he saw as its vim and good humour. In turn, we loved his Granada because it was just like we were, or thought ourselves; cool, modern, gritty, funny, anti-establishment, gutsy and warm. We even called our home region 'Granadaland' without a hint of self-consciousness. While London and the South had all those stuffed-shirt Dimblebys and whatnot, we had Ray Gosling, John Pilger, Bob Smithies, 'Happening' Bob Greaves, tiny sports guru Elton Welsby, Shelley Rohde (who the young Johnny Marr lodged with) and Tony Wilson, the actual boss of Factory Records and the Haçienda, telling us about traffic bottlenecks in Chorley. The real reason that Lancashire, Merseyside, Cheshire and bits of Cumbria were not dutifully devoted to the BBC was because we had the greatest regional TV franchise in the world, just off Deansgate. Even as children, this became clear to us the first time we ventured to Somerset, Devon and Norfolk for holidays. It was a chastening, salutary experience for a child of Granadaland, like going from the colour and vibrancy of Las Vegas to the thin televisual gruel of Soviet-era Kyrgyzstan. We had *Coronation Street*, *World in Action*, *So It Goes*, *The Cuckoo Waltz*, *A Family at War*, *Brass*, *The Krypton Factor*, *University Challenge*, *Seven Up!*, *Brideshead Revisited* and more and more and more. They had Gus Honeybun and *Sale of the Century*. How long the nights must have seemed in Barnstaple.

Given these early allegiances, it's ironic that for most of the past three decades I've worked for the BBC. That is, as a lackey of the establishment and stooge of the rich and privileged, or alternatively as an unpatriotic propagandist for the loony-left communist gay-rights feminist 'PC gone mad' brigade. People do seem to find it hard to come to an agreement on this. In the early 1990s, in a turn of events that would have surprised most of my teachers, I began to work for the most famous and revered (see also controversial and beleaguered) broadcasting institution on earth. The day I first strolled – actually, I didn't stroll, I trod softly awed and massively proud – into Broadcasting House in Langham Place, London, is still lit up in my memory. Through the revolving doors I'd seen on a thousand news broadcasts, under the sculptures by infamous perv Eric Gill, beneath the stirring slogan 'And Nation Shall Speak Peace unto Nation'. For most of my broadcasting career, it has been more like 'And Idiot Shall Talk Rubbish to Other Idiots' but the truth remains valid. I felt proud that day and most of the time still do. This is what I strive to recall when I am holding my head in my hands at the latest piece of strategic management folly or some lousily written news report or appalling daytime show about buying crap at a car boot sale or shopping your benefit-cheat neighbours. I am proud because of *Blue Peter*, *Sherlock* and *Doctor Who*, *Monty Python*, *Fleabag*, Mr Tumble, *Whatever Happened to the Likely Lads?*, *I'm Sorry I Haven't a Clue*, David Attenborough, the Proms, Barry Davies (not John Motson), Radio 3 and so on and so on. I'm proud to be associated with an organisation that marries the public sector with a national collective spirit. A massive 96 per cent of the UK population consume BBC products each week. Its services are actively chosen 140 million times a day, despite a hugely competitive, now unparalleled media choice. It has the highest audience share of any provider in UK television and radio markets with 33 per cent of the television audience and 53 per cent of the radio audience. Put simply, the BBC is the most used public service in Britain.

I have recorded BBC programmes the length and breadth of the UK. I've sat in studios in Lerwick, Shetland, and St Peter Port, Guernsey, watching respectively the Atlantic and the Channel break on the shores that bookend and span the land, all the while sipping dire BBC tea and waiting for the red light that tells me I'm on air. BBC Shetland was a tiny upstairs room off a narrow back alley above the tough, grey port of the Shetland capital. BBC Guernsey's home is an airy and spacious former TV showroom off a handsome bay clinking with sails. In Shetland the producer, a lovely local woman, gave me a steer to a secret beach where I was the only person walking the crystalline white sand as the sun set over turquoise waters. In Guernsey, I was told to take a boat out to the tiny island of Herm and walk its rugged coastal path. These places felt about as far from the jangling, busy, urban media world of idents and jingles and rolling news as it was possible to be. But in both places I was a BBC man, aware of how important the organisation is to the local communities. The presenter from BBC Guernsey, a local woman who had come back after years in London's club culture and media, told me proudly that they had the greatest 'reach' of any BBC station. I realised this later in the day when nearly everyone I met on the island told me they'd heard my interview. This is the soft and quiet power of the BBC. It unites people in a way no politician or newspaper mogul ever could, which is perhaps why so many politicians and newspaper moguls detest it.

How it wields that power though, and whether it should wield it at all, is exercising plenty of minds inside, outside and at the very top of the corporation right now. They say there is always a folk revival going on; it's tempting to say that there is always an existential crisis at the BBC. But this time they/we are not crying wolf. The new broadcast universe is a land where hostile giants and predators roam hungrily, armour-plated like stegosauri by vast budgets, freed from any public service remit, answerable to no one but subscribers and shareholders.

BBC director-general Tony Hall, in a speech to the Royal Television Society, said that he considered the opening of Media-City 'a game changer'. I think he was right, in ways both foreseen and unpredicted. Subtly, incrementally, the BBC's centre of gravity has shifted just that little bit further away from London. Not far enough, but significantly. The move has been noticed too by people with no great affection for the corporation. That space between my studio and the grey, chilly and these days crowded waters of the Manchester Ship Canal (pleasure craft, canoes, even the occasionally hardy swimmer) is now regularly colonised by every tedious, single-issue fruit-loop on God's green earth. They come in droves, with loudhailers and banners, irate and vocal, to complain about the corporation's rampant Zionism or its blatant anti-Semitism, its shockingly biased news reporting which is somehow both scandalously left- and right-wing simultaneously, either its inactivity on climate change or its hippie environmentalism, its treasonous anti-Britishness or its jingoism, its homophobia or its slavish pandering to the gay rights' lobby. Possibly all the above at once. In the last month, as I've been writing this chapter, I've had to run the gauntlet at MediaCity of Tommy Robinson's far-right bullies and a group of 'veterans' campaigning against the prosecution of the soldier accused of murdering innocent Irish civilians on Bloody Sunday. The former were encouraged by one of their braying leaders 'not to attack any BBC journalists . . . just for today', while one of the latter told me, 'We know who you are,' after I'd expressed my lack of sympathy for their cause. On another occasion, a screaming man with a frankly unnecessary loudhailer berated me for the BBC's beastliness to Jeremy Corbyn and, by extension, the oppressed peoples of the world. Depending on my mood on the day, I sometimes think that making enemies of these people, less different from each other than they would like to think, shows that 'we' are doing the right thing and are on the side of the angels. Other times I just want to go to their place of work with a badly drawn placard and shout garbage through their windows all day, harassing them and their colleagues. The reason they come to Socialist Worker and English Defence Leaguer, left, right or green, is because they think that the BBC is in some way an organ of government, a televisual *Pravda*. They're wrong.

Contrary to what opponents and even well-intentioned but misinformed friends seem to think, the BBC is not a state broadcaster. Neither is it funded by the taxpayer, nor is the licence fee compulsory. Yes, it is payable by everyone, every household, company or organisation using any type of equipment to receive or record live TV or iPlayer catch-up and, yes, that fee is set by the government and agreed via Parliament. But beyond that, the government has no editorial control over the content of BBC programmes. This has proved much to the annoyance of various administrations and politicians down the ages. Churchill thought the BBC too scrupulously fair during the Second World War when it should have been more nakedly propagandist. Alastair Campbell loathed it for trying to tell the truth about the 'sexed-up' dossier that took us to war in Iraq. David Cameron found the thought of cuts to its budget 'delicious'. Chris Grayling, never far from our thoughts in this book, thought that the BBC should always take the side of the UK in international conflicts. 'During the Second World War, the BBC was a beacon of fact, it was not expected to be impartial between Britain and Germany,' he told Parliament, completely wrongly, as we've come to expect from Chris.

The hard right has always loathed the BBC in much the same way that it loathes at some primal and pre-intellectual level the NHS, state schools and public transport. Something of its essential fairness and commonality rankles with them. But latterly even reasonable people are getting in on the popular act of BBC bashing, largely over Brexit. It's hard to argue with those who find Nigel Farage's ubiquity on the BBC irritating. James O'Brien of the LBC network tweeted, 'Imagine if [former Green Party leader] Caroline Lucas had been given the same red carpet treatment by the British media in the last 10 years as Nigel Farage. What a different place the country would be'. He has a point. The BBC did not cover itself in glory with its Brexit coverage, which even some within the organisation suspect has been flawed and mishandled. Outsiders like respected former *Guardian* editor Alan Rusbridger feel that we heard too much from Farage and the right and 'less from what we might term the rational centre or from the Michael Gove-despised "experts". Entire programmes are so obsessed with the splits within one tribe that other voices – including our bewildered European friends – are pushed to the margins or remain unheard.' On the other hand, the *Daily Express* blazed in May 2019 with 'European elections: BBC labelled "DISGRACEFUL" for election coverage – "Clear pro-EU BIAS"'. (This tide of outrage and national shame turned out to be two carping tweets from UKIP members.)

Senior figures in the industry have all opined in public or private that the BBC has handled Brexit badly and the reputation of the corporation has suffered accordingly. Of course, this is to conflate the entire BBC with its news output. To those of us in the business of making art, culture, sport, drama, comedy shows and the enormous amount of other 'content' the BBC generate, this is annoying to say the least. They also serve who only play Van der Graaf Generator and dub reggae records or animate *Peppa Pig*.

The old certainties have started to wobble and buckle in the weird heat of a new media world but the BBC still far outranks its competitors in terms of trustworthiness, as expressed in most polls. It may still be that in their hearts, when they really need accurate and unbiased reporting, the British people will still turn to the BBC, much like the rest of the world who've often listened to it under gunfire and bombs and in floods and earthquakes as the only source they can trust. But these are strange times, and we have become strange ourselves. Confronted with the icy cold shower of truth, there are many these days who prefer the warm and comforting bath of propaganda and a shallow comforting wash of opinion and half-truth that backs up their own world view. We now live firmly in the era of post-truth, a world beyond facts, where there is no objective reality, just competing biases and entrenched positions.

Truth is the first casualty of war, they say. It's certainly been led from the modern media battlefield bloodied, tattered and in need of some Florence Nightingale of the digital age. Here's a snapshot from the week that I write, but almost any week would suffice. The aforementioned Farage appeared on *The Andrew Marr Show* spluttering with indignation over being asked some mildly challenging questions regarding his past statements about the NHS, immigration and the European Union (spoiler alert: he isn't terribly keen on any of them really). Again and again, he fulminated that 'this is what we've come to expect of the BBC,' trotting out the routine denunciations about 'metropolitan elitist leftie enemies of the people' and such. But also, this very morning arch Remainer and Labour peer Andrew Adonis, in the latest in a line of increasingly unhinged tweets about the corporation, suggests that BBC journalists should be 'put in the dock' for reporting what Boris Johnson had to say during the referendum campaign. That Johnson is a duplicitous scoundrel is beyond doubt. But at that time (worse was to come of course) he was also Foreign Secretary. To not report his words, however slippery, would have been a dereliction of the BBC's role. On the other hand, to call for journalists to be silenced and imprisoned is surely how fascists talk. Why do men like Adonis and Farage hate the BBC so much? To put it simply, because it refuses to do their bidding as a matter of course or unquestioningly cleave to their opinion. Beneath their cosmetic differences, the privately educated banker and the ex-Labour peer are brothers beneath the skin in their shared entitlement and self-regard.

I've worked in the organisation for thirty years, admittedly not in the rarefied sanctums of high priestly power, the boardrooms of Broadcasting House and such, but pretty close to them, and have been deeply immersed in the day-to-day world of programme making. I have spent long, unguarded, candid days and nights with many near those fabled centres of power. I genuinely do not think that the BBC is biased to the left or the right, certainly not in any institutional way. I work and have worked with people, producers, presenters, managers who in their private and domestic life are both staunchly socialist and true-blue Tory, impeccably Green and blithely unconcerned political agnostics. Sometimes these sympathies are a matter of record. We know that Nick Robinson and Andrew Neil were both Conservatives in their politics while students, for instance, and Paul Mason, formerly of *Newsnight*, now makes no secret of his left-wing views (although this was the cause of some discomfort when he actually worked for the BBC, eventually leading him to quit mainstream news broadcasting altogether as he felt too constrained by its 'impartiality'). But it's not always so clear or so public. I have worked alongside 'posh' Radio 3 ladies as vitriolic in their diatribes against 'the boss class' as any Trot on a 70s picket line, and I've broadcast with 'men of the people' who loathe Labour viscerally and send their kids to private school. These are private matters and as long as it doesn't creep into their work, crucially so if they are news journalists or presenters, I can't see it matters. To reiterate, I don't think there is any explicit, intrinsic political bias to the left or right as such within the BBC.

What there might be though is a tacit identification and allegiance with the establishment. Tom Mills in his book *The BBC: Myth of a Public Service* argues that the BBC can never be truly independent from governments, let alone from the broader establishment, because, as he told Ian Sinclair on the openDemocracy website:

> The BBC has always been formally accountable to ministers for its operations. Governments set the terms under which it operates, they appoint its most senior figures, who in future will be directly involved in day-to-day managerial decision making, and they set the level of the licence fee, which is the BBC's major source of income. So that's the context within which the BBC operates, and it hardly amounts to independence in any substantive sense ... Does this mean it's independent? Well really the BBC's not so different to various state institutions that are afforded operational autonomy but ultimately answerable to ministers or to parliament through various mechanisms, such as the police or the Bank of England.

For Mills, a crucial and significant change occurred in 1987, the year when director-general Alasdair Milne (father of *Guardian* journalist, later Corbyn advisor, Seumas Milne) was forced to resign by the Thatcher-appointed chair of governors, celebrated uniped Marmaduke Hussey.

Milne wasn't a leftist by any means, but he had represented the more independent spirit of BBC programme making at that time. He was replaced by a BBC accountant called Michael

Checkland and John Birt was meanwhile brought in from an ITV company to head the BBC's journalism, later succeeding Checkland as director-general ... Birt wasn't really understood by his critics at the time, who seem to have been rather puzzled by his authoritarianism and his belligerent managerialism. They seem to have regarded him as a Stalinist, or something like that. But in fact, he was an out-and-out neoliberal who wanted not only to introduce stronger editorial controls over BBC journalism, but also to radically shift its institutional structure and culture away from its 'statist' character and in a more neoliberal, business-friendly direction.

Birt, as I fancy he himself may well agree approvingly, was probably the most divisive and controversial DG the BBC has ever had. I think that many of the current travails of an organisation I love, the poor morale among presenters and programme makers, the bloated, protected managerial structure, the worship of marketing, consultants and technocrats, began with a man who started off by appeasing Thatcher and wound up advising Tony Blair.

In much the same way that The Smiths, the Velvet Underground, *Viz* magazine and the *I Love the 70s* TV show can't be blamed for the dreck that followed imitatively in their wake, John Birt cannot and should not be held responsible for all the problems and occasional idiocies of the modern BBC. Let us give praise where praise is due. He foresaw the coming of the digital broadcasting universe and prepared the BBC accordingly. He fought off, or at least placated, a determinedly hostile Tory government. But he also introduced and encouraged some of the least attractive, most sclerotic elements of the modern BBC. It was Birt who swamped the corporation with costly consultants and vacuous brand advisors. It was Birt who foisted the ethos of the markets into a public service with the same baleful results found in transport and health. He introduced the murky concept of 'Producer Choice' whereby producers had to 'budget their shows' and under which it turned out cheaper to go to HMV and buy a

CD rather than take it out of the BBC Library. Like most such 'competitive' reforms (see water, railways, etc.), nothing about it ever amounted to genuine competition anyway. I tried (in order to make a point) to set up my own budget rival to the BBC Pronunciation Unit which would undercut the real one. I thought I'd do this by charging 50p a go, for which I'd just make educated guesses at foreign names. I was told I couldn't.

Charlotte Higgins claimed in a *Guardian* piece that Birt and its first director-general Sir John Reith were the two DGs who'd had most impact on the BBC, and teased out other similarities:

> Both trained as engineers. Both have lent words to the English language, neither – like their inheritances – unambiguous: 'Reithian' conveys all that is lofty in broadcasting, but comes with an atmosphere of puritanism and paternalism, of Auntie-Beeb-knows-best; 'Birtism', notwithstanding its rehabilitation as an idea, with its overtones of control and strategic farsightedness, suggests almost totalitarian levels of managerialism. Cognates include Birtspeak (convoluted workplace jargon, often expressed by 'croak-voiced Daleks', as the writer Dennis Potter memorably described Birt and Hussey), and Birtistas, the cadre of loyal shock-troops.

A word on management then. Jonathan Swift once declared, 'Principally I hate and detest that animal called man, although I heartily love John, Peter, Thomas, and so forth.' Swift has neatly summed up my feelings about the managerial structure of the BBC. I have good and close friends in management. As individuals, they are people I'm delighted to have as mates; they are gifted, funny, smart. But there is something collective in the bloodstream and the corpus, in the body politic, the wider ethos, that mildly depresses us small fry. Routinely, indeed it seems sometimes deliberately, people are appointed to senior positions who have never made a programme or even seen the inside of a studio.

Recently I was told of a high-ranking executive at CBBC and CBeebies, the brilliant BBC children's TV platforms, home to wonderful animated series like *Bing*, *Peppa Pig*, *Hey Duggee* and the rest, who 'didn't really like animation'. I know, or I'm sure, or at least I trust that all these well-rewarded, high-status individuals are talented and industrious and trustworthy. I know that management skills are transferrable. But it sends an odd message to those of us who make programmes about how we are regarded, valued even, in the grand scheme of things. It suggests that all the top positions within the corporation are there to foster, nurture and facilitate the careers of managers – often subsequently outside the BBC – rather than the Beeb and its creative ethos.

Hopefully neither a grumbling and bitter BBC 'lifer' or an unctuous bosses' nark, I thought it was important that I heard the views of that very same management in all this. So I decided to get in touch with two individuals who I didn't know well personally but I knew were seriously and actively engaged with these new challenges facing the BBC every day. I sent emails to both Alan Davey, former head of the Arts Council, now controller of Radio 3, and James Purnell, the former Labour cabinet minister who took up his role as head of BBC Radio in 2015. Both were back in touch almost instantly, both made time to see me within weeks. Both too, I soon realised, had a genuine empathy with the corporation and a belief in the centrality of the BBC to British society.

'I don't think we had a shared national culture really until the invention of the wireless,' says James Purnell when we meet in the BBC's MediaCity centre in Salford. 'Not until we could all hear the King or Churchill's speeches or dance band music. Clearly we had an English or British culture of a sort before then. But it was local and regional. I don't think it was a properly shared or democratic culture until the BBC begins to broadcast to the nation. The wireless meant we could all hear it and share in it and now the internet means we can all create it. So we at the BBC are having to learn again.'

I met with James Purnell in Dragon's Den. Or maybe it was Sports Personality of the Year. In the kind of modish move brilliantly lampooned in the TV series *W1A*, the meeting rooms at the BBC's new northern base at MediaCity have been named not 1 or 4 or 36B or even something direly 'now' like Breakout or Headspace, but after the names of famous and much loved BBC radio and TV shows. This can be a) confusing, if for instance you can't remember whether you've got a meeting about *Songs of Praise* in *Masterchef* or vice versa and b) faintly queasy, as in, 'I'll be in The Two Ronnies from about half two.' The rank and file at the BBC laugh at John Morton's aforementioned painfully accurate and hilarious *W1A*, a joyous satire on the modern BBC, in much the same way as citizens of the former Soviet Union must have laughed at Solzhenitsyn, that is to say through their fingers with a kind of black mirth. James Purnell laughs too.

'No one else would make *W1A*. That programme came right in the middle of the charter review process and no one questioned doing it. In fact there was no possible meeting or process that could have stopped it. That amazes some broadcasting organisations. But that's how we operate. *Newsnight* ran a story, again right at the heart of charter review, about the then Culture Secretary John Whittingdale's personal life. Some would have thought that very risky, given the power of his position over the BBC. But not only did no one question it or try to stop it, there was no process by which it could have been stopped. It went all through the news editorial line and we in senior management were informed just before broadcast. Some of our media partners find that very hard to understand. How can we be working with someone, an individual or an organisation, and then run a *Panorama* that's openly critical of them? But it's vital that we here can keep the two parts of our brain separate. I think politicians could learn from that.'

James Purnell studied PPE at Oxford and was a researcher for Tony Blair before becoming the Labour MP for Stalybridge and Hyde. Later he entered the cabinet first as Culture Secretary before resigning after differences with Gordon Brown's administration. He has been head of BBC Radio since 2015. Even if you didn't know any of the above, it would be obvious within a few minutes of meeting him that James is supremely bright, gallingly youthful for his achievements, and very approachable and friendly with a steely pragmatism glinting beneath.

How much is he, in his current role, still a politician? He denies it quickly and firmly. 'Not at all. The BBC is fiercely proud of its independence from government with a big G. So we are not part of the state. But we are part of the public sector and part of the job of running the BBC is concerned with public accountability. But in terms of that public sector, if government departments are at one end and then NHS England, say, then the BBC is at the other end. It is the most independent of the public services. So we're not of government but we're definitely of the public sector. Whether we're part of the state is something you could have a long discussion about. I think our relationship with government has gone up and down across the years and I think at the moment it's fair to say that we have supporters and sceptics across the parties.'

That scepticism, once largely the preserve and default setting of a particular mindset on the Conservative right, seems sadly to be spreading. Politicians from Norman Tebbit to Alastair Campbell have taken the BBC to task for telling the truth and for standing up to them. But a more modern, more serious problem is that while the corporation still rates far higher in terms of trustworthiness than any other news source, the numbers who think it biased are rising and the overall impartiality score is falling. We used to regard it as right and natural, proper even, for politicians to be given a grilling, even a carpeting by news journalists. Now the echo chambers of internet news and social media platforms have softened and warped us to the degree that we see smears and skulduggery where we used to see tough questioning and proper journalism. The left has been particularly guilty here. Laura Kuenssberg, the BBC's political editor, has been forced to take bodyguards to the Labour party conference for fear of reprisals over her perceived bias towards the Conservatives, and to watch former Labour leader Jeremy Corbyn during various campaigns being guarded like a piece of fine porcelain by his flapping minders, scuttled away from perfectly reasonable and robust questions, has been plain embarrassing.

There's a long-standing and often iterated argument used by defenders of BBC which runs along the lines that if both the left and right knock it, it must be getting things about right. I've done it myself. But Purnell is having none of it. 'I don't agree with that, actually. Because, and it's a subtle thing, I think it can become a refuge for complacency when really we should listen to people's complaints whatever they are and wherever they come from. At our best, we should be confident enough to acknowledge criticism, take on fair points and endeavour to try and do things differently.'

Roger Mosey is a former boss of mine at Radio 5 Live, now Master of Selwyn College, Cambridge. Like many ex-BBC mandarins, he weighs in regularly in the public debate over the BBC's future. Recently he claimed that the BBC's commitment to impartiality was leading it into the trap of false balance, of giving too much credence to all positions however dubious. He suggested that a better model might be 'due impartiality', which weighs the cogency of different arguments accordingly rather than simple gainsaying. He also wondered whether the BBC might be better off adopting the seemingly highly successful model used by LBC radio. Here, there's no attempt to be balanced within one programme but rather across the network. In practice at LBC this seems to mean one left-leaning presenter (James O'Brien) to counter a whole bunch of right-wingers such as Farage, Iain Dale, Julia Hartley-Brewer and Nick Ferrari. At time of writing it's certainly working for them.' At this point I did not know, though James may well have done, that long-serving Radio 4 news presenter Eddie Mair was off to join them.

'So the guidelines do allow for all that. We talk about due impartiality as well. An example would be climate change. We are not impartial as to whether it's happening. We recognise that the scientific consensus is that climate change is happening and is man-made. People who disagree with that are given the appropriate exposure. We reflect those views but we do not give them equal coverage. The BBC does not have a position but we acknowledge that the scientific position is that climate change is happening. Also, we do allow programmes that are opinionated. But that would be an *Analysis* on Radio 4 perhaps, rather than the news bulletin at ten. We have to guarantee fair treatment, the right to reply ... . That LBC model is working very well for them but we will always have to have balance within programmes.'

In the wake of the Russell Brand and Jonathan Ross scandal, when the nasty, unfunny phone-badgering of actor Andrew Sachs by two middle-aged 'lads' was wrongly broadcast, several high-ranking managers lost their jobs by 'falling on their sword'. Subsequently, what felt very much like panicky changes were introduced. Nowadays, several highly paid individuals have to sit and listen to every pre-recorded programme that goes out for fear of offending some unspecified sensibilities somewhere rather than simply trust professional and dedicated producers and presenters to do their job diligently. It is hard to conceive of a bigger waste of time and money, frankly. It also speaks, I think, to a certain fearfulness 'we' seem to have acquired. Recently I was advised (by my very brilliant and lovely producer) not to play Harpers Bizarre's recording of a gorgeous tune called 'Witchi Tai To' on the grounds that it could be seen as cultural appropriation; a Native American Indian tune played by white Western musicians. I felt I had to point out that it was written by a Native American Indian (whose livelihood we were thus damaging), that it smacked of virtue-signalling as Native American Indians are really not present in significant numbers in modern Britain, and that furthermore, from Elvis to the Beatles to Dusty to Clapton to The Clash to Eminem, the entire history of popular music is one enormous happy exercise in cultural appropriation. As Hans Keller wrote in the *Spectator*, 'at this stage in the history of broadcasting, the BBC's radio philosophy is determined by fear'. He said that in 1979, though. *Plus ça change*. But this is another common complaint about the BBC from within and without. Do nothing for years, then institute overnight revolution. Witness the haste and zeal with which right now the BBC is desperately courting the young, the licence-fee payers of tomorrow.

'Yes, the youth audience is currently occupying our thinking,' says James with the air of a man who is having these conversations daily if not hourly. 'Young people have a lot of affection for the BBC. We see this when we do surveys and consultations and meetings. But the difference is that whereas their grandparents would have put the BBC first as their "go to" source, they will put it third or fourth. Ninety per cent of young people use us every week, but some of them are not getting enough from us. The market has moved from one in which the BBC was the biggest to one in which Amazon, Netflix and Spotify have provided a much bigger ocean of content. So we have to have more special and unique stuff. Like some of our best dramas, and, I have to say, 6 Music. Plenty of people say to me that it's worth the licence fee alone.'

It's crucial and proper that the BBC is addressing these issues. But as the limping foot soldier with the pair of battered head-phones and a cup of 'uniquench' (BBC technicians' nickname for the unidentifiable hybrid warm brown liquid available in old-school studios), I have plenty of whinges/legitimate areas of concern. I understand the need to bring on new younger audiences but the current obsession with them ('replenishers' in the consultancy jargon) reminds me weirdly of the poster some student girlfriends would have on their bedroom wall, the one with the young deer captioned: 'If you love something, set it free. If it comes back, it's yours. If not, it was never meant to be.' Maybe we have to accept that some younger listeners will be lured away for a while by YouTube, Instagram and Netflix. Rather than stand Canute-like against that tide, better to simply make good programmes and hope that they will return. At the moment, it can sometimes feel that the BBC is in danger of losing the audience it has already by chasing the one it might never get.

It can lead to some painful scenarios. In late September 2019, I flicked from Sky News – where a young former Labour advisor was disagreeing cordially but analytically with a *Times* columnist about Labour's Brexit strategy – to the BBC News Channel. Here a Grime artist in a balaclava with glasses Elton John would have deemed 'showy' was delivering a rambling diatribe about climate change. After this, in an item entitled 'Flashback Friday', a flustered Buzzfeed columnist was being asked to summarise the week's politics in one minute. 'It's a tough thing to be asked to do,' said presenter Joanna Gosling, which invited the question 'Then why ask them to do it?' All over the country these past few years, I've been to festivals and events where smart, informed, impassioned young people are making their case and engaging with politics. Some within the BBC clearly think young people are more Vicky Pollard than Greta Thunberg and live in terror of being thought 'bo-ring'. As I write, Radio 4's attempts to make itself more youth-friendly are highly contentious within that network. Producers joke that it can only be a matter of time before Stormzy is presenting *Gardener's Question Time*. There's another rub too, another danger in courting youth. Nothing is as lame and painful as the failed attempt to be 'with it'. By the time you read this, Stormzy may be about as current as Roy Plomley and Wilfred Pickles. Maybe it's better to accept that you cannot be something for everyone and that Seinfeld was right when he said, 'There is no such thing as fun for all the family.'

The reason it has to try, though, is simple. It's called the licence fee.

Some years ago, I took a London black cab and asked for Broadcasting House. On hearing my destination, once installed, I was treated to a lengthy and colourful lecture-cum-diatribe on the poor quality of BBC programmes, the grotesque overpayment of some its 'stars', and the fact that it should be compelled to advertise just like everybody else. It's hard to imagine any other trade being this combative with a paying customer, but let that pass. I told him that I had some sympathy with parts of his argument, especially the latter. But just one thing, I concluded, *Columbo* style. If you do make the BBC advertise, you do know you'll put all the other broadcasters out of business overnight. Where do you think the really big-name high-end companies are going to advertise, Apple and BMW and top-of-the-range single malts? *Loose Women? Catchphrase? Take Me Out?* No, it'll be in *Strictly* and *Match of the Day, The Andrew Marr Show* and the Proms. I told him that Margaret Thatcher, who I guessed the cabbie would have some affection for, wanted to make the BBC carry ads very early in her tenure but was warned by wiser heads that this would make her friends in commercial television very unhappy and possibly out of a job. So yes, I'd be quite happy for the BBC to advertise, actually. Anywhere here will do, mate, actually.

In reality, I don't welcome advertising on the BBC. But as a pugnacious thought experiment, I like to trot out the above when some ardent free-marketeer brings it up. Of course, they don't actually care about the principle. They just want to have a pop at the Beeb, the thought of which they find 'delicious', as Cameron did. I'm not an indentured employee of the BBC and I really hope I'm not one of those BBC presenters who seem to think that they are owed a job and a platform for life. I'm a hired gun. I've lost more gigs and shows than I care to mention. Such is the freelance life. But, as one of its many freelance employees, who goes through almost daily vexation and incomprehension at the workings of the BBC, I'm always surprised at my reaction to attacks on it, which is often to jump up, fists clenched and coat off, like the punchy mate in a pub fight. It seems that the BBC, like the Catholic Church and Wigan Athletic, is one of those institutions that I am yoked to emotionally for life whatever their behaviour. There is much about life at the BBC that puts my head in contact with my desk on a daily basis. Some of it trivial, such as the obligatory sports trails comprising poetic doggerel voiced by a bluff northerner, or the mysterious Svengali-like hold Nick Knowles has over commission-ing editors. But some of it is serious, like diversity along class lines, which we'll return to, and just how the corporation should be funded. James Purnell is still firmly supportive of the licence-fee model, as he explains.

'There's a few thoughts I'd inject here. People often say that the licence fee is an anachronism and that you wouldn't invent it now, but I actually think the fee is one of the reasons the BBC works and works so well. It gives us that independence. We are funded directly through the licence fee and not the state, which is massively important. People think it's the same but it's not. Here those decisions are not made as trade-offs with other government departments. They are made directly with the fee payer. Secondly, we all feel a moral responsibility to serve because of it. Thirdly, because we all pay, it's far cheaper than a subscription service. So it supports that Reithian notion that it gives the best to everyone.'

David Elstein thinks differently and has done for some time. A graduate of the BBC's training scheme who went on to work on *Panorama* and *The Money Programme*, on moving to commercial TV he was involved in *The World at War*, *Weekend World* and *This Week*. He launched Channel 5 and is now a respected media academic. His 2004 report on the matter was admittedly commissioned by the Conservatives, tribally inimical to the national broadcaster, but even so, his later words in the letters pages of the *London Review of Books* seem to me to have a faintly uncomfortable ring of sense:

> Direct funding by its customers would allow the BBC to set its own level of charges and to escape the political control that was unavoidable under the licence fee ... the stunning success of Netflix and Amazon in recruiting more than ten million households in the UK in barely five years has further exposed the anachronistic nature of the licence fee. Because subscription funding is not dependent on either audience size or reach, but instead on take-up by people who want premium content, the services using it – such as HBO, Showtime, AMC and now Netflix and Amazon – can focus their spending

on quality productions, rather than the run-of-the-mill schedule-fillers that take up so much of BBC budgets. Yet it is those schedule-fillers that deliver the reach and volume which ... are the criteria for judging the success of the licence fee. As long as politicians of all parties (who love the control the system gives them) and the BBC itself remain committed to the licence fee, the corporation faces decline and increasing irrelevance.

Though the idealistic young Wiganer who walked into Broadcasting House thirty years ago would be horrified, I'm increasingly moving towards the above camp. Partly out of realism about the modern digital multiverse, partly to be a disruptor, and definitely to stop the BBC having to apologise to Thatcherite cabbies, appease politicians and fight with one arm tied behind its back, I see the attractions of a subscription model more sharply every day. It's taken as an article of faith within the BBC that it's only 'because of the unique way the BBC is funded' that we can do the things we do. I've never heard the merit of the licence fee questioned in studio or office, meeting or get-together, although it must surely exercise minds at the top. It's become a catechistically immutable part of 'our' faith, like the Virgin Birth or Ramadan. But lately I have become, if not an atheist, then certainly an agnostic. Current DG Tony Hall has said, with a hint of weariness I thought, 'because we're funded by everyone, we feel a moral duty to serve everyone'. But duty is not always the best motivator. Enemies of the BBC talk routinely of the licence fee as a feather bed. I think it might have become a straitjacket.

'There is no such thing as fun for all the family.' It's pertinent here. The new subscription channels are liberated from that unbearable burden of being 'something for everyone', which often results in the BBC making cheap flotsam that a privately educated commissioning editor in St John's Wood thinks a family from Hull wants. Sky subscribers pay far more than the licence fee, providing an income stream more than twice as big as the BBC. Buoyed by money and freed from the need to make formulaic filler, Sky and Netflix and Amazon Prime can get on with being part of the new Golden Age of TV. I'd argue that the BBC still does arts and culture, especially on radio, brilliantly but it's hard to imagine that the nation would be much the poorer without yet another programme where a surly bald troll tracks down some hapless fly-tippers or a plummy prannock in a bowtie prices up the pleb's knick-knacks. Also, I can't help but indulge a delicious personal fantasy that if the licence fee went, then so would much of the ponderous handwringing and the layers of bureaucracy devoted to strategy, community engagement, identity, being public-facing and the rest. Nakedly and explicitly in the business of quality rather than social policy, we could spend the money on making the best, or at least the most different and creative, TV, radio and web content.

For now though, the licence fee is here. So it's worth remind-ing people what great value it is. There's a story within the BBC of a filmed piece of internal market research which involved taking all BBC programmes away from several families of licence-fee refuseniks and BBC sceptics for two weeks. Well before the end of this period, they were desperate to be reconnected. Where had they all gone? *Match of the Day*, Mary Berry and *Strictly Come Dancing*? All those shows they had forgotten or never known were the creations of the BBC. Tearful, crazed parents were begging to have CBBC and CBeebies back, having not known or cared that *Justin's House*, Mr Tumble, *Postman Pat*, *Teletubbies*, *Peppa Pig* and the rest were products of the corporation. Before I let James go to a packed day of meetings across MediaCity's three huge bases, Dock, Quay and Bridge, briefings and one-on-ones in Poldark, Mr Benn and Antiques Roadshow I imagine, I bring up my own personal bugbear: where are the working-class voices and faces at the BBC? James gathers his papers and nods.

'Yes. Interestingly, we have trodden those issues regarding BAME and LGBT issues. For a long time if you came across a gay couple in a drama it would be about gayness as a "problem" issue; the difficulty of being gay. Or just as unhelpfully, "Oh my God!

Here's a gay couple. Isn't that revolutionary?" We should just be able to have portrayals of gay couples who are just that, a couple who happen to be gay. So we very much need to crack that on issues of class and regionality. Class occupies our thinking more and more. We measure our representation of it. It's harder to measure than gender, for example, but we have three indicators which we're using: whether your parents were of managerial class, what kind of school you went to at ten or eleven, and whether you went to university. We have four working groups at the moment and one is specifically about mobility, led by Alan Davey from Radio 3. It is really important, and yes, we are coming late to that party.'

Let's return to the BBC's flagship radio news programme, *Today* on Radio 4. Mishal Husain is an excellent presenter. During a minor on-air disagreement, she once put me gently and firmly in my place. It wasn't an entirely unpleasant experience. She has said, 'With a name like mine, my career would not have been possible anywhere but the BBC.' This is true. Also, she is supremely good at her job. But as Jason Cowley has pointed out in a *New Statesman* editorial:

> Husain is the privileged daughter of a doctor who worked in the United Arab Emirates and Saudi Arabia, where foreign workers don't pay income tax. Her grandfather was a two-star general in the Pakistani army. She attended private schools in the Gulf states and then in Kent before going to Cambridge University. International and private schools, Oxbridge and a posh accent – no one should be surprised Husain is flourishing at the BBC. As it happens, I think she's an excellent journalist. But imagine if she'd been born in Bradford, perhaps the daughter of a shopkeeper or factory worker, attended the local comprehensive and then won a place at, say, Sheffield University. Would this Bradford-born Husain, without status and wealth and with a broad Yorkshire accent and

vernacular conversational style, have been able to work her way up so smoothly at the BBC ...? We know the answer to that question ...

Mishal Husain's erstwhile colleague John Humphrys is seen by most liberals as a curmudgeonly old dinosaur whose departure from the show left it a more progressive place. Perhaps. But it's certainly left it a more unequal and elitist one. However brusque and objectionable you found him, Humphrys is from a working-class non-university background. His departure means the remaining four main presenters – and as far as I can ascertain the presenters of every BBC 4 radio news programme – were all privately educated. This is a serious indictment of the BBC's dominant culture and recruitment policy. Regardless of race, gender or sexual orientation, the BBC recruits from and reflects disproportionately the most privileged sections of our society. That means inevitably its world view is bound to reflect the collective set of assumptions of a very unrepresentative few. It is a climate, a mood music, there continually as a background hum of accents and backgrounds occasionally reaching a unignorable howl, as in when Jeremy Paxman referred to St Edmund Hall, Oxford, of which he is a Fellow, as 'Teddy Hall' throughout the last series of *University Challenge*. Short of taking his teddy bear onto the set, it's difficult to imagine a more excruciating display of elitism. One can only imagine that he wasn't told to stop by someone in production because they were scared.

Some of the Beeb's failings with regard to class are less *Brideshead* than sheer timidity and a shared set of assumptions. When Caitlin Moran was touting her sitcom *Raised by Wolves* around the networks she told me that she'd had meetings with middle-class commissioning editors at the BBC who'd initially enthused. 'I told them that it was about a girl who was fat, working class and from Wolverhampton and they were hugely excited about how great that was. Then they called me back in a few weeks later and said, awkwardly, we just have a few questions, Caitlin. Does she have to be fat, does she have to be working class and does she have to be from Wolverhampton?'

To be fair, as the footballers say, the BBC has started to address some of these issues, belatedly and conspicuously. In an attempt to reboot the mildly toxic and underperforming *Top Gear* brand, it relaunched in summer 2019 with ITV gameshow host Paddy McGuinness and laddish cricketer Freddie Flintoff, where once it was helmed by disgraced chum of David Cameron, Jeremy Clarkson, and US A-lister Matt LeBlanc. The new version is just as blokey but tellingly much more Nando's than Nineteenth Hole. But simply having a few dropped aitches from the continuity announcers does not address a structural fault within the organisation. The inconvenient truth is that genuine diversity is not served by simply 'giving the plebs what we think they want' nor by merely having more visible middle-class Asian presenters. Where are the Jamaican voices? Where are the Chinese faces? Where are the Geordie and Scouse accents in news presentation? We hear Scots burrs across the BBC's news bulletins but these are invariably the soft tones of Edinburgh rather than rich Glaswegian. To the genteel Hampstead ear, the first is still Dr Findlay while the other is Rab C. Nesbitt. Switch on Radio 4 and if you hear a Liverpool accent still it will be a comedy sketch, a gritty play about Hillsborough or unemployment. It will never be a regular mainstream play about adultery, a thriller, a ghost story or farce that just happens to feature Liverpudlians. To paraphrase a fine old philosopher, there is a spectre haunting the BBC and it is one of class discrimination. The BBC does not have a left- or right-wing bias. But it does have a middle-class one.

'Did you used to play Kerbie? Throw a football and try to hit the angle of the curve so it would bounce back into your hands? We used to play it on our estate all bloody night. Under the streetlamps. It must have driven people mad.' Alan Davey is controller of Radio

Three and, in the nicest sense, the BBC's class warrior, or rather its social mobility tsar. He's also self-professedly a child of a healthier, fairer Britain, the one forged in 1945 and besieged since 1979.

'I was absolutely a product of the benevolent state,' he says when we meet in Morecambe and Wise (or maybe it was Fry and Laurie). 'Full grant, decent education and my dad had a paternalistic employer of the old school. ICI had an educational trust for employee's kids. My dad's boss found out I was at uni and told him and from then on I got an extra five hundred quid a year off the firm. Xmas party every year and a job for life. Old school company capitalism.' Alan's dad was an electrician there. 'Not a bad job. Mum was a tea lady for Tarmac. Then what they closed down, she worked in a crisp factory in Bullingham.' He grew up on a council estate in Stockton-on-Tees in the north east.

'It's only when you get out of there and you meet people from very different backgrounds who talk about skiing or their parents second house, or you might even stay at that second house in the country, that you realise that they're the people running the country and you're an alien who has been let in. The generation before me didn't feel that because we were a meritocracy and challenging the middle-class hegemony. But it never quite tipped over. There was a window of opportunity but we didn't take it. Some of us got through to a certain level. But they are still in charge. Class is absolutely the last unspoken diversity issue in our cultural life.'

Of all the BBC's Networks, Radio 3 – dedicated to the idea of bringing non mainstream music, art and speech to the nation with no compulsion to chase ratings – is the part of the BBC that can be most sneered at as 'nanny statist'. In much the same way as I've been called a snob for not finding *Cash in the Attic* the most brilliant and creative use of the licence fee, so I'm called elitist for enjoying Radio 3 a lot more. But it was as important and influential a 'state education' to me as schools or libraries. I was not alone in this. Peter Maxwell Davies described how, as a boy on a council estate in Swinton, he would listen to the Third 'every evening, more or less from the moment it started till the moment it shut down, while I was doing my homework. And it was the best education I could ever have got.' Writing in the *Guardian* on Radio 3's fiftieth birthday, Davey made a case for the network that is refreshingly at odds with some of the sheepish self-consciousness of some at the corporation. 'John Reith's dictum for the whole BBC – "give the public slightly better than it now thinks it likes" – might have a whiff of loftiness to some, but as an ideal for public service broadcasting it's still hard to beat. For 70 years now, this network and its orchestras have been more innovative and less hidebound than their reputations deserve. This great cultural achievement of the post-war era is still going strong. And it's all yours.'

I came away from my day of meetings with Alan Davey and James Purnell feeling invigorated, inspired, delighted still to be part of 'the state broadcaster' (even if it isn't really) and reassured that there are people of real competence and vision still in the higher echelons of power. When I grumble about the Beeb and its moods and caprices, its obsessions and foibles, I do so while still thinking that people like Alan and James are the best kind of public servant, doing their job with the best of intentions and with great ability. Out there though, beyond the arms of Auntie and her old-fashioned belief in principles, ethics and a national good, there is another kind of media now and another kind of broadcasting. Don't be evil, they implore you, which is a bit rich I think, as it's their world where the real nasty stuff lies.

In 1998, 9 per cent of British homes had access to the internet, most of these inhabited by geeks, weirdos or the professionally obligated. Twenty years later it was over 90 per cent. No one has embraced the online world as passionately as the British. Per capita, we shop and surf more than any other country. Not that anyone says 'surf' any more, of course. The idea that being on the internet might be a separate, chosen leisure activity like golf or knitting rather than a permanent all-consuming state of being is almost quaint. We live online, connected umbilically by our phones, our watches, our TVs and even, had the stupid idea taken off, our glasses. We are the wetware that moves through a grid of machines. We have given ourselves to it utterly like willing slaves. The idea of going on holiday to somewhere without Wi-Fi or a mobile signal is for many, and not all of them teenagers, akin to vacationing naked and blindfolded inside a dormant undersea volcano in the Baltic.

On every day of 2018, Apple sold 600,000 iPhones, Amazon made more than $500 million, 1.5 billion people logged on to Facebook and there were 3.5 billion searches on Google. What tech writer Farhad Manjoo called the Frightful Five – Amazon, Google, Apple, Microsoft and Facebook – have colonised our waking life in a way that Orwell would recognise with a shudder. I'm not a Luddite or a Unabomber. I believe in better living through technology. But I also worry. As I mentioned in the Introduction, Billy Bragg said recently that capitalism is like fire: controlled it can give you heat and light and energy; but uncontrolled it will consume and destroy everything in its path. I fear that the same can be said for technology. When the only limit to what can be invented is what can be imagined, we are left with only ethics and morals to guide us. And I'm not at all convinced about Mark Zuckerberg's.

According to academic David Runciman, Facebook 'is both the most and least democratic thing ever, a community of 2 billion people that is the plaything of a thirty-something billionaire. It makes no sense.' James Ball in *Prospect* magazine suggests that the internet 'poses the biggest threat of monopoly in a century' and cites how America dealt with the threat of a rail monopoly by the Sherman Anti-Trust Laws and Teddy Roosevelt's actions as a trust-buster back when America (and the West) was rightly mistrustful of big business rather than in thrall to it. But why all this here in a book about the state and the public realm?

Because – and brace yourselves, comrades – I believe that the time has come to nationalise the internet. Or at least some of it.

Surprisingly, Chris Hughes, co-founder of Facebook, agrees. Sort of. In a *New York Times* article entitled 'It's Time to Break Up Facebook', Hughes says that 'From our earliest days, Mark used the word "domination" to describe our ambitions, with no hint of irony or humility.' While eulogising Zuckerberg's down-home ordinariness, the 'regular guy playing softball with his kids' angle, he paints a rather more chilling picture. 'Mark's influence is staggering, far beyond that of anyone else in the private sector or in government ... The American government needs to do two things: break up Facebook's monopoly and regulate the company to make it more accountable to the American people.'

On stage in front of an audience in Manchester I put all this to someone who has thought and written great deal about it recently. Paul Mason is a former avant-garde composer, northern soul dancer, economics editor of the BBC and Channel 4 and now respected, polemical writer of the left. Tonight I'm hosting a Q&A session at Manchester's Dancehouse studios, the same stage where the lithe young Take That once polished their routines, to talk with him about something a little less ebullient. In his latest book, Mason examines the possibilities and the perils facing humanity from technology and artificial intelligence. I ask him how the privatised world is affecting not just our systems but our humanity.

'Well, the French sociologist Michel Foucault writing at the dawn of the neoliberal system understood what we would have to become in a privatised, highly competitive and impoverished society,' he explains unhesitatingly in full sentences delivered crisply in his rich Lancashire burr. 'We'd have to become "entrepreneurs of the self". By privatising not just industries but all the risks formerly dealt with by a benevolent state – vaccinations, ill health, unemployment or workplace injury – the new system forced everybody to start calculating risks at the front of their minds in a way my parents' generation never had to. All this leads to a kind of evaporation of consent for democracy as surveillance capitalism and algorithmic control by big corporations grows. Loss of faith in human self. That's what we've got to get back. You can fight it.'

In his book, *Clear Bright Future*, Mason outlines some of the small but crucial ways you can fight back against the rise of the machines and the tyranny of the algorithm: never use the automated checkouts, always wait for an assistant, look your barista in the eye and engage with them, not your phone. 'I'm not a technophobe. But I understand what capitalism's objectives are. Four hundred and fifty thousand men in this country drive vans for a living. I'd love driverless cars to become standard. I'm excited for them and I would love to find them something better and more fulfilling to do. But I am not excited about the economic tragedy that will happen unless all this happens under the control of an enlightened state not capitalist big tech. The promise of internet is lower prices, complete symmetry of information. But the internet is trapped by the social relations it's been born in. We need to free it for us all.'

It sounds like a case for nationalising the internet. Every time I utter this phrase, I'm aware it sounds like something only the most doctrinaire Mao-book-carrying, blue-serge-suit-wearing communist would say. When Labour's 2019 manifesto called for free broadband, there was apoplexy. When Liz Truss said at the Tory conference in 2018, 'Jeremy Corbyn wants to nationalise the internet,' she did so secure in the knowledge that the room would be scandalised and appalled, even if half the delegates in the room were probably still on AOL dial-up and use block caps in their emails. She wailed like Cassandra. 'That is what he is saying. [It wasn't.] He wants to run it. He will be deciding the messages.' She added: 'Things like Facebook and Instagram, they are privately owned companies and that is what he is against.'

Perhaps. Or perhaps like me, faced with a new Dark Age where Facebook helps rig elections, where creepy fugitive narcissists breach national security with selectively leaked information, where fictitious statistics emblazoned on buses and fake news online aid the nastiest people in our society, he just thinks that all that precious information and data, the new power source of the world, would be safer in the hands of dull, disinterested but principled civil servants than Zuckerberg, Assange and Bannon?

Former US President Bill Clinton told a Chinese trade delegation in 2000 that attempting to state-control the internet would be 'like trying to nail jello to the wall ... good luck'. As it turned out, the Chinese didn't need luck. They had political will. The standard, vaguely utopian western view of the internet and social media is that it is, inevitably, a powerfully liberating and democratising force, anarchistic even. *New York Times* columnist Thomas Friedman touted it as a 'nutcracker to open societies' and dissident artist Ai Weiwei gushed 'The internet cannot be controlled. And if it is uncontrollable, freedom will win. It is that simple.'

The truth is never that simple. The Chinese government have managed not just to control the internet, but to actively employ it as a tool of the state. They have instituted what they refer to as a system of 'cyber sovereignty'. Essentially, they have their own independent version of the Internet with its own features and platforms. They have their own version of Google (Baidu), their own Amazon (Alibaba) and a kind of cross between Facebook and Netflix called Tencent. (They are good at these odd hybrids; their version of WhatsApp, WeChat, also contains features of Uber, Deliveroo and online banking and bill paying.) Because China is so big, these Chinese counterparts now often dwarf the American originals.

Let's be under no illusions about the Chinese Communist Party's motives here. The Chinese internet is one huge surveillance and control exercise. People have been sent to prison for posting the wrong kind of message on WeChat. No one is suggesting this is a good thing. But what the success of the Chinese internet, the sheer effectiveness of their 'cyber sovereignty', proves is that this kind of state regulation is entirely possible. With the right intent, it might even be highly desirable at least to a degree. Unless you really believe that the amoral billionaires of Silicon Valley and Harvard are the best custodians of all our societies' future and the nature of our public discourse. Some degree of state involvement of, say, social media might seem deplorable to Julian Assange and possibly Ai Weiwei. But it might prevent a situation where a contestant on a ballroom dancing talent show receives astonishing abuse culminating in death threats simply because someone didn't rate his paso doble.

'There are two practical things I think we could do immediately,' says Mason. 'At the moment, there is no social contract between you and Google or Facebook. This has massive ethical issues. The day is coming when, with their brilliant AI, Facebook will know the date you are going to die. Once they can know that, and once Facebook has its own major insurance company, well, it's goodbye insurance for a lot of people. We need them to have a social contract with us. So some of us, and even some of them, think it would be better to have a publicly owned data registry of who we are and our health and all that vital information and they have to compete to use it, on grounds of price, ethics, social good, etc. So that's a kind of nationalisation, a publicly owned data registry.

'But I'd go further. I'd introduce some good old-fashioned capitalist competition into it. You don't have to go to your bank's ATM for your cash. Why not have a Facebook-type interface like that but behind which you choose what services you want and what social network you want? You could choose the one without ads, or the one that doesn't give your data to the Russians, or you might not care. You might choose the one where they pay you to use them. But you'd have the choice. There's a famous quote from Fredric Jameson who said that 'it's easier to imagine the end of the world than the end of capitalism'. Sometimes it's easier to imagine the end of world than Zuckerberg telling us what the algorithm does. You're not allowed to know that or his business goes ping. We have perfectly good competition law, but we haven't used it because they are too rich and powerful. But we are getting wise. In America, the genie is out of the bottle because of Elizabeth Warren. I think one day soon maybe one of them will be broken up.'

Elizabeth Warren, who as I write is the Democrat's favourite contender to unseat Trump, may well be the next president of the United States. Mark Zuckerberg will probably do everything in his murky, data-harvesting, email-leaking, algorithmic power to stop her though. As Paul Mason says, she has the tech giants in her sights. 'Today's big tech companies have too much power – too much power over our economy, our society, and our democracy. They've bulldozed competition, used our private information for profit, and tilted the playing field against everyone else.'

Their enormous, head-swimming wealth puts them on a par with nation states. Apple's cash reserves in 2017 were roughly double those of the Federal Reserve in 2016. Facebook is shaping and twisting the outcomes of democracy. The Frightful Five have become bigger than governments without any of the sense of moral purpose or principle that even the worst governments have. Nailing the squelchy, amorphous, shifting, queasy 'jello' of the internet to the stern and ethical wall of the state might be difficult. But it is surely not impossible. We should certainly try. Because this is the next and maybe the last great battle for the state and its citizenry.

So delete your Facebook account, turn off your phone, and come with me for some fresh air.

CHAPTER 10

I LOOK FORWARD

'SELLING ENGLAND BY THE POUND'

'It is difficult, if not impossible, to combine the citizens' rights and interests and the private enterprise's interests, because the private enterprise aims at its natural and justified objective, the biggest possible profit.'

Joseph Chamberlain

'Greed is good.'

Gordon Gekko

The Upper Derwent Valley, Derbyshire. A fine, calm, April evening, the air warm and still, the kiss of breeze very welcome. The journey up here out of Manchester through the city's weekday rush hour is never something you'd call pleasant; smothered in the damp armpit or bulky backpack of a fellow traveller on a stifling privatised train, or tail to tail in the fuming cars that crawl through the winding bottlenecks of the A57 to Glossop and Sheffield. Worth it though, when you arrive. The crystal freshness of high moorland air, the plangent music of curlew and lark, dark, lovely waters reclining languorous and seductive in the hollow of green hills. Even the occasional gladdening tinkle of an ice-cream van.

I'm walking above the handsome, slightly forbidding dam. It stands at the end of the middle of the valley's three reservoirs, built between 1902 and 1943 by the Derwent Valley Water Board to

slake the thirst, fill the baths and power the pumps and turbines of
the great northern and Midlands cities of Sheffield, Leicester,
Nottingham and Derby. After a prolonged dry spell, the kind of
dry, hard, hot summer that British people crave in March and curse
in August, something of the past awakes and re-emerges here.
Decades ago, the villages of Ashopton and Derwent were drowned
under the deep, black waters of the lowest reservoir, Ladybower.
Their inhabitants were moved to the very cities that their homes
were engulfed to serve. They went willingly, if sadly, servants of a
greater good, putting themselves second to the needs of the many.
In this obeisance to the stern demands of the state, they were like
the villagers of drowned Mardale in the Lake District, now under
the waters that feed Manchester's homes and industries, or the tiny
villages of Imber in Wiltshire and Tyneham in Dorset, where the
villagers were given a month's notice to vacate in 1943 when their
beloved home was turned into a tank firing range in preparation
for D-Day.

Perhaps the exiles came back to Ashopton and Derwent in
drought. At these times, when water levels fall, the skeleton of the
village is laid open to the sky like an exhumed corpse's bony
ribcage; the outline of a church and a wall, the arched bridges
over the mill brook, the jagged stumps of the old wood. The
students of Chesterfield College have digitally recreated the drive
through the now-drowned Ashopton online. It's a brilliant if
eerie evocation, the slow glide past the door of the Ashopton Inn,
the stables, the garage, the tearoom with its Lyons advertisements,
the toll house and the Methodist chapel.

I walk along Ladybower's bosky eastern shore, the water
glittering away down to my right, the ridge of hills charcoal blue
against the sky. I walk past Fairholmes Visitor Centre, locked now
as dusk gathers and the 'gloaming' creeps across the north shore.
Seven decades ago, on April nights like these, young men in huge
planes skimmed low across the long Y-shaped lake as the moon
rose over the deserted submerged farms and houses of Ashopton
and Derwent. The farmers and locals grumbled at the nightly

disturbances from those joyriding RAF johnnies. Didn't they know there was a war on? When, before long, they found out just what had been happening those April nights, they never grumbled again about their spooked hens and their dislodged roof tiles.

We ought to be grateful to those young men in their noisy, low-flying planes. And like the displaced of Imber and Tyneham, we should remember and be thankful for the sacrifice of those Derbyshire villagers, those who were sent away and those who stayed, those who had to make new lives in crowded Sheffield and Manchester, whose nights were disrupted by the low, guttural roar of Lancasters. Because this newly built reservoir and the old commanding Derwent dam were the perfect choice for the practice ground for Operation Chastise. For six weeks in the spring of 1943, flying low over the cold, still waters, this is where the RAF's 617 Squadron tested, in conditions of absolute secrecy, Barnes Wallis's 'bouncing bomb'. Just days later, 617 Squadron would use these bombs to breach the Eder and Möhne dams causing ruinous floods across the Ruhr Valley and wreaking significant damage to the Nazi war machine. Forever after 617 Squadron would be known as the Dam Busters, immortalised in the film of 1955 and its comically stirring music.

There are no stirring marches and no romantic movies about the Derwent Valley Water Board. Their reservoirs and dams may have helped us defeat Hitler and win the war but its serious-minded public servants are under the ground now, like the inns and farms of the valley. In 1974 the Board was taken over by Severn Trent Water, then in turn in 1989, that was privatised along with all the water boards of England and Wales. Since then, in a bewildering series of mergers, demergers, acquisitions and sell-offs, Severn Trent has bought and sold the waste company Biffa, developed a private laboratory wing in America which it then sold to global giant HIG Capital, and gone into partnership with United Utilities in preparation for further deregulation of the water 'industry'.

Severn Trent Water has been subject to its own chastising operations of late. During the floods of 2007, a Tewkesbury water-treatment plant became contaminated and enormous numbers of people across Middle England were left without running water. James Meek in *Private Island* provides some interesting extra detail.

> In July 2007, a few days after the floods arrived, with 350,000 people still cut off from the first necessity of life, Severn Trent held its annual general meeting. It announced profits of £325 million, and confirmed a dividend for shareholders of £143 million. Not long afterwards the company, with the consent of the water regulator Ofwat, announced that it wouldn't be compensating customers: all would be charged as if they'd had running water, even when they hadn't. Colin Matthews, chief executive of Severn Trent at the time of the floods, left the company soon after this to run another private monopoly, BAA ... In his last year as head of Severn Trent, he was paid £1.2 million.

Between 2001 and 2011, Severn Trent had the worst leakage record in England and Wales, losing 27 per cent of the supply, or half a billion litres a day. In 2008, Ofwat confirmed that it had fined Severn Trent Water £35.8 million for deliberately providing false information to Ofwat and for delivering poor service to its customers. The same month, in the first conviction and fine of a company for such criminal behaviour, Severn Trent pleaded guilty to reporting and covering up misleading leakage data after a Fraud Office investigation uncovered a web of orchestrated deception. They were fined £4 million, later commuted to £2 million. On 11 March 2016, thousands of Severn Trent customers in Derbyshire were left without a clean, reliable water supply after high levels of chlorine were discovered.

Guy Gibson, dashing hero of 617 Squadron, the Dam Busters, was killed in action in 1944. He was awarded the Victoria Cross and a marble monument commemorates him beneath the huge

Derwent dam and above the silent moonlit water where he flew his Lancaster seventy-six years ago. If he and the Dam Busters wanted to fly there now though, preparing to face some foreign foe, they would have to go, RAF caps and MOD chequebook in hand, to a very particular band of civilian brothers: the besuited board of a private company floated on the London Stock Exchange and part of the FTSE 100, namely Severn Trent Water PLC, a corporate umbrella name for a cluster of companies across mainland Europe, the USA and the Middle East. Depending on who were fighting, getting permission could be tricky, I suppose.

Wise council, like that of Joseph Chamberlain noted above, has always been that placing essentials like our water supply in private hands is folly. But for forty years, greed has been trumping wisdom. The new Gekkos – or should that be 'geckos'? – have slithered into every corner of our national life. Water privatisation has been perhaps the most difficult to justify on any moral or societal grounds. It's difficult to square with the celebrated ethos of competition, that mythical beast beloved of the free-marketeer. The customer has no choice, can't take their business elsewhere, has to pay the price set by the monopoly provider and thus loses on every count. So much for the benefits of competition. It is absolutely emblematic of what Frank Cottrell-Boyce spoke of when he excoriated the corrupt, effete version of capitalism that now holds sway in Britain. 'The phase of capitalism that we're in is not remotely competitive. Where are the dynamic venture capitalists? Who's in the driving seat of our economy? Is it entrepreneurs? Is it customers? Is it workers? No, it's hedge fund managers. Ours is an economy run by retired dentists in the Cotswolds. That's not a lively virile capitalism.'

Not virile, not dynamic and certainly not transparent or accountable. The darkness of privatisation has spawned a mushrooming of opaque and baffling foliage far more impenetrable than it ever was under the state, as Cottrell-Boyce says. 'With the state you knew who was to blame for things going wrong. If your bins weren't emptied, you rang the "corpy". They were responsible for the bins, not some vague offshore trust or hedge fund. Nowadays Amalgamated Holdings/Wile E. Coyote is emptying your bins, based somewhere in France. No one knows who's answerable. It's like "Find the Lady". One of the results of moving public assets into private hands has been a kind of sleight of hand where you don't know who's responsible. In the old days, you could ring the actual man responsible when British Rail screwed up. Today, well, you could try Branson, but even he can just say, sorry, I don't own the tracks. There is nothing more disempowering than not knowing who's answerable.'

Needless to say, all this has proved beneficial for the new management of our hastily, recklessly privatised utilities. Take water again. The executives there have pulled off the enviable trick of commanding the highest salaries in Europe for delivering the most costly, fattest-profit-making water supply on that continent. It may be leaking pipes, hosepipe bans and polluted water for us but it's trebles all round in the boardrooms of United Utilities, Affinity Water, Veolia, Icosa, Severn Trent and the rest. In 2019, the latter's share price rose nicely and profits were up over 6 per cent. According to the BBC News Market Data section, Severn Trent 'confirmed the final dividend will be 56.02p. But the firm warned once more about the impact of any future nationalisation of the industry on its strategic goals.' Whatever those strategic goals might be was not recorded, but I imagine increased dividends to shareholders, attractive bonuses and bigger profits would be high among them, higher perhaps than safe, reliable, cheap drinking water.

It's not just water, of course. In this book, I've looked at how schools, hospitals, houses, transport – essential life resources for us all that should be owned by us all – are now in the hands of a few for private profit. But there's something particularly dismaying and pernicious that water – water that falls from sky on the just and the unjust alike, the rain that raineth every day according to Shakespeare in *Twelfth Night* – that something so basic, pure and natural, should have been hived off and privatised. That seems both barmy and immoral to me. For who can own the spring rain, the mountain streams, the dancing becks?

Who? Well, once it's got into Ladybower, it's Severn Trent's, mate.

Even the land beneath our feet, like water, has been taken into private hands by a kind of theft, stolen by enclosures and land grabs throughout history and since 1979 sold off in utterly scandalous numbers. Brett Christophers in his book *The New Enclosure* estimates that since 1979 10 per cent of the land mass of Britain has been sold by the state to the private sector. That amounts to some 2 million hectares worth at today's prices £400 billion. That's £400 billion of your money. This was your land too: woodlands, moors, railway tracks and sidings, parks, playgrounds, swimming baths, sports grounds, school playing fields, golf courses, old barracks, dockyards, allotments, cabbage patches and waste ground, fields and meadows, greens for putting and bowling, all sold to the highest bidder, or the crony, without your consent or even your knowledge. We didn't realise until it was too late. This new narrative was a lie with a name. Quite a nice name. Tina. Not such a nice sentiment though. There **Is No A**lternative.

The phrase 'there is no alternative' is attributed originally to the classical thinker Herbert Spencer, but it will forever be associated with Margaret Thatcher. It was one of her deadening catchphrases, along with 'the lady's not for turning', 'the enemy within' and the other zingers. She fell back on it whenever it was suggested that there was another way to run a country except wholescale deregulation, savage spending cuts, a dismantling of the welfare state and enslavement to the markets. It was codswallop, of course. There were and still are any amount of alternatives, from full-scale command-state Maoism and Soviet Communism to mixed-economy social democracy to anarcho-syndicalism to plutocracy to absolute rule by plutocratic budgerigar (never yet tried but worth a go). There was an alternative. There still is, though we have left it late and lost much. For a lesson in how we could live happier, healthier, safer, be more sane and more productive, let's revitalise one of George Osborne's fatuous old slogans. Let's visit a real northern powerhouse.

I was an odd kid in many ways. I would develop raging curiosities, obsessions even, and in an era before the internet this would lead me each week, maybe even each day like the Morans in the summer holidays, down to Powell Street Library to feed this niche craving with book after book. Maybe I wasn't so odd, actually. Maybe you did this too. What were your fixations and fads? In my case, there was heraldry, then Romanian football (Come on, you Petrolul Ploieşti!), but most of all there was my all-consuming passion for Norse mythology. As I mentioned in Chapter 4, I worked backwards from the terrible Marvel versions in the *Thor* comics to the real, icy, misty, bleak and fire-breathing deal. I still love them for their grim, strange evocations of a harsh and indifferent universe, awe-inspiring landscapes, existential heroes and villains living lives lit by danger, chance and celebration. Later this passion for all things Norse would spread and sublimate itself into a love of Abba, Björn Borg and the detective stories of the eccentric Swede Agaton Sax.

My Norwegian and Icelandic friends find this weird but cute. Anne Hilde Neset is a music writer and broadcaster who felt the pull in the opposite direction. Drawn from her native Norway by the UK's experimental music scene, she lived in London from 1995 to 2012. Now she's back in Oslo with her husband, the music writer Rob Young, and their two children. She's director of a civic art gallery, formerly an artist's collective, in the café of which we sit eating pizza listening to 70s Ethiopian jazz. Each slice probably costs more than a three-course meal at your local Harvester or Spoon's, but it is delicious. Also, the breath-taking price of a Quattro Stagioni is something maybe worth paying for living in a country that is fairer, more generous, more forward-looking, more human than modern Britain. There are alternatives to how we've done things this last half-century. One of them is the Norwegian way.

'That phrase "nanny state" was so weird and shocking to me when I first came across it in Britain,' says Anne Hilde. 'Not even in our most populist tabloid press is there ever talk of a nanny state here. It would be ridiculous. We assume the state is there for its citizens. Not even our far right would say there's no such thing as society.' Like most Norwegians I know, Anne Hilde can indulge in a little eye-rolling exasperation at the painfully fair and decent nature of her society. Most at some point will bring up with a wry smile a celebrated piece of literary satire by Aksel Sandemose from the 1930s. He formulated the law of Jante or *Janteloven*.

'We refer to it time and time again. It's the Norwegian love of mediocrity, I guess. You are not allowed to stand out. You must not think you are better than your countrymen. Some people think there is a downside to our love of equality, in that it is hard to be other and that we are suspicious of anything that's not bog standard. But in Norway that bog standard is pretty good, I have to say. We make fun of our country, affectionately. But we are proud of it. That word "nanny" is so pejorative, so full of hostility. We would never say that or think like that.'

During her time in London, Anne Hilde was particularly shocked and scandalised by one British trait and topic of dinner party conversation. 'When I lived there, the UK seemed to be full of people obsessed with not paying tax and not being remotely embarrassed about that. You get accountants to help you avoid paying tax. Here if you call yourself a grown-up, you would be ashamed to act or talk like that. It would be like bragging that you do runners from restaurants, or boasting to your friends that you go to Top Shop and steal clothes. It is not something that a grown adult would do or ever be proud of doing. The Norwegian just thinks' – she makes a scowl of disbelief – 'okaaaayyy ... so you don't pay your proper tax. That's kind of weird. So do you have kids? And do they not go to school? And have you never been to the doctors?'

She continues: 'You can live in England as a single city girl and be a Marxist intellectual living in a right-on bubble. You can live in your own zone of your great job and cultural wealth and the BBC and the *Guardian*. But when you have a family, you have to deal with it. As a parent you come right up against the UK class system. Before their kids were born my London friends were researching schools and preparing to move to get into the right catchment area. It was hard enough for me understanding breast feeding let alone plotting a trajectory for a little thing still in nappies. To move house in Norway to get a better school is unthinkable. Schools are all the same. It would be like moving to get a different water supply. It's just there. Education is on tap. When we moved back with our London values and we asked to have a look around schools, you could tell they thought we were weird. You just move to the area you like and go to the local schools.' Beyond 'specialist' areas of education like Steiner and Montessori and outside of a few schools for the kids of foreign diplomats, there is no private education in Norway. The thought of it makes my Scandi friends snort with derision. It is yet another example of the bizarre way we do things here.

That night I eat out again (and again with punishing effects to my bank balance) with my friend Joakim Haugland, who runs the excellent Norwegian record label Smalltown Supersound.

Joakim is by any definition a small businessman, an entrepreneur and a successful one. But in Norway thriving businesses and a decent welfare state don't have to be mutually exclusive. He has none of the lazy, entrenched attitudes that seem to come fitted as standard with our business leaders, the threadbare rhetoric and the sullen self-centredness. Joakim, like Anne Hilde, sees himself as a product of a benevolent state, not a selfish and insular elite. He would never be as silly or arrogant to call himself, as our business class does with such blustering bullishness, a self-made man. Joakim knows just what he owes to the Norwegian state and its people. 'High taxes don't bother me. I love to pay my taxes. Last year I had a back problem. I slipped a disc, as I think you say. I was in so much pain. An ambulance came immediately and got me and paramedics took me to the hospital ward. I was in the hospital for fifteen days and I was given the best of care for free. And as well as that I got paid fifteen hundred pounds for my loss of earnings.'

How can they afford it? The same way we could have done. With the black gold of the North Sea. Oil. But, unlike us, the Norwegians used their resources for the good of the people. In May 1963, Einar Gerhardsen's government proclaimed sovereignty over the Norwegian continental shelf, declaring that the state owned any natural resources on there. But the Nordic oil boom really began in 1969 with the discovery of oil on the mighty Ekofisk field. Joakim takes another bite of cod and a sip of a really rather nice organic red wine. 'We Norwegians, we are a nation of stupid farmers really who all of a sudden got oil. We don't have an aristocracy or hierarchies. What we did have was a clever guy in the Labour Party called Jens Evensen who thought this new oil we found should be for everyone.'

The Norwegian government though were not just principled, they were savvy. 'We were smart,' says Joakim. 'We let the Americans dig and stood next to them and learned how to drill for five years. Then we said, "Your licence is up," and we threw them out. But the Americans were happy. They had five good years and made shitloads of money. Then Evensen did a deal with the Danes too. They had some rights to the oil but their guy was always drunk so Evensen gave him a few extra beers and he gave us Ekofisk and billions of pounds of oil revenue.' The Dane incidentally was called Per Haekerrup and he is infamous in Scandinavia for this boozy mistake.

Norway put their enormous North Sea oil revenues into a sovereign fund. It became literally a national treasure, funding a world-class welfare system and the needs of an aging population. Venezuela, under Hugo Chávez, used their oil wealth to help the poor. We, naturally, did no such thing with our oily windfall. Margaret Thatcher used our revenues to alleviate a balance of payments deficit, fund costly tax cuts and unemployment benefits, and soften the blow of her vengeful industrial restructurings. All of this played well with the electorate of Middle England – Tony Blair remarked in 1987 that North Sea oil was 'utterly essential to Mrs Thatcher's electoral success' – and some of it may have been necessary. But had we had the foresight and will to put even a small percentage into a sovereign fund we could now be living like Joakim and Anne Hilde; secure, happy and equitably rather than debt-ridden, fearful and ill. With this, that different attitude to taxation and the government investing in its people, we could embrace the nanny state again and could all reap the benefits.

Joakim is a football fan. He supports the great industrial club side Stavanger Viking, so our conversation naturally goes to the most famous footballing exchange between England and Norway, the World Cup qualifier of 1981 in Oslo which Norway won by two goals to one. At the final whistle the Norwegian commentator Bjørge Lillelien went into a wonderful and crazily triumphalist rant which Joakim, like every Norwegian football fan, knows pretty much by heart. It is a mad roll call of now humiliated celebrity Aunt Sallies, all English figures from our national life. Joakim can easily manage it, even after those glasses of good red.

'We are the best in the world! We are the best in the world! We have beaten England two – one in football! It is completely unbelievable! We have beaten England! England, birthplace of giants. Lord Nelson, Lord Beaverbrook, Sir Winston Churchill, Sir Anthony Eden, Clement Attlee, Henry Cooper, Lady Diana – we have beaten them all. We have beaten them all.'

The conclusion is oddly fitting. 'Maggie Thatcher, can you hear me? Maggie Thatcher, I have a message for you ... Your boys took a hell of a beating! Your boys took a hell of a beating!'

Sitting in this chic Oslo restaurant, thinking of home, our failing healthcare systems, our decrepit trains, our pot-holed roads and underfunded schools, looking at Norway today and Britain today, it's hard not to hear an echo of that speech, which doesn't sound quite so crazy and vainglorious now. Our boys, and our girls, our young and old, our cities, our towns, our people.

We have taken one hell of a beating.

Another celebrated modern rant goes like this:

You are not special. You're not a beautiful and unique snowflake. You're the same decaying organic matter as everything else. We're all part of the same compost heap. We're all singing, all dancing crap of the world.

So says Tyler Durden in *Fight Club*. Although some claim 'snowflake' has been an insult aimed at the fuzzy liberal since the American Civil War, it was the usage in the 1999 movie adaptation of *Fight Club* that led to its becoming one of the many cheap, knee-jerk rebukes of the US alt-right. In their grubby armoury, it is aimed solely at, as they see it, limp and shrilly, oversensitive, easily wounded millennials, their prissy values and sappy sense of grievance.

I loathe the demonisation and mocking of the young that's become the hallmark of a protected and petrified older generation. Like Paul Mason, who originally wanted to call his new book 'The Snowflake Insurrection', I think the young people of today are showing courage by taking on the great injustices of our age, from Extinction Rebellion to Black Lives Matter. But there's another dimension here that I'm going to warily explore. Anyone of my vintage and gender who dares say that there may be something deeper and more meaningful in that phrase 'snowflake' than just a pat swipe risks opening up a front in the culture wars Mason refers to. But I think there is something there, and it's at the crux of what this book is about. It involves a certain serious scepticism about the rise of identity politics and the primacy and sanctity of the individual, this relatively young religion and the new theocracy of the West. What has this individualism done to our sense of community?

Here's Eleanor Penny in a *New Statesman* piece boldly titled 'All Politics Is Identity Politics'.

All politics requires that we build coalitions around a shared picture of reality, a shared image of the future, deeply rooted in our image of ourselves, and what justice or progress might look like. Racial or ethnic background will shape how you experience the criminal justice system. Your gender shapes how you experience work, or how you experience violence. If you're disabled, you're more likely to be at the frontline of austerity. These aren't indulgent departures from real politics – they are rooted in concrete realities of who has power, who has resources, who is exposed to violence and who is sheltered from it. They are cultural frameworks for understanding, organising and indeed changing the world.

I agree with pretty much all this. But I don't agree with another line in the piece describing calls to unity as 'bleary-eyed nostalgia'. I think that unity, rather than a focus on the individual, can be what helps save us – and is what has always underpinned the idea of a national welfare state. Unfettered individual liberty may seem like a paradise, but it's incompatible with a society that's fair, decent and supportive. Laws, taxes, schools; all are potentially restrictive to one's individual freedom. But without them, the strongest succeed and the weakest go to the wall. Just as, as the saying goes, there are no atheists in the foxhole, there are few libertarians in the workhouse or the soup kitchen.

Jonathan Rutherford is an academic associated with the Blue Labour school of left thinking which believes Labour's drift from traditional class roots to bourgeois liberalism has undermined it fatally. The electoral disaster of 2019 would seem to bear this out. He identifies not millennials as the vehicle for this, but a cast of mind called 'cosmopolitanism'. Also writing in the *New Statesman*, he said:

Cosmopolitans believe that their obligations to others should not be confined to fellow national citizens, but extended to include all of humanity. Yet in committing to everyone as part of a universal humanity, we commit to no one and nothing in particular. Under the influence of this abstraction, progressive and left politics in the

1990s turned away from class politics and solidarity in favour of group identities and self-realisation. It rejected forms of membership that make a claim on people's loyalty ... the logic of cosmopolitan liberalism has turned identity politics into a competitive struggle of one group identity over another. In place of solidarities, there is a kind of Hobbesian war of all against all and a narcissistic preoccupation with the self.

I think individuality is over-rated. That chilly misanthrope Jean-Paul Sartre may have felt that 'hell is other people' but in many ways Sartre was an arse, as Simone de Beauvoir could attest. Heaven can be other people as well. Let's take a moment to celebrate the communal joy of Christmas crowds, football stadiums and dance floors, of rubbing shoulders at work and school. The trend towards self-expression over connectivity and communality is a movement, but it may not necessarily be progress. David Hepworth captured something of this perfectly in a Radio 3 essay about trends in funerals and weddings. 'We now live in the world of customised vows where the off-the-peg solution no longer seems equal to people's needs, where the standard musical selection is too confining of everybody's presumed giant personality. Just as a wedding is increasingly all about personal fulfilment rather than a commitment to continuity and is marked by songs like "I Will Always Love You", less a vow than a boast, so people who've lived lives of blameless anonymity are now delivered into the hereafter to the strains of Frank Sinatra's ridiculous "My Way", a song which is the very definition of building your part in life.'

Deprived of any real power in our lives, any proper strength and solidarity in our communities, we've been encouraged to try the opium of self-aggrandisement as a sop. I rarely agree with John Lennon but the most famous line from 'Working Class Hero' does seem to have some brutal resonance here: 'You think you're so clever and classless and free, but you're still fucking peasants as far as I can see'. Maybe we should embrace the joy of our communal peasant-hood, rise with our class rather than out of it, celebrate sometimes our warm sameness as well as our felt uniqueness, love it rather than deny it in favour of a narcissistic self-regard.

For the forty long years of the dismantling of the post-war consensus, playwright David Hare has been chronicling it all in a series of acclaimed 'state of the nation' plays. Early in 2019, he gave his cold and sobering take on where we are now.

> At this point, I cannot imagine my country being civilised until it is back in the hands of people who believe that the state has a duty of care to all its citizens, and most particularly to the most deprived. If that is not possible, then, as second best, I would still be ready to accept a version of capitalism that was continually revitalised by offering open access to newcomers from outside. What I will never accept is the idea of rich nations imprisoned inside rotting gated communities, with right-wing politicians barking through the railings like mangy guard-dogs. Too many walls are being built, creating too many strongholds for people who have no vision in life except to hold on to what they've already got and kick everyone else in the face.

The mood of pessimism and defeat can be contagious. When I watch the smirking faces and the posturing of the bullies, liars and incompetents currently helming our political class, hear how debased and pathetic, ugly and brutish, whingeing and self-absorbed the tone of our discourse is in the streets and the media, it's easy to feel deeply fearful about the future. These are the times when the mountain bothy or the Shetland croft seem most attractive.

But perhaps there is, as I wondered a few hundred pages ago, a new mood abroad. We've all heard a lot about 'the will of the people' these last few years. So perhaps it's worth noting that, in polls, a sizeable majority of the British people still favour state control of our essential services, the building of more council houses, an end to charitable status for private schools, accountability for bankers and traders and a whole raft of related progressive ideas that the *Sun*, *Mail* and *Times* rarely credit. Frank Cottrell-Boyce saw evidence of it at the 2018 World Cup. 'There's a hunger for decency these days. You could see that in how people warmed to Gareth Southgate. He seemed a decent, thoughtful bloke. It was refreshing. Essentially it was about him not being a wanker.'

There is an alternative. It doesn't need to be repressive command-state totalitarianism or destructive laissez-faire neo-liberalism. It could be the enlightened social democracies of Scandinavia or New Zealand, which under Jacinda Ardern is the first major country to abandon growth as a political priority in favour of wellbeing. Billy Bragg tells of once being on a TV debate show with a Conservative cabinet minister. When asked whether child maintenance should be increased, he replied, 'Well, we'll have to wait and see what the bond markets say about that.' As Bragg says, no one voted for the bond market. The bond market has no nation, no community, no love or loyalties or duty. It is unpatriotic. It – not the striking miners Thatcher slandered with the phrase – is the enemy within. We need to start seeing the untrammelled free market of the twenty-first century for what it really is; a bully, even a traitor. For the market has no loyalty, no responsibility, no fellow feeling.

Only a few miles from Ladybower is another Derbyshire village, synonymous with duty, service and sacrifice. I visited Eyam on a freezing deep winter day just before Christmas. Icy rain fell all morning but even on the balmiest July afternoon, there is always a chill and a pall about this lovely place. In 1665 a tailor from Eyam ordered a box of fabric from London, intending to make it into clothes for the villagers. Fatally, the cloth bore fleas that carried bubonic plague and 260 Eyam villagers would die from it – more than double the mortality rate suffered by the citizens of London in the Great Plague. But the human cost would have been unimaginably worse were it not for Eyam's extra-ordinary and enduring self-sacrifice. After the first death, Eyam sealed itself off from the world at large to prevent the disease spreading. Between September 1665 and October 1666, the villagers quarantined themselves. No one entered or left. Food was left for them by neighbouring villagers on the isolated hillsides for Eyam's residents to collect. They left coins soaked in vinegar to prevent infection as payment. The individual stories are heart-breaking. At pretty Rose Cottage on the main street, all nine members of the Thorpe family died. Two lovers met in secret in the wooded Delph until Emmott Sydall could no longer risk her beloved Rowland Torre's safety and enclosed herself within Eyam's walls to die. Roland lived into old age unmarried. One woman, a Mrs Hancock, buried seven members of her family in eight days.

The village information board and map, a little crassly perhaps but in an attempt to lighten the mood, jokes, 'Welcome to Eyam, it's infectious'. Though Eyam's atmosphere may be sombre, it is not ultimately depressing because the story it tells about humans' capacity for selflessness and altruism is powerful and positive. The ordinary people of Eyam condemned themselves to death so their fellow men and women might live. Interestingly, the local landed gentry, the Bradshaws of Bradshaw Hall, its forlorn and overgrown ruins still visible, discreetly slipped the cordon and fled. They were not typical though. Most of Eyam acted in the common good and put themselves second. It's tempting to pronounce, with a sigh and a shake of the head, that this would not happen now, that another Eyam could never happen in our atomised and self-obsessed world.

But apparently it could. The popular American podcast Radiolab had a recent episode called 'How to Be a Hero' devoted to the Carnegie Hero Fund, established to recognise persons who perform acts of heroism in the United States and Canada. These acts are measured against six criteria: the recipient must be 1) a civilian who 2) voluntarily leaves 3) a point of safety to 4) save the life of another human being for whom they have 5) no responsibility and which 6) risks their own life. In the show, we learn of a twenty-one-year-old female college student who jumped from her car to scale an electrified fence enduring thousands of volts of charge to physically stop a 150lb Jersey bull goring a woman to death. She risked her own life to stand the huge enraged animal down by hitting it in the face with a pipe. Also honoured was a thirty-seven-year-old man who jumped from his bed in the middle of the night wearing only sweatpants to go three times into a blazing car to pull three teenagers to safety. Finally, a fifty-year-old construction worker who left his young daughters on the platform to jump onto the subway tracks and lay atop a convulsing epileptic man as a speeding train passed over them. Each afterwards said the same thing, as indeed every recipient of the Carnegie Hero Medal does: 'I did what anyone would do.' I know that this isn't true, because I know that I cannot honestly say I would do any of the above things. These heroic ordinary men and woman are surely rare and getting rarer as we become more selfish and insular.

But no. The Carnegie Hero Fund is having to make its criteria more difficult and exclusive faced with ever-increasing numbers of candidates being put forward. There are more and more instances of extreme and extraordinary heroism every year. The director told Radiolab, 'We are fortunate to be living in a society, regardless of what you hear elsewhere, where people do look out for other people, even strangers.' If however you believe that there is no such thing as society, then there is no explanation for the heroism above. It is aberrant. It is stupid. It is pointless. The above individuals were just not looking after themselves or their families first – Thatcher's mantra – they actively risked their own and their loved ones' health, safety and happiness to do something for others. No intellectual theory of complete free-market liberalism can ever really deal with the pesky concept of altruism. No Hayek or Friedman, no Keith Joseph, no Institute of Economic Affairs, no right-wing think tank can ever properly explain the behaviour of the selfless, the volunteer and the hero.

What has this to do with the state? Because, as Caitlin Moran said, the welfare state is love made institutional. Yes, our state can do wicked things. We've seen that at Orgreave, at Hillsborough, at Amritsar in 1919 and in Derry in 1972. But that is when we let the levers of state fall into the hands and the minds of the zealot and the entitled. Between the end of the Second World War and the entry of Thatcher into Downing Street, the state generally did what it thought was the best for the very best of reasons. It was progressive, imaginative, adventurous, caring and responsible. The years since then have seen not salvation but a shrinking, the slow sour closing of the English mind and heart, as we turn to worship at the altar of the private sector.

The modern boasts of self-actualisation and empowerment are all very well, the talk of pride and identity. But the state is there for you when you do not feel proud or sexy or empowered. It is there for you when your self-belief has evaporated and when there are more important things than pride at stake. There are the simple joys of brotherhood and the common herd. There is such a thing as society. Its fabric is ragged and threadbare but it holds, just. Its institutions have been enfeebled, under-resourced, starved even. But it is still for most of us the glue that binds us together, the apparatus that will keep us safe. When the private sector has left you stranded and alone, when you cannot pay your way, when you are tired and heartbroken, the state, though a diligent, tireless and underpaid worker, will help you stand and carry on when the businessman will only ask what's in it for him. When the market has left you friendless and alone, the state will still be there.

I hope.

I'm writing these words on the north-eastern fringe of the Lake District in the summer of 2019. As I write, a multimillionaire old Etonian, sacked twice for dishonesty, firstly by his newspaper, then by the leader of the Conservative Party, a man who described black people as 'piccaninnies' with 'watermelon smiles', compared Muslim women to bank robbers and letterboxes, gay men as 'bum boys' and the EU to the Third Reich, the man who has lost the taxpayer £43 million in the half-baked vanity project the London Garden Bridge, abandoned without a brick being laid, Alexander Boris de Pfeffel Johnson has just become the Prime Minister of Great Britain.

With that shaming and humiliating news for my country, it's difficult to feel much in the way of optimism or enthusiasm for the next few years. Looking up from my writing, I can see the misty, lonely, beautiful summits of High Pike, Carrock Fell, Blencathra and Bannerdale Crags. It's tempting to throw a few items in a rucksack, pack the lightweight tent, head up Bullfell Beck to Bowscale Tarn, pitch a bivvy by the deep, cold, ancient water and stay there for a few years till we have come to our senses.

Maybe we will. Maybe we'll be somehow tempered by the purgative fires of Brexit and emerge like a phoenix. Maybe we'll realise that we have spent four decades believing in the lies of the rich and insulated, gulled and hoodwinked, swallowing lie after lie until we could not see the plain truth of what was right and good about ourselves. Perhaps a truly chastening humiliation, an economic and political catastrophe, the like of which Boris is eminently capable of delivering, is the slap in the face we need to wake us from our queasy hankerings for lost empires and foreign adventures and to realise just when our finest hour really was. Back when having helped save the world from the new Dark Age of Nazism we moved for a while into the broad sunlit uplands of the post-war consensus.

Those few decades have been alternately mocked and romanticised but from here it's hard not to see them as a Golden Age, the years of the NHS, the Arts Council, the National Parks, the Open University, the Third Programme and wonderful Radio 1, of the Beatles and the Stones, mods and rockers and folkies and hippies and punk, of soul and ska and roots rock reggae, of Larkin, Hughes, Pinter, Delaney, *Saturday Night and Sunday Morning*, Finney, Courtenay, Tushingham, Bates, Burton, the Festival of Britain, Olivier and the National Theatre, the '66 World Cup, the achievements of an enlightened and responsible establishment in tandem with bright, brilliant generations of working- and middle-class kids raised on rationing and free school milk and orange juice, free specs and dentures, cheap buses, grammars and comprehensives and the whole flawed but beautiful public realm.

The people who complain about the nanny state are the people who had nannies. They continue to divide and rule, to buy and sell, to trade in our future for their profit. As I write these words at the very end of 2019, partly due to the lack of any real or capable opposition, partly because of their strength of networks forged at schools and clubs, they have bought themselves more time and more power. These rich and privileged figures, mostly men, have no need of the simple things this book celebrates. You will not find them in doctors' waiting rooms, on the muddied pitch, on the swings in the park or in the noisy chaos of the baths on Saturday morning. They will be somewhere else, in their private world of old money and secret ties. They have their nannies. We have the nanny state: kind, brisk, more concerned with fairness than fashion, with decency rather than dogma. The struggle to save her goes on, but the appetite is there.

The nanny state made me. It made you too. We have never needed her more. It's time to bring her back.

ACKNOWLEDGEMENTS

I'd like to thank the following individuals who gave their time so freely and brilliantly for this book. With the hugest apologies for any omissions – corrected in any future editions I promise – they are, loosely, in order of appearance:

Matron Julie Treadgold and Lauren Flanagan at Trafford General, Margaret Scargill and Jim Logan, Dr Susan Bowie and Tom Morton, Dr Anna Olsson Rost, Frank Cottrell-Boyce, Caitlin Moran, Francine Houben, Julie McKirdy, Simon Armitage, Hunter Davies, Jarvis Cocker, Richard Hawley, Jeremy Deller, Nigel Blackwell, Lynsey Hanley, Nadia Shireen, Andy Burnham, Christian Wolmar, Alan Davey, James Purnell, Paul Mason, Elizabeth Alker, Anne Hilde Neset, Joakim Hauglund.